The Alignment Quotient

How to Create and Powerfully Live a Life You Love

Christopher Ancona

Copyright © 2020 by Christopher Ancona

All rights reserved.
Published by Ugly Professor Publishing
Ann Arbor, MI

No part of this book may be reproduced, scanned, or distributed in any printed or electronic form without written permission from the copyright holder or a stated representative. To request permission or for information about bulk purchases, please email:info@uglyprofessorpublishing.com

This book is sold with the understanding that the publisher is not engaged in rendering psychological, financial, legal, or other professional services. If expert assistance or counseling is needed, the services of a competent professional should be sought.

Cover design by Alex Head
Book design by Alex Head
Cover image by Line and Circle and Shalla Mar Mugot

ISBN: 978-1-7343444-0-0

Library of Congress Control Number: 2020901381

DEDICATION

This book is dedicated to my son, Samuel James and my good friend Patrick Ryan. In very different ways, both inspired the writing of this book, which I hope allows for the possibility of peace and purpose in both their lives.

I also want to dedicate this book to my Grandma and Grandpa Pasciak. Without their willingness to take a stand for me, and turn their own lives upside down, I am not sure I would be here today – and I certainly would not be the person I am. Thank you Gramma and Grandpa.

TABLE OF CONTENTS

Acknowledgments xi
Foreword xiii
Introduction 1
The Hole. 2
What to expect in this book. 3
The Alignment Quotient. 5
Franz Stigler. 5
What is Alignment?. 7

PART 1: THE FOUNDATION

Beginning as Being 13
Rethinking Being: from Abstract to Real 15
Being in Relation to Everything (Else) 16
Adding Information and Causal Flows 18
Making the Model Real: An Example. 20
Information Flow, Filters, and the Game of Perception . . . 21
A Dangerous Game. 23
The Trap 24
Another Paradigm: The Escape 26
For the doubters. 27
Intuition, Consciousness, and the Idea of Mind. 28
Three Fallacies about Being. 32
    Fallacy 1: "Being" and "values" are the same thing . . . 32
    Fallacy 2: Your Being is Fixed at Birth 34

Fallacy 3: Your Being Cannot Be Chosen or Changed,
Only Discovered. 38
Proposition: Being is a choice. 40
Conclusion. 41

PART 2: THE PATH TO SELF-CREATION

Re-examining past, present and future 45
For the love of quantum weirdness 46
    The double-slit experiment 47
    Quantum Entanglement 50
    Future First? 51
Opening up New Possibilities: Freedom in Uncertainty . . 52
The Power of Declarations 54
The Power of Declaration and Alignment. 56
The Alignment Commitment: Declaring Your Being . . . 57
    What kinds of words do I use?. 57
    The time-benefit of using a noun 60
    "Being" as a noun 61
    The role of role models 62
    Using impermanence as a brainstorming tool. . . . 65
    Bringing it home 66
The Being Salad 69
Creating your Purpose 70
    Why do you need a why? 70
    Developing your "so that" statement. 72
Creating a SPICY Purpose. 72
    Stable 72
    Personally Meaningful 74
    Inspirational 76
    Community. 78

"Y" = WHY 80
The Purpose Statement in action 80
Creating your personal Purpose Statement. 82
    SPICY Path #1:The reflective route. 82
    SPICY Path #2: The viral route: 91

PART 3: MOUNTAINS AND BOGEYMEN

Purple is not a real color 95
Creating reality 97
Beyond lions, snakes and bears. 99
Unhelpful responses: Your meat suit tools gone wrong . . 100
The STUPID Brain 100
    Should-ing. 101
    Tragedy Seeker. 101
    Unholy Martyr 103
    Pessimistic Forecasting 103
    Indecent Labeling 104
    Deceptive Emotions. 105
    Black-and-White Thinking 106
    Right-Mongering 106
    All about Me 107
    Idiot Oracle 107
    Negative Nelly 108
Your meat suit strings: SAFETY 109
Dealing with You 112
So what's the point? 114
What is self-awareness? 114
Integrity: The Key to Alignment 116
Rediscovering Integrity 118
Declaration of being as mantra 119

    Your declaration as a mantra 120
    Resilience: An unintended benefit beyond
    self-awareness. 121
    The power of journaling 123
        The science of journaling 124
        My journal 125
        Getting started. 129
        Tool 1: Random Being Check 129
        Tool 2: Micro-Feedback 133
    Conclusion. 141

PART 4: WRESTLING WITH ALLIGATORS

    The experience of being aligned with integrity 145
    Seeing only what you are focused on 145
    Don't fight against not being, just be 147
    Failures in alignment—clean up your mess. 148
    Patrick's Rule: Being with what is so 148
    Accepting what is so and focusing on what is possible . . 150
    Reality and Deception 151
        Dan's misunderstood declaration of generosity. . . . 152
        Claus's self-deception 153
        The "She's a witch!" effect 156
        Obligatory interdependence: Stay negative, Jeremy! . 158
    Leveraging your meat brain: Creating your community . . 160
    Leveraging your body: Creating helpful stories. 161
    The body-mind connection unveiled 162
    Replacing unhealthy stories. 165
    Living your SPICY Purpose 166
        Way #1: I Spy with my little eye a SPICY Perspective . 167
        Way #2: Little SPICY treasures 170
        Way #3: The SPICY Passion Project 172
        Way #4: A SPICY Life Revolution. 177

Managing impermanence (creating meaning as we age) . . 179
    Nancy's prison 180
Death is imminent—but every minute can be SPICY. . . . 181
Conclusion. 183
Author's Note: How I See It 185
    The elephant in the room 189
    A root of the problem. 191

APPENDIX 1: REASONABLE DOUBT IN A MATERIALIST VIEWPOINT 195

    Beyond Body to Brain 198
    Emergence Theory: From Brain to Consciousness. 199
    The definitional problem 200
    The Measurement Problem: Behaviors 201
    The Animation Problem: The OpenWorm project 202
    The Calculation Volume Problem: Human Awareness . . . 203
    Split Brain Research and Consciousness. 204
    Artificial Intelligence and consciousness. 205
    The Chinese room argument 206
    We have reached the limits 207
    Revisiting the Definition Problem 208
    The Materialist approach fails to even
    understand material 209
    Conclusion. 211

APPENDIX 2: BEING DEFINITIONS AND QUESTIONS 213

    1. Enthusiasm 214
    2. Joy 215
    3. Inspiration 215
    4. Excellence. 216
    5. Love 216
    6. Compassion. 217
    7. Freedom 217

8. Self-Expression 218
9. Integrity 219
10. Resilience 219
11. Dependability 220
12. Courage 220
13. Responsibility 221
14. Authenticity 221
15. Present 222
16. Cause 222
17. Grace 223
18. Peace 224
19. Hope 224
20. Ambition 225
21. Persistence 225
22. Curiosity 226
23. Adventure 226
24. Creativity 227
25. Conscientiousness 228
26. Generosity 228
27. Abundance 229
28. Determination 229
29. Fun 229
30. Passion 230
31. Humility 230
32. Optimism 231
33. Thoughtfulness 232
34. Kindness 232
35. Unreasonableness 233

ENDNOTES 235

ACKNOWLEDGMENTS

A very special thank you to Sally Collings. Without her unending positive energy, passion, dedication, drive, and smarts this book would be a disorganized shadow of its current self.

A special thanks to Lisa Osswald for allowing me to pry away some of her precious time to help me with the wording and sense of the book from start to finish, to help assure it makes sense to folks who don't speak English.

To my friend Gregory Rump, without his thorough review and challenging of my underlying logic to assure I leave no unexplained gaps, I am sure to have missed many important points that impact the completeness of this work: Thank you for your unending support and encouragement!

Another big thank you to Patrick Ryan for being a sparring partner and co-creator of the "being" definitions in the appendix – thank you for all of your arguing with me on these topics over the years.

A special thanks to John D. Shaw and Valor Studios Inc. for their willingness to allow me to use the painting "It's a higher call", and their generosity in sharing the story of Frantz Stigler and Charlie Brown.

And not to forget all the people who read parts of the book and gave feedback including Leonie Hull, Alexandra Deutsch, Tobias Kiefer, Richard Bentley, and Robert Kulp.

Thank you to Draft Lab for your work in making this book shine with your design work and your help coaching me to make bring this all together for launch. Last but not least, thank you to Jason Williams for his great and timely work on proofreading. Your eagle eye and grammar smarts were critical in making sure the text communicated my meaning and logic as intended.

FOREWORD

2010 was the year we founded the company Q595. To my surprise, some of my neighbors still believe it is a radio station. The name represents the one thing that keeps us going as we work with individuals, teams, and organizations to support them in becoming better leaders for better results. By focusing on 5 Quotients (Q5) of success, we get them 95% of their way to success. The rest is up to them.

Alignment is one of the 5 Quotients, and it was clear from the very beginning that this is a tough nut to crack. It could easily come across as esoteric, spooky, not relevant for tough businesspeople (who, in my experience, are most often not aligned at all with what they decide, do, and think). This book proves through extensive research what alignment is all about and how it works. It is the answer for those who believe alignment is rubbish or a luxury to think about.

This book is like a really good cookbook, opening your eyes and your senses to an approach that could transform your life. But like a good cookbook, it does not only talk about the spices and how they work—it gives very clear instructions on how to find your being, how to declare it, and how to become the person you love to be.

Sounds scary? It is! And it is THE chance to get you—and hopefully a large portion of our society—back on track. I can see this book helping millions of people to have less stress in their life, make better decisions, interact with more humility, and become strategically future-oriented all guided with their own will-power. It will help to activate those brains that blindly follow rules that were established decades ago and which no longer make any sense—especially important given the challenges the human species is facing these days.

Last but not least, I have witnessed my friend and business partner Chris—the author—in easy and in difficult times, and I can say: yes, he changed. Yes, he is clear in his purpose. Yes, his actions follow his purpose. Yes, this is integrity.

This book is for those who care about their own lives and the lives of their colleagues and families. This book is for those who are ready to make a little bit of an investment in order to get back a huge amount of fulfillment.

While you read this, know that we have helped many people in our training and coaching programs to become fully aligned—and by being aligned, to make a significant positive difference in the world.

Tobias Kiefer
December 2019

INTRODUCTION

The Alignment Quotient is inspired by a philosophy of living based on a cross-disciplinary study of science, math, religion, art, and practical logic dating back to Socrates. When I make a claim that some may find radical, or that one may not have had a chance to previously consider, I will be sure to justify that claim with an appeal to the best thought from multiple branches of science and philosophy for the purpose of both removing doubt and personal enlightenment on topics. This means when I give a technique for taking a step forward, I assure you, the reader, that the path is clear and logical with vivid examples and references. It means I will lay out a philosophy that is not meant to be believed, but instead tested and lived.

The goal is to lay out a well-argued, practical and pragmatic path for you to follow in order to reach a state where you are living a life you love, which will include powerful living with purpose and meaning that minimizes regret. There are many books that cover some of the ideas in this book, including life's purpose and meaning. While I don't believe this book is perfect or will be the last book ever written on this topic, it proposes *a way* forward, and not *the* way forward. Anyone who claims their own work as the latter is selling you something you don't need or working to recruit you into a religion – neither of which are the goals of this book. If a tool or process works for you, keep it and improve on it. If you test it and it's not working for you, discard it.

The Hole

Although education is supposed to help build young people into functional citizens able to fully contribute and add value to society, lessons dealing with how to create a life filled with purpose and meaning are completely missing from core school curricula at all levels of education. While a handful of universities, including Harvard and the University of Southern California, and smaller colleges such as Oberlin and Pomona, offer individual classes on the subject within religious studies or philosophy departments, specific lessons in purpose and meaning are not offered as part of any K-12, college. The same holds true for any corporate training programs, as far as I am aware. According to the International association for K-12 education Online Learning (iNACOL), students should be "able to articulate a vision for their futures, exercise agency in pursuing that vision and effectively navigate their own paths,"[1] indicating that purpose and meaning are critical components of such an education. But the curriculum is totally lacking this part of education. At best, there are career planning services that attempt to approach this topic.

Meanwhile, in a very unscientific survey, I asked about 150 of my Facebook friends about meaning and purpose in their lives. Fewer than one quarter reported finding meaning and purpose in their careers—which makes sense, as most people tend to look at jobs as a means to put food on the table and a roof over their head, rather than as a source of meaning and purpose. As education becomes more focused on ensuring employment, it is unlikely that many Meaning and Purpose 101s will appear, despite their potential for addressing many of our social ills—from depression to anxiety to negative stress.

Some may argue that purpose and meaning fall within the realm of religious institutions, and though research shows a correlation between religion and purpose and meaning in life[2], it is evident that simple participation in religion does not guarantee an inviolate sense of purpose or meaning in life[3]. Moreover, religion is in decline in the Western world. In the U.S., 35% of Americans say they have no religion or are not religious, and this increases to 43% for millennials according to a 2018 American

Family Survey[4]. In Europe, the percentages are even higher: Over 70% of young Northern Europeans identify themselves as religiously-unaffiliated; those in the Czech Republic outpace the group, with more than 90% of young people saying they do not identify with any specific religion[5].

For much of history, church and religion played an important role in helping people find purpose and meaning in life, which helped with happiness and well-being and buffered them from the inevitable storms of life; storms that would have otherwise led to hopelessness, anxiety, and depression. The decline of religious identification and practice has left a sizeable hole in Western society—a hole that, if not filled, will continue to grow, causing unnecessary pain and suffering. I wrote this book in an effort to fill that hole with science and philosophy.

The Alignment Quotient is designed for anyone who is lacking connection to a life of meaning and purpose and who wish to change that situation through philosophy and science.

For those of you who are struggling, this book offers a paradigm that is supported by thousands of years of human philosophy, supported by multiple branches of science, and tested for years by real people—including myself. I hope, if you decide to adopt this paradigm and act on it, that it leads you to the same level of freedom and success that it has provided me and others who have taken similar journeys.

If you already feel that your life has meaning and purpose—if you are happy, that is - don't let better become the enemy of best. Stick to what you are doing and keep following your path. However, you may seek a deeper level of engagement. If so, *The Alignment Quotient* can present additional paradigms and tools that will allow you to supersize what you are already doing, making your purpose more effective for you and those who matter to you.

What to expect in this book

The Alignment Quotient book is laid out in four parts with additional material at the end. Each part of the book builds on the previous parts.

Part 1 introduces you to the Alignment Quotient and lays the foundation of *being* so you can understand the base of where to start. It is reasonably philosophical with some supporting science, but introduces you to important paradigms that are critical to your success on the journey to powerfully add meaning and purpose into your life.

Part 2 continues with some new and necessary paradigms to set the stage for the work ahead. In the middle of part 2, you will begin creating and testing your own unique path. By the end, you will have walked through a complete journey to lay out a personal foundation for living a life you love.

Part 3 is called "Mountains and Bogeymen" because you will learn about all the things that will get in your way. You will also be introduced to tools and methods to discover and overcome those mountains and bogeymen.

Part 4 is called "Wrestling with Alligators" because it lays out how to manage the day-by-day realities of real life—which are not always pleasant. Part 4 also introduces you to practical and beneficial ways to begin building your alignment quotient while integrating your path into your life so that you can live a life you love.

After the four parts, I have added supplemental material, including an author's note that tells a little bit about my own journey. I have also included an appendix with a brief argumentation against materialist and reductionist views, which supports the paradigms in part 1.

My sincere hope is that this book makes you think and reflect and helps you to create and live a life you love.

If you seek to explore more, you may consider looking into the information in the endnote section of this book, or checking www.thealignmentquotient.com for additional information, tools, and training programs.

THE ALIGNMENT QUOTIENT

"In looking for people to hire, you look for three qualities: integrity, intelligence, and energy. And if you don't have the first, the other two will kill you. ... If you hire somebody without integrity, you really want them to be dumb and lazy."

WARREN BUFFETT—BUSINESSPERSON, INVESTOR, AND PHILANTHROPIST.

Franz Stigler[6]

The date was December 20, 1943: Lt. Franz Stigler, a fighter pilot in the German Air Force, was just one downed Allied Forces bomber away from qualifying for the coveted Knight's Cross issued for bravery on the battlefield. Stigler had landed to refuel and reload when he heard a B-17 bomber flying low and slow directly towards the airstrip. After years of risking his life for his countrymen, today he would attain recognition for his heroism. He flicked away his cigarette and climbed into his plane, ready to claim his prize.

Knowing that the B-17 was heavily armed with a dozen guns that could carpet the sky with enough firepower to take out a whole squadron of fighters, Stigler approached the bomber like a predator hunting dangerous prey. He needed to get close, unload, and get out: whoever fired first and true would live.

As he had done many times before, he aimed his sights square on the plane. But just before squeezing the trigger that would unload his 20mm cannons, he noticed something strange: the crew did not raise their guns to fire. The tail gunner was dead, his position completely destroyed. The left stabilizer had been shot off, the rudder was mostly gone, and the bomber's skin showed massive holes and was peeled back in places. Only one engine out of the four seemed to be fully functioning. Stigler was shocked the plane was still flying. He decided to inspect the plane and as he pulled up on its side, he saw crewmembers huddled together, tending the wounded. In that moment, he no longer saw the plane as a bomber. In this state, it was no different than a parachute for the imminently perishing men inside.

Stigler followed an uncommon code that required him to pursue victory in battle, not death. To stay true to who he was in that moment, a few thousand feet up in the air, in the heat of battle, and with his coveted Knight's Cross on the line, he did not shoot down that bomber.

It's A Higher Call by John D. Shaw, courtesy of Valor Studios Inc.

Stigler's deliberate inaction was undoubtedly an act of treason under the Nazi regime, punishable by firing squad.

Nevertheless, Stigler did not stop there. Aware that the B-17 crew was retreating to Allied territory, which required them to pass through a wall of anti-aircraft batteries, Stigler knew their only hope was for him to escort the plane from German airspace. The expert German gunners would recognize the shadow of his plane as a Bf 109 fighter and would not fire on their own countryman. So, Stigler took position over the wing of the B-17 and accompanied it safely across German air-defense lines until the plane was out of the risk of being shot down. Once over the North Sea and headed towards England, he waved to them and turned back to Germany.

Despite serious known risks, Stigler chose in those moments to align his actions with his personal rules of honor: rules independent from the actions of his enemies, the orders of his political leaders, his own desire for recognition, or even his own personal safety. Stigler chose instead to follow the rules that allowed him to keep his integrity and humanity intact.

What is Alignment?

The story of Stigler's incredible act is an extreme example of how the concept of "alignment" works, and how important alignment is to personal integrity. In our own personal and professional lives, the choices we make may not feel any less profound. At times, we may put our relationships and careers at risk in order to ensure we are living with integrity, and that risk can feel as grave as facing a firing squad.

Stigler fought for the German air force until the end of the war, serving among elite pilots as one of the first to fly jet fighters, never saying anything about that dramatic day in the sky. The world would only find out about his act of integrity when Charlie Brown, the American pilot of the B17 whom Stigler had escorted to safety, tracked down and contacted Stigler 40 years later.

Whatever may be known about Stigler's decision, the story remains his alone. We may daydream about what we would have done, but he actually did it. Stigler's actions were his exclusively, a true expression of who he was and who he chose to be. These are the key characteristics of alignment.

A quotient—the degree or amount of a given quality or characteristic—is a useful measure for thinking about personal and professional attributes. The Intelligence Quotient (IQ) test is a well-known aggregation of measures related to the ability to think analytically, logically, and quickly. It is also a test of short-term memory. The Emotional Quotient, or EQ, popularized by journalist Daniel Goleman in 1995[7], is based on a combination of measures that include the ability to: recognize emotions in oneself and others, discern and label different feelings, use emotional information to guide thinking and behavior, and manage and/or adjust emotions to adapt to environments or achieve one's goal. While IQ and EQ are both recognized as important indicators of "success" in life, we also know that neither—either together or in combination—can determine what makes a life worth living, what makes one love the life they have, or what allows a person to live a life without regret. For Stigler, neither IQ nor EQ appropriately captures the qualities he harnessed to take action, which went beyond the circumstances of war, the politics of the time, or his own aspirations. Anyone familiar with his story sees there was something special about him beyond IQ or EQ that influenced the actions he took.

It was Stigler's Alignment Quotient.

Alignment Quotient

"One's ability to declare and maintain integrity between who one is (being with purpose) and one's thoughts, emotions, behaviors, and actions regardless of the situation or circumstances."

The Alignment Quotient is a fresh take on old concepts. Terms like "being," "integrity," and "declaration" are so overused that they have practically lost their meaning, and thereby their connection to our experience of living. Using a combination of philosophy, science, and my own and others' life experience, this book breathes new significance into these terms, allowing their full potential to be seen, as well as how they are forged together as a key to self-empowerment.

By developing your Alignment Quotient, you exercise a freedom that can never be taken from you without your permission. Though alignment does not guarantee an easy life path—it can't make you rich, or popular, for example—it does guarantee to push you outside your comfort zone. It ensures that you will choose your own way forward with honesty and responsibility. Just as Stigler exhibited the skills necessary for living a life he loved while holding his head high, *The Alignment Quotient* will give you the specific tools to create the stories that both honor yourself and inspire others.

PART 1: THE FOUNDATION

BEGINNING AS BEING

*"First say to yourself what you would be; and
then do what you have to do."*

—EPICTETUS

The first question that may come to mind when presented with the concept of alignment is, "*What* does a person align to?" Alignment requires some reference point with which to align, and that referent needs to be something solid and secure: something that can stand the test of time. Because we are human *beings*, the first distinction we should explore is in the description we have given ourselves—the distinction called "Being." Being is the foundation on which we will build our Alignment Quotient. But what is it?

To answer that question, consider the following situation. You want to hire a caretaker for someone whom you love deeply, and who has dementia. You have interviewed two people. One exudes patience, kindness, and a quiet fortitude—she has some experience, but no formal education. The other has all the right degrees, including one specifically for managing people with dementia, and has the same amount of experience as the first caretaker, but does not display the same warmth or competence. Who do you choose?

Based only on that simple description, most people tend to choose the first caretaker because of *who she is*—her "being"—also referred to as her character, personality, nature, disposition, reputation, or temperament. But we are not human *temperaments*, or human *reputations*. We are human *beings*. But what specifically is a *being*? It seems such an obvious question, but I would bet that a clear answer doesn't pop into your head. Though its importance may not be fully appreciated, the answer is the key to a door to freedom we did not have before: the key to mental, emotional, relational, and even financial health and wellness.

What is Being?

The dictionary describes **being** as[8]:

*The nature or essence of a person where **essence** means the intrinsic nature or indispensable quality of something, especially something abstract, that determines its character OR a property or group of properties of something without which it would not exist or be what it is (or who we are).*

At first glance, this definition seems fairly obvious and understandable; but it also holds some mysteries—which makes understanding it less like using a fork to skewer a firm apple, and more like picking up soft, wobbly Jell-O. For example, if I ask you to identify the "indispensable" quality of a knife, you will probably answer "blade" pretty quickly—for without a blade, a knife is not a knife. But if I ask you what the indispensable quality of love is, you might have a much harder time answering, because love is an abstract concept without any immutable physical characteristics.

If you attempt to write down a definition for love, you may find that parts of your definition are in conflict with other parts. For example, you may think love implies a certain gentleness—as with our love for young children—but you may also realize that love sometimes requires a certain harshness, as when that same child is a teenager and you catch them skipping school. Christians can turn to the New Testament's 1 Corinthians 13:4 for this definition[9]: "Love is patient, love is kind. It does not envy, it does not boast, it is not proud." Or maybe you turn to artists like the Everly Brothers, who captured the harsher side in the title of their 1961 classic song "Love Hurts."[10]

Because love is an abstract concept and not a tangible material object like a knife, our conceptual framework for it are limited. We form its definition by setting boundaries, describing what it "is" and "is not," because in this universe, this is the best we can do. Knowing that the concept of our "being" is intangible will be important as we define and then translate into action the characteristics we seek to define as part of our Alignment Quotient. Understanding that a definition of "being" will be less like describing a knife and more like describing love, here are a few thoughts on the structure and nature of being.

Rethinking *Being*: from Abstract to Real

In the 1630s, philosopher and mathematician René Descartes proposed this question[11]: What if there was a demon who had created an illusion of "the sky, the air, the earth, colors, shapes, sounds and all external things," in effect deceiving Descartes into "considering himself as having hands or eyes, or flesh, or blood or senses, but as falsely believing that he had all these things?" What if the illusion was so perfect that he was unable to determine it was an illusion? (Yes, Cartesian philosophy predated *The Matrix* by more than 350 years.) The thought experiment led him to admit the possibility that everything he was experiencing may not be real, including his experience of other people. But in this scenario, in which the demon has deluded Descartes, the philosopher concluded that, at the very least, he himself must be real. If he weren't, there would be no point in the demon tricking him. Rationalizing that "we cannot doubt of our existence while we doubt," Descartes wrote, famously, "*Cogito, ergo sum*"—or, "I think, therefore I am." Or, captured more accurately, but less famously in his posthumously published work: "I doubt, therefore I think, therefore I must be."[12]

Imagine you are in a simulation and that simulation is so perfect you cannot tell you are in a simulation. Everything you think you know would, in fact, *not* be real: your house, car, family, even your own body. If all of these figments, as it were, were taken away—if the demon halted the simulation and everything disappeared—then what would be left? What would you be? *Who* would you be? What does a consciousness all alone floating through an empty void look like? It would be very hard to visualize.

Without material things, devoid of the stories about your past, free from social pressures, with no physical body to behold in the mirror and then love or hate—without mirrors, in fact—you are left only with you, a simple conscious being. In this state, the best analogy for what *being* is, is the color, shade, texture, flavor, or vibration of this sole consciousness. *Being* is what imbues consciousness with the properties that, in turn, allow others to experience that consciousness. Let's assume the consciousness, even in a vacuum, would exude something. If there was an outside observer looking at the consciousness that was you, and they possessed the senses to perceive your consciousness, it would plausibly come across as something like a color, shade, texture, flavor, or vibration. No one can know definitively what consciousness is, as no one has "seen" it firsthand, and neither scientists nor spiritual leaders have a common definition of it (though scientists are seeking to define it[13]). But, despite there being no widely accepted definition, I think this thought experiment can explain "being" in a way that can provide utility as it is related to "you" and your life.

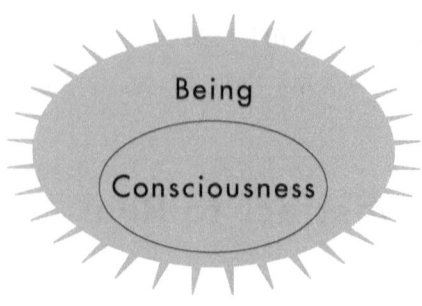

Figure 1: Consciousness exuding being absent the physical universe as we know it.

Being in Relation to Everything (Else)

Stepping back from Descartes' demon-driven thought experiment, we can start assembling, layer by layer, the elements beyond our consciousness and being that make up our reality. This model is a compilation using the underlying philosophy of existentialism (existence = consciousness, which precedes essence, i.e. being), and then leverages what we know from neuroscience, social psychology, and other related branches of science to create a visual representation of layers which make up reality both as we know it via science and and as we experience it it every day. It is a model of utility, not meant to define absolute truth, as this is not currently known.

The model includes a set of concentric circles with consciousness at the core, our being surrounding consciousness at the most proximate level, internal thoughts and behaviors represented by the next ring, followed by the material body (our "meat suit"), and finally, the outermost ring, which represents our interactions with the world.

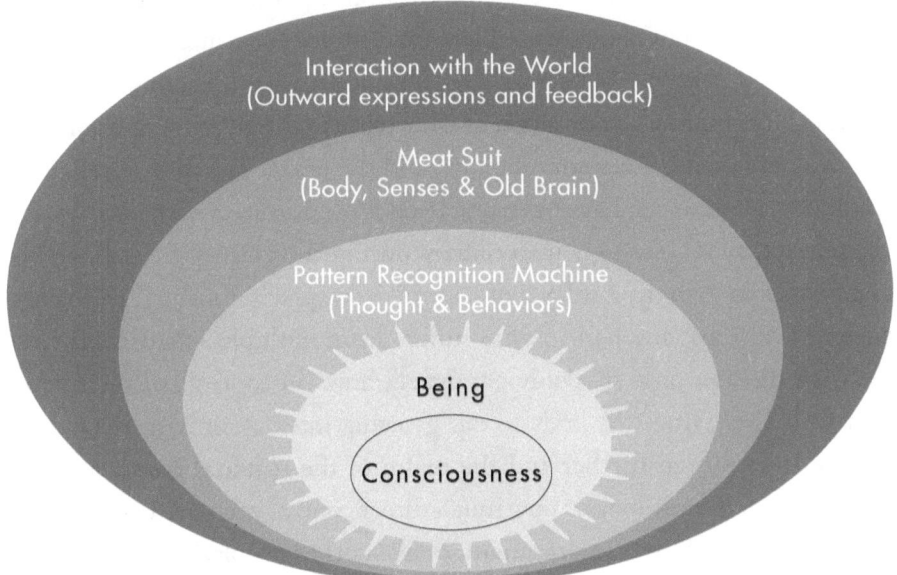

Figure 2: The layers coating consciousness which enable it to entangle with the known universe.

Note that I create a filter between the pattern recognition machine and the meat suit (including brain), not because there is scientific evidence suggesting that these things are separate, but because it helps to visualize the separation between the abstract and the truly physical. I have done this to allow space for the strange and currently unexplained phenomenon that materialist scientists call "the brain that changes itself." Note also that materialist scientists do not believe consciousness exists outside the physical brain. The decision to separate these two components recognizes that there is more to know about the meat suit. It also leaves an opening for the possibility of consciousness as a thing separate from the brain that can, using guided thoughts and behaviors, make physical changes in the meat-brain—as evidenced by neuroscience-founded studies into mindfulness[14].

Though consciousness is not fully separate from being, and neither consciousness nor being are separate from the material body, they are also not necessarily defined or limited by them, which gives them a true distinctness. Notice that the further the ring is from consciousness, the more physical the layer becomes and the less control we have over it. The least physically-defined space, from consciousness to being, is where we have the most control – we will discuss this in detail in the next sections. We have less control over our thoughts, which are abstract constructs of the mind, and still less over the behaviors that flow from them. There are myriad methods for improving our levels of control, including the meditation and mindfulness used in Eastern religions, and the prayer of Western religious traditions, all of which have been practiced for centuries upon centuries. As the physicality increasingly materializes during the journey from thoughts and behaviors to body, our level of control drops precipitously. If this is not apparent, just ask any person who suffers from multiple sclerosis, or Lou Gehrig's disease, or is suddenly paralyzed, how "in control" of their body they feel. Then, from the body to our growing interaction with the world, control lessens even further and the realm of the material is exhibited in full splendor. Simply look at how much direct control you have over society, government policy, the environment, or even other peoples' opinions about you. Of course, you do have *some* control over these things, but nothing in comparison to how much control you have over your body, and still less than what you have over your thoughts and behaviors.

Moreover, when it comes to the control you have over your being, no one can touch that unless you allow them to. It is yours and yours alone. It is the basis for your freedom.

Adding Information and Causal Flows

The next step in the process of developing our Alignment Quotient is to add information flows and causality. The next graphic illustrates informational and causal flows: one from the conscious "I" (out through the body and into the world) and another from the world (through the body and to the consciousness). Both are basic flows, albeit in opposite directions, in which each layer is a filter that modifies the flow of information in some way.

You will notice that there are two outward flows. One is an "aligned flow of choice," and the other is an "automated response." It is important to realize that much of our lives are lived as an automatic reaction to stimuli—this is the "automated response." Those reactions include everything from simple un- or sub-conscious (thankfully) breathing, to our non-conscious drives to and from work (like that time you drove home and forgot how you got there), to the automatic ruminating thoughts you have regarding a time you were dumped by a former lover (wondering what you did wrong and thinking negative things about yourself, your former lover, or both).

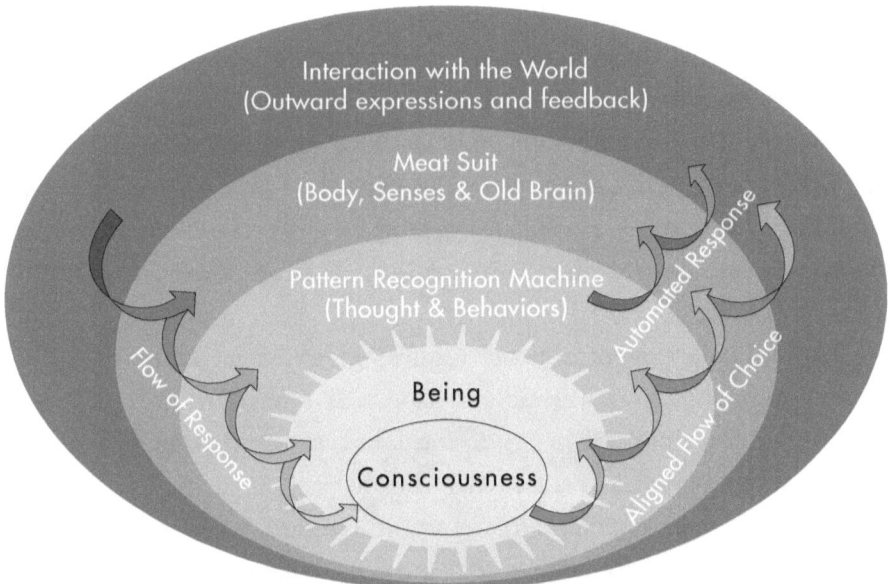

Figure 3: Model of self with filters, causal actions and informational flow.

Neuroscientists suggest the "automated response" flow behaves like autopilot, somewhere between 95% and 99.99% of the time. So, though we have a consciousness that can make choices, our autopilot does most of the reacting to outside stimuli automatically and habitually, without any input from the "I" that makes up who we are.

This setup is very practical. It relieves us from the burden of thinking about boring or repetitive tasks, like listening to that friend complain about politics for the umpteenth time. It also automates important tasks, like scanning our environment while walking to help avoid stepping on a poisonous snake or in a pile of dog poop. We would not have evolved to be able to cede control of our thinking without there being serious benefits to this capability; in this way, our meat suits are wired and trained for near automated survival. That being said, the success of this automation means we have grown to trust our bodies and brains to do right by us. They do what they do, we follow along, and the vast majority of the time we are content with this arrangement because it is practical and easy—it works. We accept near total dependence on this automation and just move through life.

But this automation has a downside too. Our meat suits (which include our brains) don't only respond to low stakes, everyday risks and occurrences, they also react to things that *matter*, things that we should be considering at a deeper level. Even when we can interrupt the automatic response—and often we do not—our automatic brain can take our trust in it and skew our decision-making. Using the filters it has developed through evolution, our automatic brain creates a life of short-term survival reactions, rather than the conscious, integrity-filled, and inspiring decisions that will lead us to a life we love.

Notice in the flow of response (figure 3) that for each level the information flows past, a modification is made to that flow. Information never reaches our consciousness in "pure" form, but instead it is filtered at each stage of flow. As we process external information, our bodies' senses feed signals to our brain, which then interprets those signals via its filters, making the messages we ultimately receive anything but pure. In part 3, we will talk about some of the many filters that exist in the brain and body, and the effect they can have on your ability to maintain integrity with who you choose to be.

Making the Model Real: An Example

Imagine you buy a coffee for a friend. This is a decision to be generous, made by your consciousness and guided by your being, to take a specific set of actions (give money to a shop in exchange for a coffee; gift the friend the coffee). The results of those actions show up in the world as 1. a shop sold a coffee, and 2. a friend received a coffee. That is how simple the flow of choice is. There are at least two simple interactions that came from this flow of choice or causality: the interaction with your friend and the interaction with the coffee shop. Let's focus on the interaction with the friend. When you hand her the coffee, she may be happy and give you a smile, which then feeds back as information to your body, causing a feeling of warmth in your body that is observed by "you." Your body reacts with an automated, habitual smile. Your friend sees this smile and then stops and asks you, "Ok, what's the catch? What do you want?" This response is new information that feeds back to your body, causing a different type of physiological reaction that makes you feel upset. An internal monologue begins, fueled by what the "you" observes: "Why would she think that way?" you ask yourself, sinking into an unpleasant state of uncertainty.

For most everyone, this type of interaction happens continuously throughout the day. Notice, in this example, how the consciousness chose a way to "be" first, then a particular set of actions flowed from that being. Then, once you witnessed your friend's suspicion, which was filtered by your brain, the automated responses took over and the conscious choice of being generous was dropped. All the while, the "you" was able to observe these causes and effects and, more or less mindlessly, signed off on your brain's automated reactions.

Information Flow, Filters, and the Game of Perception

As our meat suit lacks a sensory input to directly view a "being," it relies on proxies provided by information flow to the senses we do have. Sometimes, those proxies are smiles, scowls, vocal intonations, or body language. Other times, they are physical actions like the generous act of buying a coffee for another person or the abrasive act of taking a decision that was known to be counter to your own preferences or expectations. Still, other times, the proxy is a material thing, like ownership of a particular house, car, or business. In the case of a person we know intimately, a best friend or a life partner, we may use our years of familiarity (history) as a proxy for who they are.

In none of these cases do we have direct access to the *being* of the person being judged. Our judgments are based on the mostly automatic actions of their beings' brain manipulating their meat suit, some of which enter the world and are picked up by our meat suit and delivered to us via our information filtration systems, which tend to focus on how those things make us feel. Most of the time we don't even have enough information to make any legitimate judgment at all, but that does not stop our brains from making them anyway. Those judgments are masquerading as a description of being and likely have nothing to do with who the other person is. Despite this, we have confidence in our judgment.

Take these examples of judgment versus reality:

- *She is so patient and kind*, the man on the subway thinks as the woman lifts his wallet from his pocket.
- *He is such an insensitive jerk*, the exhausted salesperson says to herself after being brushed off by a man who was just fired from his job.
- *She is so judgmental*, says the woman being talked out of continuing an abusive relationship by a friend.
- *He is such a caring and understanding person*, says the elderly woman about the insurance salesperson who is overcharging her.

This process happens quickly and automatically—similar to how a lightning strike causes a startle response, and with the same potential for a devastating effect on a person or a relationship. First impressions are a great example of this process in action. Research on first impressions shows how quickly snap judgments take place, how little information our brain requires to solidify those judgments, and how long-lasting they are—even when the first impression is later shown by new evidence to be incorrect. This is a type of bias called the "Primacy Effect,"[15] whereby we tend to "remember the first piece of information we encounter better than information presented later on." It is one of many similar biases caused by the brain's information-filtration and meaning-making machine.

Our descriptions based on our experience of a person are flawed: by contextual experience, cultural particularities, and myriad other human biases. Humans use the only method available to determine who we are, employing the limited labels offered by our native language and culture that most closely match our flawed perceptions of observed behaviors and actions. We know we do this, and we know others do the exact same thing to us.

Does this mean we should disregard all judgment by others and live as though we were impervious to, or independent from them? Of course not. Firstly, we do not live in isolation. What others think of us matters, and it hurts when they think poorly of us[16]. When someone says, "I don't care what other people think of me," they are likely lying to themselves. Secondly, we are susceptible to delusion and the tendency to think of ourselves as something we are not (typically, as being better than we are[17]). Serial killers may see themselves as compassionate "artists" bestowing freedom on their victims; frauds may see themselves as purveyors of hope and excitement in a life of boredom; a 25-year-old living in their parents' basement, smoking weed all day, may see themselves as an underappreciated genius. Just because these people perceive themselves in a particular way does not make their perceptions true. Who we are and how others experience us are interconnected, and, often but not always, interdependent. We cannot completely ignore outside impressions of ourselves, even if we know them to be flawed.

A Dangerous Game

Snap judgments aim to determine and label our being, that is, the root of who we are. If their message was simple—if they communicated "friend vs. foe," or "safe vs. dangerous"—these judgments would have a clear evolutionary advantage. To survive, we only need to know whether to go towards a person or stay away. But our brains go further, concocting descriptions with abstract, complicated, and fuzzy meanings. People are labelled *generous*, or *thoughtful*, or *passionate*, or *inspiring*. In other cases, they are a *jerk*, or an *idiot*, or a *moron*. Our brains can come up with myriad descriptions in very little time, with very limited information.

Since we know the judgment of others is important, and yet we recognize that judgment to be flawed in very particular ways, we can manipulate it. Our awareness of our ability to manipulate others' perceptions of who we are sets us up to play what I call the "Have Game." In this game, we use our knowledge that the information flow to our judgment center begins with the outer ring—the world—since what exists in that world provides us the information we need to be able to judge who we are. Of course, as I prefer positive social judgment, I have a strong desire to control your judgment of who I am. This drives where I put my energy and sets up a very dangerous trap, one that plagues our society.

This process sets us up for failure in the most critical aspects of life. It causes missed opportunities and diminishes our physical, emotional, relational, and even financial health and wellbeing. Here are two tragic but common examples of how this trap is set.

The Trap

John was a technician at an automotive company. He grew up in the Upper Midwest of the United States and had a traditional upbringing. Married to his high school sweetheart, they had two children and lived in a suburb outside a large town. Ever since he was a boy, John dreamed of having the perfect family. He was the sole provider for his family and worked hard to provide a solid middle-class lifestyle; he had always wanted to *be* a good husband and father. John both believed and took pride in the fact that he was the kind of person who *is* a good father and husband because he was such a reliable provider. He had learned that being a good provider was the essence of being a man from his father, who had done the same for him. Then the economy soured and John was abruptly laid off. After applying for jobs every day and exhausting his network, he was still unemployed and unable to provide for his family. So, his wife went to work. John became terribly depressed, which caused his behavior to change. He no longer played with his children with vigor or spent intimate time with his wife. John escaped by watching TV or playing video games. John was no longer the good husband or father he had always yearned to be.

John had lost "who he was"—his being, or his essence—because he equated it to his job or his income, things that he "had" rather than something he fully controlled. John had fallen into the trap by playing the "have game," defining his *being* using the flawed perspective he had developed in his upbringing. It turns out the shaky foundation on which John's world and personal view was based is common across most contemporary cultures.

I call this the *Have-Do-Be* model of seeing the world.

Have ⟶ Do ⟶ Be

John needed to "Have" a job and money, so he could "Do" the things that he imagined a good father and husband does, like providing resources for his family, so he could "Be" a good father and husband. John learned to tie *who* he was to his job, which was not, ultimately, in his control. When the job disappeared, "who he was" disappeared with it. He lost himself.

Here is another example—again, one that is quite common around the world. Jackie's mother was always very hard on her, pushing her to look pretty and proper so she could find a good man and have a family. Jackie loved children and had an idealized view of marriage, so she always worked hard to live up to her mother's expectations. Jackie went to college and got a great job after graduation—something her mother viewed as important to both finding a good husband and being a good partner. Jackie spent a lot of time looking for her perfect man, eventually fell in love, got married, and had a daughter. Jackie was very happy with life, but her husband did not share her positive experience. After years of trying to work things out, Jackie's husband informed her he was dating another woman and filed for divorce. Jackie was devastated; it was as if her life was over. She stopped taking care of herself and turned her focus to taking care of her daughter, always seeking approval from her daughter and being terrified of her daughter leaving her.

Jackie had fallen into the same trap as John. Jackie needed to "Have" a family and "Do" the things that she had idealized in order to "Be" worthy. When she lost her husband, she did not only lose a husband, she lost her sense of self-worth, her confidence, her inner strength. Who she *was* was tied to something—a relationship—she had.

Another Paradigm: The Escape

The foundation on which a person's *being* rests can be formed differently if the order is reversed. This foundation will be strong, secure, and controlled entirely by the person who "is."

Be ⟶ Do ⟶ Have

In this form, a foundation can *be* created so that full control always remains with the person themselves. In *Man's Search for Meaning*[18], Viktor Frankl writes about the importance of this foundation. Frankl was a prisoner in a concentration camp during World War II, along with thousands of others from all walks of life. People of every kind of background—from respected lawyers to wealthy shop keepers, accomplished professors, husbands, fathers of five children, and high-performing athletes—were not protected by their accomplishments, roles, or titles. Upon entering the camp, they were stripped of these labels and identified only by numbers tattooed on their forearms. Frankl, who was educated as a psychiatrist, was put in charge of the camp hospital, basically taking care of those who were dying. In the camp, most of the people were worked to the bone, given only one piece of bread and a small amount of water daily. He observed prisoners taking bread from those in the hospital who were dying—not a shocking occurrence considering food equated to survival for most in the camp. What did surprise Frankl were the few people who would give up some of their bread for those who were sick or dying in the hospital. These prisoners did not allow the situation to control who they were—they maintained the alignment between who they were and the experience others had of them,

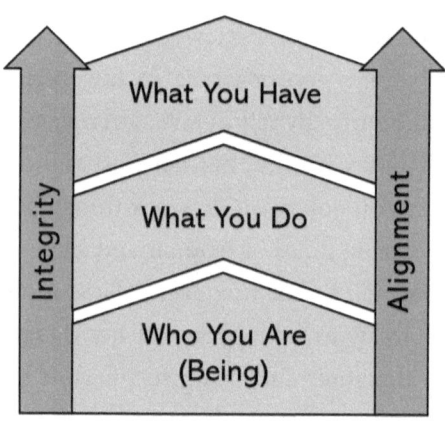

sometimes at the expense of their own life. This led to Frankl's famous observation, "Everything can be taken from a man but one thing: the last of the human freedoms—to choose one's attitude in any given set of circumstances, to choose one's own way." For our purposes, Frankl's use of the word *attitude* can be substituted by the word *being*.

Frankl was one of only two people in that camp who survived, mostly due to luck. Those who stole food from the sick and those who gave food to the sick died just the same. This shows an ultimate truth: whether we let the situation control who we are, or we have integrity with our being independent of the situation, we will still all die in the end. I contend that the former is to die a slave to situation and the latter is to die free with the least regrets. And the choice is always our own.

For the doubters

Many people reading this book may identify themselves with the idea of soul, or subtle consciousness, or some sense that who we are goes beyond our brain and body. If you were asked to point to yourself, you would likely not point to your head. Instead, you might even point to your heart or your gut, yet still know that you are neither your heart nor your gut. For you, we will continue the journey to explore the nature of being.

Other readers may look at the *Be-Do-Have* model and conclude that it conflicts with their existing belief that who they are is located inside their skullcap and between their ears and goes no further. These doubts about the *Be-Do-Have* model are pervasive throughout Western culture based on the Materialist paradigm. In scientific thought, Materialism is not about the need to buy the latest model mobile phone or to have the biggest house, fanciest car, or most toys. It is simply the belief that *matter* is fundamental, and nothing, including being and consciousness, exist outside of material interactions. Or to put it another way, there is no world beyond material things—things we can touch, taste, hear, *physically* observe, and measure.

If you subscribe to the materialist argument, but are still open to being persuaded that consciousness may lie outside the confines of your meat-suit—hence, the possibility that Being can come before Having—or you simply have an interest in the scientific debate around this topic, please turn to the appendix of this book to the part called "Where Materialism is not working." There you will find an outline of the materialist case made by elite mathematicians, engineers, and scientists suggesting the argument that consciousness is located only inside the brain is not as compelling as a materialist may have you believe. I use no religious or spiritual arguments or language, nor do I use any woo-woo science. Instead, I dig into scientific knowledge and philosophical thought from highly reputable sources, which I cite throughout so you can follow the argument and do your own research into the topics. If you are in doubt, this may be a useful read before you move on to the next part.

Intuition, Consciousness, and the Idea of Mind

If you are still reading, I assume it means you are willing to consider that being can come first and are ready to dig further into this paradigm. As Frankl suggests, our only real freedom is to choose who we are in any given situation. So, the *Be-Do-Have* paradigm is an important piece of the puzzle on the journey of living a life you love.

With a little reflection, we intuitively know that we *are* not our bodies, or our thoughts, or our feelings. We *are* not our history or beliefs or opinions. We *have* all those things, and we consider these things to be part of us, and can even be quite attached to them, yet they are not us—they are not who we are.

The "I" who is me can choose to seek out new perspectives and paradigms despite what information my senses feed me. The "I" who is me can even change and direct my intentions independent of what is happening around me. The "I" who is me is distinct and separate in a certain way from all that I *have*. We have all had the experiences of "I" as separate from what we *have*. We have had this experience no matter what the graphics earlier in this chapter show, and independent of the scientific justification of consciousness that is discussed in the appendix. We have the experience that the "I" who is me is what animates body and mind—it observes, examines, and reflects on life. Yet at the same time, we know we are intimately connected to our body and to the world. We cannot deny this connection.

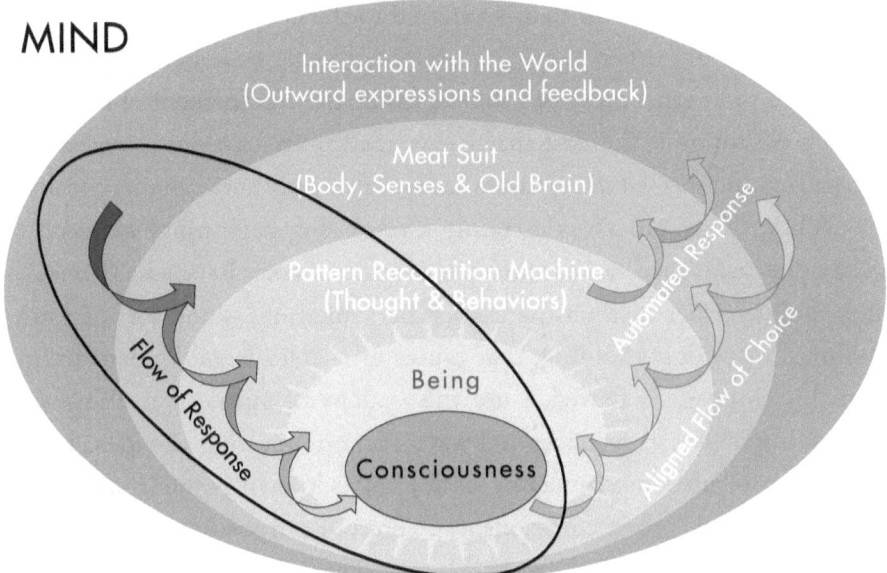

Figure 4: The model of self with the areas included in Dr. Siegel's definition of mind highlighted

In an attempt to fill the gap in our experience and understanding of consciousness, Dr. Dan Siegel, clinical professor of psychiatry at UCLA School of Medicine, and founder of the field of interpersonal neurobiology, has come up with a definition of the mind that highlights an important part of our model from earlier in the book (figure 4), and will serve as a tool later as we move into the practical aspects of alignment. According to Siegel, the mind is:

> *"all that relates to our subjective felt experience of being alive, from feelings to thoughts, from intellectual ideas to inner sensory immersions before and beneath words, to our felt connections to other people and our planet. And Mind also refers to our consciousness, the experience we have of being aware of this felt sense of life, the experience of knowing awareness. Mind is the essence of our human nature, our deepest sense of being alive, here, right now, in the moment.[19]"*

Siegel's definition of mind recognizes the importance of information transfer between our subjective felt experience and the external world. It suggests that we are not limited by the brain, since our consciousness has an interdependency on all that is external to the body, such as objects, our environment, and other people, while at the same time being intimately connected to internal processes that lie inside the confinement of the skull. Siegel's definition is the first that I have read from a serious scientist that recognizes and sets out to capture what we intuitively know about ourselves.

While this approach is certainly a promising beginning, we need to go further before we can capture the essence of consciousness. If *mind* is as Siegel describes it, then there must be something, some sort of formless machinery or scaffolding, that causes or enables *mind*. Understanding that this language is flawed, I use the analogy of formless machinery or scaffolding merely as a conceptual way of communicating the idea. In the West, this formless machinery or scaffolding is known as the "soul"; in the East, it is called "subtle consciousness." For our purposes, we will use the term "consciousness" for what comprises the base of our model of the mind, mainly because science has yet to agree on clear language for what we are discussing.

This, or any other kinds of thinking, should never be taken at face value. Rather, my hope is that it will open you up to the possibility to honestly, openly, and fully explore this idea for yourself in your own life—for the sole purpose of exploring and discovering new things that will in turn transform your life into one that you love.

Here is a simple exercise for exploring your own consciousness, and all of the filters that Siegel defines as part of the mind. If you have never done this before, please take the time to do it now. You may already believe I am right about this, but there is nothing like the first-hand experience you get from doing it.

Mind Exercise:

Find a quiet place to sit (not required, but helpful). Set a timer for 3 minutes and commit to completing the full 3 minutes. Close your eyes and clear your mind. Do not allow yourself to focus on any particular thing. After you clear your mind, simply observe any and all thoughts that automatically bubble up into your conscious awareness. What are those thoughts about? Are they intellectual ideas? Are they thoughts about your relationships with other people? Are they reflections of your past, or ruminations about your future? Are they stimuli from the environment—a sound, a smell, or a sensation on or from your body? Notice what thoughts are randomly coming into your awareness, and then gently push them out of your mind to get back to a clear mind and start over.

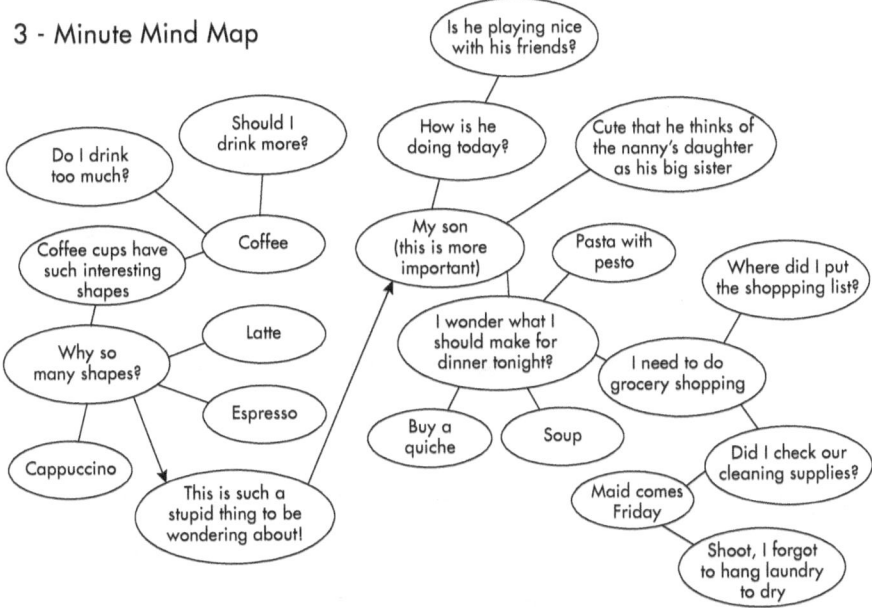

Figure 5: Example mind map from 3-minute exercise

At the end of the exercise, reflect on which parts were the conscious "you" and which parts were due to automatic and habitual information flow between the filters that exist between your consciousness and the world. Feel free to take a piece of paper and draw a mind map (example figure 5) from this experience as a record of what "you" observed from your brain (Don't worry if it looks a bit disorganized and crazy, this is just how our brains naturally work). This simple exercise is all it takes to understand the model in Figure 4, and Siegel's definition of mind. Notice how the "you" can both observe and clean out those automatic thoughts: one can both observe *and* control thoughts. This is one of the abilities you can build that is critical to developing alignment.

Three Fallacies about Being

Even when we are intellectually and intuitively in agreement with the concept of *being* as the starting point, the entrenched beliefs that are part of many cultures can make our views difficult to reconcile completely. These incorrect cultural paradigms include:

1. Being equates to values
2. *Who we are* is fixed at birth, and
3. *Who we are* is only discoverable—it is neither choosable nor changeable.

All three of these ideas are incorrect and damaging to our health and well-being. Therefore, it is worth the time to weigh these belief structures against scientific and philosophic knowledge, and see how they fall apart when held up to scrutiny.

Fallacy 1: "Being" and "values" are the same thing

Values are important, but they are separate and distinct from what we call "being." The Lexico online dictionary defines "values" as: "principles or standards of behavior; one's judgement of what is important in life[20]." In her book, *Values-based: Career and Life Changes that make Sense*, my friend Christine Locher simplifies it further. "Values are *THINGS* that you value (no kidding)[21]," she writes.

Both definitions point out that values are something you *HAVE*. This means that different values may be applied based on different situations. You will use different values in making different decisions. You may have conflicting values depending on the issues you are confronting. In contrast, who you *are*, your *being*, should remain consistent independent of the situation. Who you are, your being, should determine which values to apply in a given situation. Who you *are*, if correctly understood and powerfully chosen, will not conflict with your s*elf*.

Think back to John, who, if you remember, lost his job and lost himself. John held the "values" of hard work, dedication, and commitment. These values did not go away when he lost his job. These values may be the very reason he stays with his family instead of running off and starting over. If and when John does find a new job, he will undoubtedly work hard, which is evidence that his values can remain intact, though they are situationally dependent. John does not exude his values; he maintains them as concepts to be executed based on the situation. This is how values work and makes sense.

Now imagine that John's "being" is one of his values—let's say his being is hard work. As such, what he exudes will be "hard work." Now, how does that manifest when John is on vacation with his family? How will John be able to "live his values"—"hard work"—when his wife wants him to sun on the beach next to her, or his children want to splash with him in the sea? I think we can agree that John would not want to apply his "value" of hard work during these situations.

Now, contrast what we just learned about values with "being." You should not desire to turn off who you are, your being, based on the situation. *Being* is inseparable from your self. It is who you are in each and every moment.

Going back to the example of the caretaker who we were hiring to take care of the dementia patient, we do not say, "She *values* kindness or patience." Rather, we say, "She *is* kind and patient." Kindness and patience are *what she exudes*, not only things she values. This distinction between who a person *is* and what values they hold is significant and important. It is the difference between knowing and appreciating a path and *being* the person who walks the path.

When I say I "value" something, it means I seek it out, I search for it, and I also want to find it in others. I may value family, money, beauty, nature, my relationship with my partner, history, friends, and many other "things", but they are not me. Who I am is me, and what I value are simply preferences that I have. Some of those preferences may strongly engage body and mind, but this does not make them who I am. Who I am—my being—is separate and distinct from my values.

Fallacy 2: Your Being is Fixed at Birth

Many people believe that who you are is fixed at birth. This theory dates back to the Middle Ages, when many Western societies were stratified in such a way that if you were born a baker or a farmer or a nobleman, that was the role you inhabited for the rest of your life. Old ideas die hard, even when they are wrong and damaging. Hence, this ideology still exists today in many cultures around the world and, unsurprisingly, has anchored itself to scientific debate—specifically, nature versus nurture. The parallels between the details of some of these debates and the ones focused on *who we are*, make this argument worthy of review.

Genetic Determinism and Epigenetics

The theory of genetic determinism came about with the discovery of genes and the field of genetics more than 150 years ago. Since then, the theory that genes, and only genes, determine what we are, who we are, and what we will be has been widely accepted. This theory has only been seriously challenged in the last 20 years with the advent of epigenetics: The study of biological mechanisms that will switch genes on and off. The discovery of epigenetic effects led scientists to the understanding that environment affects genes. There is evidence that in many cases, our grandparents' and parents' environments have had impacts on our genes, and that our own environments can have impacts on our children and on their children[22]. These findings provoked serious philosophical debate within the scientific community, raising the question: Does the discovery of epigenetic impacts contradict genetic determinism?

The question of which characteristics a child is born with versus which are determined by parent/child interaction, local culture, life experiences, and other environmental factors is the subject of a great deal of scientific study. Interestingly, parents of multiple children often observe how different their children's personalities are, and how soon after birth these differences became apparent, which suggest some evidence for genetic determinism.

The Ramifications of Genetic Determinism

Once scientists discovered genes, theories quickly emerged claiming genes accounted for all our behaviors. (No doubt, scientists' personal experience with their own children had an impact on these hypotheses.) These theories kicked off interesting and important policy and ethical debates about how we should manage society if genetic determinism could be proven correct. For example, if criminals have a genetic makeup which predetermines their likelihood of becoming criminals, would we, as a society, be morally obligated to label these people at birth, and immediately imprison them? There do exist some data on prison populations showing higher rates of psychopathy[23], and other data linking the MAO-A (monoamine oxidase A) gene, also known as the warrior gene, to violent criminals[24]. These seem to support the argument for genetic determinism. Would identifying people with the MAO-A gene and segregating them at birth benefit the greater good of society and make it safer? If your answer is "yes," then why stop there? If we believe in genetic determinism, then we may decide to organize society in any number of ways, by sorting people into groups upon birth and labeling them for life. Why not stratify society based on genes alone, creating gene classes, and directing resources where they are predicted to help the most?

Research suggests that if we took this course of action, it would likely have mixed results for the well-being of individuals and society at large. Many experiments have found that once a person is labeled by society, they tend to modify their behaviors to match that label[25]. Hence, a child who is labeled a "troublemaker" will tend to make more trouble to fit that label, and a child who is labeled "smart" will work harder to fit that label. Why? Because we all tend to bow to social pressure and live up to—or sink down to—what is expected of us (and others unconsciously assist to realize these self-fulfilling prophecies). Therefore, due to this bias, if we were to take this route as a society and label people based on what their genes show, we would likely find people would tend to fit the labels given to them. But would we be correct to take this action?

Epigenetic Influence

Thankfully, scientists have continued to do studies before such policies could ever be implemented on a large scale. With the discovery of epigenetic effects, we understand that having a gene does not pre-determine our future. Let's take one example: the case of a person who has a brain deformity shared by many psychopaths, as well as the MAO-A gene, making him a clear case, according to genetic determinism, of someone who should be classified as a dangerous criminal. Yet this person has never killed, is not in jail, and claims to have never even considered killing anyone. This person is Dr. James Fallon, the neuroscientist that discovered the brain deformity that causes psychopathy, and author of *The Psychopath Inside*[26]. A father and husband, married to the same woman for decades, Fallon has made significant contributions to our scientific understanding of the human mind—hardly what a genetic determinist would expect from a psychopath with the warrior gene.

The Flaws in Genetic Determinism

This example is one of many that highlight the logical fallacies inherent in some genetic determinism arguments. First, just because criminals may have high rates of psychopathy and the MAO-A gene, does not mean all people with psychopathy and the MAO-A gene are criminals. Second, genes share some characteristics with scratch-off lottery tickets. If you don't have a scratch-off lottery ticket, you cannot win. However, if you do have a ticket, there is no guarantee of you winning, even if everyone playing a scratch-off ticket knows they have 1-in-4 odds that they will win something. This analogy is important as it highlights that "who we are" is not predetermined, and especially not by genes. Some things are, indeed, determined by our genes—our hair color or our height, for instance—even though growth can be stunted through childhood malnutrition and hair color is eminently changeable.

When it comes to characteristics that are measured by psychologists, things like neuroticism, extroversion, agreeableness, openness to experience, among others, the connection to genetics does not seem to be very strong. Though some twin studies suggest that genes may account for upwards of 40% of a person's personality[27], further gene studies have challenged such findings. For example, dopamine genes and oxytocin genes were expected to be the culprit into a gene-personality connection, but in fact oxytocin showed no conclusive impact on personality, while dopamine showed only a 6.6% connection[28]. When it comes to genes and personality, when you tell me that my genes are 6.6% responsible for my personality, then it seems they only play a minimal role since that would mean 93.4% of my personality is determined by other factors, including the choices we make. We have more control than we realize.

The Evidence for Change

Neuroscientists long-ago rejected the early belief that the brain is "fixed" after age 24. Since discovering neuroplasticity—the brain's ability to change and reconfigure itself—neuroscientists have been publishing papers on the brain's astonishing ability to rewire itself constantly until the moment we take our dying breath[29]. Some of the new research around brain training shows that active measures like mindfulness training can change the brain and even impact gene expression. This work is documented in Daniel Goleman and Richard Davidson's book, *Altered Traits: Science Reveals How Meditation Changes Your Mind, Brain, and Body*[30]. The authors, both psychologists, show that the parts of our personality that were once considered "stable personality characteristics"—such as neuroticism, conscientiousness, and agreeableness—were not hardwired and could be rewired with focused attention and practice. These are the exact type of traits that a genetic determinist may argue could not be changed.

So, there is strong and irrefutable evidence that your destiny is not determined by your genes, and even that your choices can alter your DNA. And there is strong and irrefutable evidence that you are capable of changing traits that were otherwise considered fixed. So, though we are born with some characteristics, our meat-suit has the ability to be molded by both our environment and conscious choices such that we are prevented from being condemned to a genetically determined fate, i.e. who you are is not fixed at birth.

Fallacy 3: Your Being Cannot Be Chosen or Changed, Only Discovered.

Hans Christian Andersen's fairy tale "The Ugly Duckling" lays a great foundation for the wrong-minded belief that a person's *being* is anything but discoverable. A homely baby bird is born to a family of ducks, who tease him for his strange appearance. He truly believes there must be something very wrong with him. After much torment, the baby bird matures into a swan, the most beautiful of all birds. Once he has recognized what he really is, thanks to the help of some adult swans, he settles in to a life of luxury, being loved and fed cakes by humans.

The key to the story is that the baby swan only finds happiness once he discovers his true self. The story's strong message is that we cannot change our *nature*, or *essence*, or *being*—we can only *discover* our true self. This fallacy is one of the most dangerous, yet one of the most widespread. Moreover, it is terribly flawed on both philosophical and scientific grounds as well as theoretically and in practice.

Philosophical Issue

If "who I am" does not change and can only be discovered, then I am condemned to wander through life inauthentically, including in my most intimate relationships. Until I discover who I am, according to "The Ugly Duckling," true happiness will evade me. As most of us will never discover who we are, or can only hope to late in life, we are destined to look back on our lives with regret and anguish because the majority of our lives would be lived both unhappily and inconsistent with who we *are*. How depressing.

Scientific Issue

Scientifically, we know this viewpoint to be very damaging. Dr. Carol Dwick calls this the "fixed mindset" and connects it to higher levels of anxiety, lower levels of life satisfaction, less positive relationships, and a lack of resilience and performance compared to those with a "growth mindset," which is the converse belief that we can change and grow our basic abilities.

The research on mindset is profound and very well established. For example, studies have shown that socio-economic background is strongly related to achievement[31]. Basically, if you are born poor, you are likely to stay poor; if you are born rich, you are likely to stay rich. If your parents went to college, you are more likely to go to college; if they didn't, then you are less likely to as well. This makes sense, and we all know it to be truer than we would like. However, we are also intrigued, inspired and tend to root for those who go beyond the life they were born into and move up the socio-economic ladder. The standard belief is that it takes hard work, determination, and some luck to move up in status. However, Carol Dwick and her colleagues were able to show a clear and compelling argument that uncovers that which causes a person to work hard and be determined so that they can take advantage of the luck that comes their way.

Dwick and colleagues had the unique chance to study 75% of the 10th graders in Chile[32]. To be clear, this is an almost unheard-of sample size. It's so close to being fully representative, it should almost not be called a "sample." It cut across all possible socio-economic groups while controlling for age to assure a clear comparison regarding achievement. Amazingly, what they discovered is that the children's mindset—in other words, what they believed about themselves and their ability to learn and develop—completely flattened the effects of socio-economic factors regarding achievement. The research found that "the belief that your basic qualities are things you can cultivate through your efforts" allowed a poor person (lowest 10%) to have the same level of academic achievement as the richest 20% of students. Wow. How powerful are our beliefs if they can modify outcomes that most people believe are determined at birth, in this case, intelligence, which manifests as academic achievement?

If 10th graders can use their beliefs to bolster their academic achievement, then imagine how easily one might modify such things as generosity, passion, excellence, and love. The science clearly shows that you are the master of both who you are and your fate.

Practical Issue

The scientific evidence is compelling, but there is also a practical aspect to this observation. Suppose we *couldn't* change who we are, then how would we be able to grow out of childhood into adults? If we were born who we *are*, then growing up would seem superfluous and impossible. If people cannot change who they are, then how can anyone have autonomy? Without the ability to change, one would be a puppet to a self that one does not yet know. We know this cannot be true as there are many stories of people making great changes: transformations that include growing up. The belief that who you are is only discovered falls apart.

Proposition: Being is a choice

Being is your essence. It is so fundamental, so prevalent that you probably do not realize that you are already always *being*. Who you are does not get shut off. As long as you are alive, you are exuding who you are in everything you do and in everything you think. The *being* that you are exuding is causing other people to have an experience of you with every interaction. The *being* that you are exuding is impacting your thoughts and intentions about your own future. But what about changing your *being*? Is choosing who you are even possible? As fundamental as being is, I contend that you can create it by choice.

In fact, you already do it. Every time you stop yourself from getting angry and reacting and tell yourself you are not going to let this person get to you, and you move forward in your own personal way, you are choosing who you are being independent of the situation. Every time you continue to push forward despite the barriers you confront, you are choosing who you are being despite the situation. Every time you stay true to who you are even when you know the consequences can be difficult, you are choosing who you are going to be despite the situation. You are a conscious moral causal agent[33] who can choose and create your being separate from your *having*—a separation which gives you control over yourself in ways that no other known thing is capable.

Hence, *being* always comes before *doing* or *having*, which is one of this book's fundamental paradigms. The next step is to codify that commitment to being and make it a personal point of reference. We will walk through this together in Part 2.

Conclusion

In this section, we have understood the dangers of the paradigm *Have-Do-Be*, and introduced a different way of looking at life: *Be-Do-Have*. We have explored what *being* is, and how it interacts with the world. We have reviewed fallacies about being, highlighting the distinction between being and values, and the misconceptions of genetic determinism. We have learned why it is incorrect to think that people cannot change. And we have set you up to understand that you can—and already do—choose who you are.

I hope this chapter has opened your mind to the possibility that we each have the ability to choose who we are and then change our lives in fundamental ways towards whatever new direction we set our sights on. Now, let's move into Part 2 where we begin making this "real".

> *"I know where I'm going and I know the truth, and I don't have to be what you want me to be. I'm free to be what I want."*
>
> —MUHAMMAD ALI

PART 2: THE PATH TO SELF-CREATION

RE-EXAMINING PAST, PRESENT AND FUTURE

"Mieux vaut une tête bien faite qu'une tête bien pleine."
("a well-formed mind is better than a well-filled one.")
—MICHEL EYQUEM DE MONTAIGNE

In order to be sure the concepts in this book are practical to implement, it is worth examining a few basic concepts that are often taken for granted or misunderstood. This way, we might avoid confusion and unnecessary internal conflict during the execution phase of *The Alignment Quotient*. After reading this part, you should be able to newly consider your world in a way that will free you from your past and give you the power to generate your future. Both of these are prerequisites to developing your Alignment Quotient. I am not telling you anything you do not have the ability to explore for yourself: these new perspectives are thought experiments designed to shift your thinking in a direction that will allow you to be successful in the journey ahead. In addition, these paradigms are all evidence-based.

The first paradigm we can reexamine is the concept of "causality," also understood as the flow of time. We are taught to look at time through the lens of a timeline in which past comes first, causing and followed by what exists in the present, and then proceeding into the future. This paradigm allows teachers to fit history into a neat and clean causal story. It takes all the craziness and chaos that is the reality of people and their lives and lines them up like so many dominos, all so our meat suit can absorb the information and regurgitate it in standardized tests. This paradigm is a very practical way of learning, though, so it ends up pervading our thinking and stays with us throughout our lifetimes. For our *experience* of life, however, this paradigm is a handicap which impedes our choices about our futures.

Our lived experience shows us that the future does not flow seamlessly from the past the same way dominoes fall one by one. As we live in the present, we have knowledge of the past. We understand that while the past impacts the experience of the present, which domino the future yields cannot be known with the same certainty. Instead, the future holds many options, some we can see and others we can't, and each with a different probability of becoming real. This makes practical sense, as most of us know the anxiety that comes with doing something unknown: like asking out that person we've had a crush on for years, or going to that impending job interview, or deciding to buy that house, or changing jobs, or any of the other big life decisions we have made or will have to make. We would love to think that we could perfectly forecast the future if only we had enough information. But this is an impossible dream, because in order to meet the goal of the "perfect" forecast (which exists in theory only) we would need *all the information in the universe, which astrophysics has shown is impossible*[34]. Thankfully, we do not need that level of knowledge to prove that this way of thinking is incorrect. We can simply look at our practical and theoretical understanding of quantum physics.

For the love of quantum weirdness

The results of physics experiments must be replicable to be of value. To make replicability possible, scientists set up dedicated hardware to run an experiment and then collect their data. Once the experiment is run by one scientist, the setup can be used by many other scientists to verify the results on their own. This replication of the results of an experiment is what makes the scientists' findings noteworthy. This is evident especially in experiments pertaining to the concept of time. Three different experiments—the double-slit experiment[35], quantum entanglement[36] with the quantum eraser[37], and the

Wheelers delayed choice experiment[38]—reveal important things about how our universe works and the role consciousness plays in our lives.

The double-slit experiment

In 1801, Thomas Young decided to shoot a beam of light at two slits in a panel. This seemingly basic experiment generated the first answers to a question that had been debated for generations: is light a wave or a particle?

As far back as 2,500 years ago, it was commonly believed that the gods bestowed humans with sight by giving eyes the ability to emit something like laser beams from them, which would in turn illuminate everything visible. Plato called this "emission theory." Then, about 1,000 years ago, Hasan Ibn al-Haytham proposed that people saw because light bounced off objects and into the eye, debunking the theory that light beams were shot out of eyes. Finally, in the 17th century, Sir Isaac Newton proposed that light was, in fact, matter that bounced off things and was perceived by a person. If light was matter, then it must be made up of little bits of things—like little balls. Young's experiment a century later complicated Newton's theory by showing that when the light was shot at the slits in the panel, the pattern produced on the target behind the screen was an interference pattern (see fig. 6).

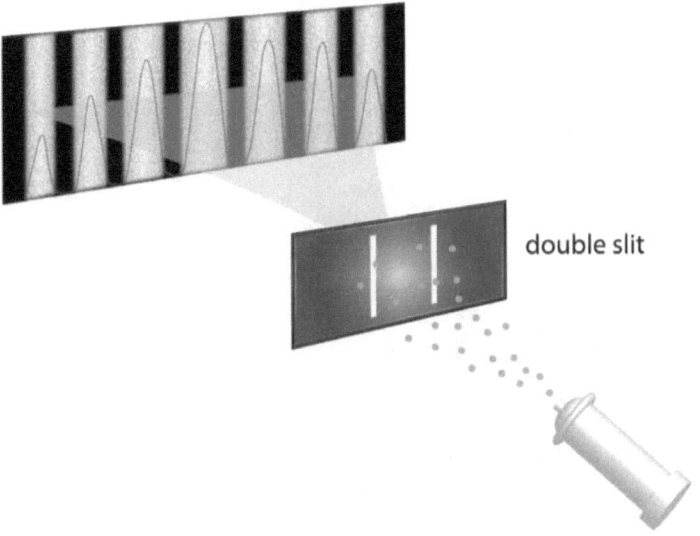

Figure 6: An interference pattern generated by light being shot at 2 slits

If light was matter—in other words, little balls—you would expect the target to show two lines, one for each slit. To illustrate this point, if a machine gun shoots a round of bullets (bits of matter) at a solid sheet of metal with two slits in it and a target behind it, you would expect most of the bullets to hit the metal. On the target behind where the slits were, however, you would expect a distinct grouping of bullet holes behind each slit. 2 slits = 2 groupings of bullets on the target. When Young did this experiment with light, he did not observe two groupings of light behind the slits, but instead many groupings—what is known as an interference pattern. This experiment showed that light was not made up of little pieces of matter, but instead acted like a wave: if a wave were to hit the two slits, it would create two waves on the target behind the panel. When the top of one of those waves combined with the top of another, they would double in size; and when the top of one wave hit the bottom of another, the waves would cancel each other out, creating multiple markings across the whole target, which we call an interference pattern (figure 7).

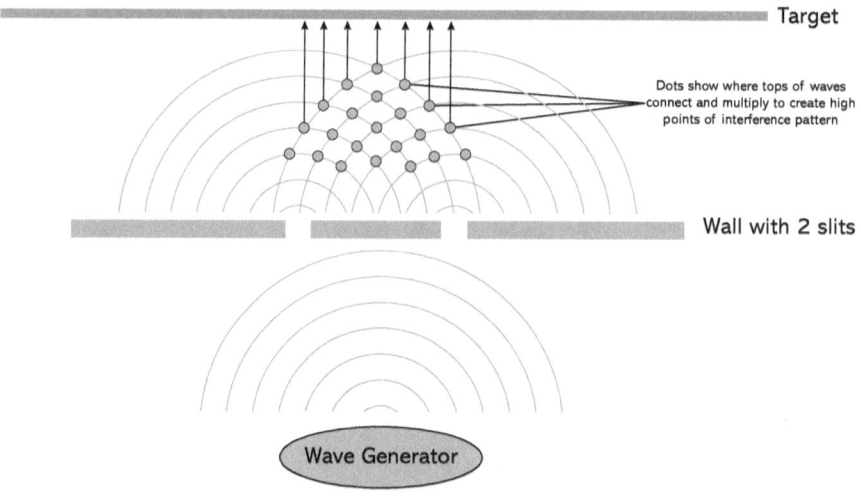

Figure 7: How a wave hitting 2 slits creates an interference pattern.

This was revolutionary: there was now direct evidence that light was a wave, not a particle. In 1961, Young's experimentation, which had only been done using photon particles, was furthered by repeating it with electrons: subatomic particles that are commonly considered to be "tiny bits of matter". In fact, it's likely that as kids in science class, you drew electrons on atoms as little orbiting dots. When the experiment was completed, the electrons also created an interference pattern, confirming that they were acting like waves, not particles. This experiment has also been successfully completed with atomic-size soccer balls composing 60 carbon atoms, and even a chain of amino acids[39]—obviously small pieces of matter and even the building blocks of life.

Skeptics in the scientific community immediately started looking for theories that would disprove this finding. In one, scientists posited that the electron was somehow going through one slit and then interfering with itself on the other side. They decided to see if they could peek at the electron before it went through the slit to understand which slit it went through, and set up a detector to see the electron's position. They ran the experiment again with this important modification, and—bam!—the target showed only two lines. The interference pattern was no longer visible. The electron had acted like a particle. Make no mistake, this is bizarre. It shows that an electron is a wave until you want to measure it, and then turns into a particle. This bizarre experiment has been reproduced many times over decades, and still amazes physicists.

Gurus the world over have appealed to this experiment in quantum physics in their discussions of the nature of reality, using it to raise questions about whether things are real unless we can observe them. This is a rabbit hole no different from the age-old question, "If a tree falls in the woods and no one hears it, does it make a sound?" If you want to test the absurdity of the idea that things don't exist until we view them, just put your laptop on an active train track in the morning, and go back the next day.

Instead of spending time contemplating the absurd, what if we accept this experiment as showing an obvious truth, not about the reality we already know, but about the reality that is soon to come: the future. What if it simply suggests that the future exists as a set of possibilities—unfixed until we observe and experience it. Even the best forecasting, then, would never be one hundred percent correct, one hundred percent of the time. No matter how much you could know about the past, you would never be able to perfectly predict the future. Determinism is dead; long live uncertainty!

Having come this far down the quantum physics rabbit hole, let's not stop here. In order to get to our main point about time, we need to briefly discuss a strange quantum phenomenon that Albert Einstein, in a personal letter written to another famous scientist, Max, Born on the 3rd of March 1948 called "spooky action at a distance."[40]

Quantum Entanglement

If you are interested in quantum computers, you may have heard of quantum entanglement. Very little is known about how this phenomenon works, only that it does and that it can be reproduced in different ways. That it works at all is strange, as it seems to contradict physics as we know it. What *is* clear is that quantum entanglement is critical to the functioning of quantum computers like IBM's 20-qubit quantum computer that anyone can learn to program.[41]

Entanglement is a "bizarre and counterintuitive phenomenon" in which the quantum state of one particle cannot be described independently of the other. Moreover, if one particle's quantum state is changed, the other particle's quantum state is also changed—*instantly*—no matter how far away those two particles are from one another. The current record for the distance measured between human-generated entangled particles is about 1200 kilometers (about 750 miles)[42]. Because the changes happen immediately, the interaction seems to break the rule that information between objects travels at the speed of light, and no faster, which is why Einstein called it "spooky".

This would be like having twin children who lived perfectly synchronized lives. In these conditions, a parent could take one twin on a business trip to Tokyo while leaving the other in Detroit, and by observing the one in Tokyo, they would know exactly what the twin in Detroit was doing in that instant. Conversely, the parent would have to hope the twin in Detroit was not jumping on a trampoline while they were on the airplane to Tokyo.

But entanglement's most important distinction is that it allows scientists to measure one of the entangled particles and gather information about the other without observing it directly. This distinction introduces questions about our whole way of looking at time and causality.

Future First?

Scientists understood from the double-slit experiment that a particle could not be measured without causing the probability wave to collapse, forcing the particle to act like matter. Curious by nature, they decided to set up an experiment using entangled particles, whereby one particle would go through the double-slit and the other could be measured. By measuring these entangled twins, those sneaky scientists were looking to hack the quantum system—to see if they could come up with a back-door method to measure the particles without collapsing the wave.

Experiment #1

First, they wanted to reproduce the double-slit experiment and send one of the entangled particles towards the double-slit, and the other to a special setup with a semi-transparent mirror. The idea was to make the semi-transparent mirror such that about half of the particles would go into a detector where they could be measured, and the other half would bounce off and go into oblivion where they could not be measured. Unsurprisingly, when they measured the entangled twin, its sister particle reached the target and acted like a tiny bit of matter, but when they did not measure the entangled twin, the sister particle reached the target as a wave and produced an interference pattern. The backdoor the scientists had hoped to open now seemed closed. This was an important discovery, however, allowing scientists to create entangled twins and then prove their connection. They pushed further—and this is where it gets strange.

Experiment #2

Scientists wondered: what if they allowed the first particle to go through the double-slit and hit the target, and then—only after it made impact—measured its entangled twin? The scientists used an experimental setup which allowed them to measure all the particles and randomly "lose" the measurement information on about half of the particles. All measurements would occur only *after* the sister particle had already gone through the double-slit and hit the target. The results were baffling. If the entangled photon was measured afterwards and the information about which slit it went through was retained, the first photon had already hit the target as a tiny bit of matter, not a wave. But if the entangled particles' measurement was "erased," the particle was observed to have hit the target as a wave, generating an interference pattern. It is as if the first particle was already aware of the future of its entangled partner. To be clear, this is totally bizarre. It means that, from the perspective of the scientists, an event that was to happen in the future had an observed effect on the past.

An unavoidable conclusion of this experiment is that the future may, somehow, in some strange way, affect the past. For the purpose of this discussion, this suggests that the prevailing paradigm that the past always *precedes* the future is flawed. It also suggests that the future may have the ability to *cause* the past.

Opening up New Possibilities: Freedom in Uncertainty

These two paradigms may seem to fundamentally conflict with each other, but with careful consideration, it is clear they do not. The first paradigm, illustrated by the outcome of the double-slit experiment, suggests that the future is fundamentally uncertain until we arrive there and view it. This should be comforting—it means our futures are not pre-destined. The second paradigm, illustrated by the twin-particle experiments, should also be empowering as it suggests that we can play a creative role in our as yet undefined future. Sure, there are some probabilities that change instant by instant based on the last choice we made, which can be limiting, but overall, it means our approach to our future can be more like that of a sculptor carving stone to unveil our masterwork. The stone's final form is not determined: the sculptor has a vision and carves in pursuit of that vision. Each chisel does not remove a piece of stone exactly as the sculptor intended due to the fundamental uncertainty involved in the interaction between the sculptor's hand, the tool, and the stone. Yet every stroke creates a limitation for the strokes that will follow. This suggests that neither fatalism nor determinism rule our lives; instead, our vision, intentions and action—in other words, our free will—have an outsized influence on our life's outcomes. We have both power and responsibility that can be harnessed. Or, in William Ernest Henley's words in the well-known poem, "Invictus," "I am the master of my fate, /I am the captain of my soul."

Adopting this new paradigm opens up possibilities. The "future first" paradigm is not the only way to look at time, but it does bring new awareness—awareness that makes our perception of time complement our experience of living in the world.

I say "awareness" because this idea should not seem foreign or radical. When we are young, we declare our intentions: to go to college, to get married, to move to a new city. It is those declarations that determine our future before it exists; we start living *into* them until that declared future manifests, or doesn't. As young people, we brazenly declare many things about our futures. Then, we retrospectively find ourselves surprised at what we had been able to accomplish having realized we had no idea at the time of declaration what we were getting ourselves into. Some declarations are realized and others go unrealized: maybe we were going to rule the world, or be independently wealthy at 30, or eliminate world hunger. It is natural for conscious causal agents, like ourselves, to make any declarations we choose, regardless of whether they end up being realized and free from whatever is in our past.

History hinges on conceptions of the past. Yet there are many examples of leaders who envisioned the future not from the perspective of previous events, but with an eye to possibility for the world we live in. For example, take the U.S. Declaration of Independence:

> *We hold these truths to be self-evident, that all men are created equal, that they are endowed by their Creator with certain unalienable Rights, that among these are Life, Liberty and the pursuit of Happiness. That to secure these rights, Governments are instituted among Men, deriving their just powers from the consent of the governed*
>
> —PREAMBLE TO THE DECLARATION OF INDEPENDENCE

In 1775, at the time Constitutional Congress met in Philadelphia to draft the Declaration of Independence, no such country existed: not in concept, practice, and scale. The United States was considered a great experiment. Even King George III of England, who had "allowed" the American colonies their independence, worried that the U.S. might suffer from the lack of a monarchy. It was new, something that had never really existed before, hence it could not come from the past, though obviously there were past events that set the stage and allowed for the declaration of the future creation of the U.S. to be possible. That future was guaranteed not by the past, but by the integrity of the people in their execution of that declaration.

Another example comes from the speech given by John F. Kennedy on May 25, 1961, declaring:

> *"I believe that this nation should commit itself to achieving the goal, before this decade is out, of landing a man on the moon and returning him safely to the Earth."*

Again, no one had ever done anything like this, and when Kennedy gave this speech no one really knew how it could be done. In fact, when NASA was given the mandate, they didn't even know what type of staff they would need, what building they would use, or what technologies might be involved. Again, it was the declaration of the future that came first, the vision that was to be manifest, a future that a whole country began to live as though it would certainly happen. History was made future first.

The Power of Declarations

We can find an endless number of examples throughout history in which the paradigm that future came first is evident. This paradigm can be difficult to accept, as we are also aware of the failures of declarations: things that did *not* happen due to unforeseen or contradictory circumstances, or because there existed competing declarations and only one could become the future.

I don't claim that the future first paradigm allows you to simply declare an intention for something into a complete void, and that it is then going to create a future where that declaration magically manifests itself. You are not the only conscious causal agent in the world, so your declarations may be competing with others. And there are also other processes happening, like earthquakes and random illnesses, which are among billions of other things out of your direct control.

This paradigm only serves to give you access to a new way of looking at time that can open you up to possibilities within yourself and your life. These possibilities will open doors to autonomy where you see none, security where there is none, esteem that is not provisional, and most importantly: a growth mindset. Science shows the growth mindset to be one of the healthiest mindsets that a person can have across various spheres of life: personal health, career, and relationship.

I use the word "declaration" to articulate the critical tool we can use to take advantage of the future first paradigm. What is a declaration?

The dictionary defines a declaration as[43]:

"a formal or explicit statement or announcement of the beginning of a state or condition or intent to act."

A declaration is one of those simple, overused, and underappreciated terms that I talked about in the introduction of this book. Because declarations are exactly what we use to create our future, when we look at their role in relation to the future first paradigm, their importance takes on near mythical proportions.

Humans are unique in that we can declare a future for ourselves that is somewhat independent of simple causal outcomes. In other words, we are moral agents able to discern and guide next steps in our lives rather than simply causal agents who are a mere part of a chain reaction. While we *can* choose to ride the wave of time like a feather on a gust of wind, we also have power to mold the future into our own creation.

So much of what we do starts with a declaration, whether it be a vacation, a surprise party, or building a new business unit. A declaration can be as basic as "I am going to bed," or as profound as a declaration to put the first man on Mars or free an entire citizenry from tyranny. What all declarations have in common to be effective is one contingency: You must use your declaration as a tool to align your thoughts, behaviors, and actions in order to bring it into existence. This should be common sense, but as we all know, common sense is not necessarily so common. And though this contingency seems simple, it is anything but as we will discover in part 3.

The Power of Declaration and Alignment

You may be thinking, "This is all good and well, but what's the big deal?" The "big deal" is your life. You already use declarations, but probably not to set you on a path of living a life you love. Chances are, you are instead allowing self-limiting beliefs to rule your life, so you fall into a trap you will find difficult to extricate yourself from. The arrow of time keeps pushing you into the future whether you like it or not. Each day you do not grab the reins of your life, declare a future, and then live into that declaration is not only time lost, but time to build up regret for who you could have been, but did not become.

In her book *Regrets of the Dying*, Bonnie Ware[44], who worked in end of life care for many years, writes that the number one regret for people who are facing death is not having had the courage to *be* oneself. At the end of life, many people realize how much power they gave up by letting other people, or situations, or their own fears and biases dictate who they are—and ceding this control also dictated what they did. What a pity to discover that you lived other people's lives, other people's dreams, and other people's expectations instead of your own, only to regret it when there is no time left to change, no time left to explore, no time to realize the full expression of yourself.

Thankfully, if you are reading this book, you have learned that you do have a choice, and now is the time to declare and begin living fully self-expressed through alignment with your declaration. With that in mind, let's uncover the most important tool in your journey to living a life you love, your declaration of self and purpose: Your Alignment Commitment.

The Alignment Commitment: Declaring Your Being

The Alignment Commitment is necessary for developing our Alignment Quotient. This is the first and most critical step towards alignment. And it starts with the simple and fundamental act of creating a declaration of being. The declaration is striking in its simplicity: "I *am* [insert your *being* here]." Remember, being is the foundation of alignment and the first layer in our model—the part we have the most choice and control over. But this format is also very practical. But before we get into that, let's establish some rules and procedures for conceptualizing a declaration.

The language you choose for your declaration is critical. You may wonder what types of words are appropriate for the "I am" statement. Which words will keep you from falling into the *Have-Do-Be* trap? Which will prioritize *being*? How do you write your declaration in a way that allows you to live your future first? Knowing how challenging this decision may feel, I have outlined two "techniques" to guide you to your answer. I have also included a dictionary of 35 of the most commonly used *being* words to inspire you.

What kinds of words do I use?

In order to describe our *being*, it is best to use a noun. Yes, that part of speech that describes "a person, place, or thing"—a fact we have had seared into our minds since grade school. The reason for this guideline is to make a clear distinction between what I *am* versus how I am seen and labeled by others, by the world around me. That description would be made using an adjective: the part of speech that serves as a modifier. Our *being* cannot be modified. Of course, there is nothing saying that how I *am* and how I *am seen* by others cannot be in alignment, but this declaration will benefit us most when there is an apparent *misalignment* between who we are and how others see us; when we can say, *I am wrongly described by the world.*

There will be times in your life where others describe you in ways consistent with who you are. My grandmother was a good example of this: she was a generous person who cared for her family and participated fully in her church community. She lived life abundantly and was, by all accounts, seen by the world for what she was: a good person.

But the alignment between *who* my grandmother was and others' assessment of her is not universal. Many of us have faced times when our intentions were misjudged, misunderstood, or recast as something they were not. During these times, being clear and maintaining integrity over your declared being is critical, as the story of Ignaz Semmelweis shows[45].

Dr. Semmelweis was a Hungarian physician working at Vienna General Hospital in 1847. Like all doctors, Semmelweis took the Hippocratic Oath[46] to "use treatment to help the sick according to my ability and judgment, but never with a view to injury and wrong-doing." In Vienna General's obstetrics ward at the time, pregnant women were inexplicably dying from puerperal fever (commonly known as "childbed fever") at rates 5 times higher than at a similar hospital next door. Following years of research and investigation, he was able to definitively show that the simple act of washing hands with a chlorinated lime solution (what we call a disinfectant today) reduced the rates of death by more than 90%. He was also one of the first physicians to isolate sick patients to prevent disease spreading by "little particles traveling in the air." These were revolutionary ideas at the time, and he had clear evidence that they worked. In maintaining integrity with his oath, he was compelled to share his discoveries with other doctors.

To say that Semmelweis' news was not welcomed by his fellow physicians is an understatement. Seeing his ideas as an indictment of themselves, Semmelweis' colleagues thought he was blaming them for their patients' puerperal fever. They rejected and ridiculed both his ideas and him as being the height of insanity, and in 1865 his wife had him committed to an asylum where he died two weeks later. While germ theory was developed by Louis Pasteur by the early 1860s, it would not be widely accepted until after Semmelweis' death.

Of Semmelweis, Sir William Sinclair (1909) wrote: "Many men have been endowed with clear intellects and hearts full of love for their fellow men, with the enthusiasm of humanity, and they have been enabled to achieve some signal service for the human race in their day and generation; but in the whole history of medicine there is only one Semmelweis in the magnitude of his services to Mankind, and in the depth of his sufferings from contemporary jealous stupidity and ingratitude."

Despite the personal cost of Semmelweis' monumental discoveries, he knew who he was, and he maintained integrity with his commitment and himself until the end of his life. These are the times that our declarations are critical to us. Sometimes, those around us are trapped in a paradigm that makes them unable to see us for who we truly are, unable to see that our actions are coming from a place that is closer to love than hate. We have all had these experiences, whether it was trying to help a friend escape an abusive relationship, an act of generosity that was misconstrued as a greedy search for power, or even an act of honesty meant to edify.

You may ask why I am using an example as extreme as Semmelweis' experience. The reason is that the integrity associated with your Alignment Commitment is not just about surviving—it's about living a life you love while minimizing regret. If you simply want to survive, just listen to your meat suit: it's designed to ensure survival. But if you want to thrive and minimize your regrets in life, you need to go beyond the programming of this meat-based survival suit towards something greater in nature: your choice of who to *be*, independent of anything you *have*. Your Alignment Commitment may, at times, put you in conflict with the intimate relationships in your life, your professional colleagues, or even society at large. It is in these times, when how other people describe us is incongruent with who we have defined ourselves to be, that having a noun in our "I am" declaration becomes useful. It is useful because others will tend to throw adjectives at us in an attempt to define who we are. Knowing that those adjectives are descriptors of other people's perception, based on all of their biases, gives our brain a logical method of flipping the script, putting these descriptions into their own box, and keeping that box separate from the noun chosen to declare who I *am*. It's nothing more than a mental trick to help your brain maintain independence between others' descriptions of you, and your declaration.

The time-benefit of using a noun

The human meat brain is very good at not changing. Any excuse to put off until tomorrow what can be done today usually works. When it comes to our being, using a noun in the declaration is another trick to coerce the brain to stop resisting your will. If you describe yourself as an adjective, then you give your brain lots of ammunition for avoiding implementation. Adjectives are descriptors that are assigned based on past behaviors, but applied in the present. You cannot declare your past, and you cannot declare, independent of the past, a description of who you are. So, if you declare *I am excellent*, but you know that yesterday you sat on the couch and wasted the whole day watching stupid YouTube videos, your brain then says, "Well, I am obviously not excellent, so Mr. or Ms. Consciousness, your claim is all a sham, you can't fool me!" Then your brain gives up and motivation dies.

When you begin with a noun, time is not as critical. A knife in your kitchen was a knife yesterday, is a knife right now, and will likely be a knife tomorrow. It may not have been sharp yesterday, but I can sharpen it today and it will be sharp tomorrow. Either way, it will still be a knife. When I declare "I am *excellence*," rather than "I am excellent," yesterday does not matter. Only right now matters. My declaration is refreshed each time I declare it. My meat suit may have been on autopilot for a period of time, but when "I" wake up and take the reins, I can immediately align myself in the direction of my declaration.

Whenever the brain or society is an impediment to you, the noun form of the word you choose for your *being* is particularly helpful. These times include when you are rightly described by the world based on your past behaviors but are initiating change (Changing Reputation), or if you are being held back by your own past behaviors but want to move forward differently (Personal Redemption). In these cases, the noun form along with what I explained above can help you through the process of realigning your meat suit.

"Being" as a noun

Here are some examples of a few nouns presented with their adjective forms. Note the difference:

Noun	Adjective	Noun	Adjective
Passion	Passionate	Creativity	Creative
Inspiration	Inspiring	Adventure	Adventurous
Excellence	Excellent	Compassion	Compassionate
Curiosity	Curious	Love	Loving
Freedom	Free	Persistence	Persistent
Generosity	Generous	Reliability	Reliable
Joy	Joyful	Self-Expression	Self-Expressed

I have also included a list of 35 "being" nouns and their definitions in the appendix, along with an interpretation of each noun in its "being" form. Here are several examples:

1. Passion: One who can generate powerful or compelling emotions or feelings.
   Being Passionate: A way of being that can generate directional energy (towards or away) that goes beyond purpose, stays unreasonable, and requires no justification.

2. Enthusiasm: Intense and eager excitement, enjoyment and approval; something that inspires zeal or fervor.
   Being Enthusiastic: A way of Being that supports one's own eagerness in pursuit of a passion and an intensity of purpose and direction.

3. Love: Feeling of strong or constant regard for and dedication to someone or something.
   Being Loving: A way of Being that takes a stand for and is dedicated to others' experience of life, including the experience of peace, love, joy, and freedom.

4. Excellence: The quality of being outstanding or extremely good. The fact or state of excelling; superiority; eminence.
   Being Excellent: A way of Being that propels one to a level of mastery, to accomplish one's task for every reason possible, not just the perceived reasons as stated by others.

I have devised two paths for you to declare your being. Both are equally valuable; however, I expect that many people will find the second path more difficult to follow. You may be tempted to say, "I'll read this now but not do it until later because this declaration is so important to me." This instinct has both right and wrong origins. Right, in that the declaration is important to you, and wrong, because that does not mean you should do it later. Don't wait to declare your being. I don't recommend reflecting on it all that much either. A solid hour is likely to work for most, but you can probably do it in as few as five minutes. The goal is not to be perfect. Don't let the search for perfection prevent you from moving through your life in your own powerfully chosen direction. Never forget that you are already moving through life, so every minute you are not doing this consciously is lost.

The role of role models

> *"When you see a role model, what you see is a person who has the courage to be who you wish you could be. Stop wishing and just be."*
> —ANONYMOUS

When thinking of role models, we tend to think about their behaviors. What they have done makes us respect them. Nelson Mandela was a freedom fighter against overwhelming government repression; Mother Teresa was unstoppable in her fight to help the poor; my grandmother was always dependable and willing to help. While they inspire us as role models based on their "Doing"—because observed behaviors and outcomes are what we can see—in the end, it is *who* they were that inspires us.

It's not the doing

> *"I have a dream that my four little children will one day live in a nation where they will not be judged by the color of their skin but by the content of their character."*
>
> —MARTIN LUTHER KING, JR.

Though Martin Luther King, Jr., is a role model for many, few, if any, would go back in time and experience the pain and suffering he went through. Those who would want to live his life would only do so if they were guaranteed knowledge of his myriad achievements. But time does not work that way. If you are going to relive a life, you must do it without knowing if the outcome will include your success, or conversely, your being forgotten after having accomplished nothing. When we desire to relive a famous or successful person's life through their doing or having, it is more about removing the uncertainty that comes with not knowing the outcome of our own path. It is a satisfaction akin to the fun a person has when buying a lottery ticket and dreaming about all the things they would do and buy if they won. Though those fantasies are fun, once the daydream is over, we have a real life to live. Though the *doing* or *having* may be the inspiration for choosing any particular person as a role model, it is the *being* we are seeking.

It's all about the being

When we choose a role model, it is because we want to emulate their lives—we want to *be* MLK-like. We want to embody the spirit of the person: who they *are*, their *being*. We seek this alignment with the being of role models so we can use it to estimate the behaviors they would take in a given situation that we face. Our interpretation of their actions, all their behaviors, from the situations that they might face to the way they carry themselves, the words they speak or do not speak, and the decisions they make in their own life, inspires our choices about who we will be.

Role models align what they do with who they are (Be-Do-Have). Their behaviors flow from this unseen being, and that alignment resonates for those observing them. When someone seems comfortable and confident in their own skin, we call this charisma—they exude who they are. Alignment of action with being inspires.

The Latin root of "inspire" is *inspirare:* "to breathe or blow into." [47] Today, the word has several meanings, one of which is "to give rise to, cause to be, bring about, beget." [48]. This is exactly what role models do to us: they give rise to a particular type or flavor of "being" in others, acting as a valuable tool while doing so. Choosing a suitable role model is a key element in the first technique for creating your declaration of being inside of your Alignment Commitment.

Research and Writing Break

Name three people you hold in high respect, and who you hope to emulate in your life.

1. _____

2. _____

3. _____

Now write down what each of the people you identified above have *done* that is inspiring. Take care not to focus on what they *have*. You can write as much or as little as you like. Enjoy the process and describe the inspiring actions as clearly as you need to for yourself. If you do not know the person well, you may decide to interview them if they are alive, or talk with people who knew them or read about them if they are not.

When you have finished writing about each one, see if you can come up with 2-5 *being* words that you could reverse engineer from their observed behaviors and how those behaviors made you feel (your experience of those behaviors). Feel free to use the dictionary of *being* words in the appendix to support this process if you are having trouble.

Person 1:	Person 2:	Person 3:
1. _____	1. _____	1. _____
2. _____	2. _____	2. _____
3. _____	3. _____	3. _____
4. _____	4. _____	4. _____
5. _____	5. _____	5. _____

Now you have a solid list of *being* words that can serve as a place to start for your own declaration. You may wish to circle words that show up for more than one role model; where there are consistencies between role models you may find a being that inspires you.

We will leave these words alone for now and come back to them later. The next important part of your search will start with *you*.

Using impermanence as a brainstorming tool

In the next part of this journey, you will look at your own life from a somber vantage point—your own funeral. I recognize that this type of exercise can make some people deeply uncomfortable. In response, I paraphrase the words of Elisabeth Kübler-Ross, author of *On Death and Dying*:

> *It is the denial of death that is partially responsible for people living their life as a reaction to the situations around them; for when you live as if you'll live forever, it becomes too easy to postpone being who you know you must become.*[49]

With this in mind, imagine you are able to be at your own funeral. At the ceremony, someone comes up with the idea to describe you with only a few simple words. The two people who are closest to you start. They can be family, including spouses (current and past) and children, but should not be your parents or grandparents because they have special biases and are usually not part of your social tribe per se. They can also come from your community of friends and colleagues. They need only to be people who appreciate you. What would they say using a maximum of three adjectives? Would they use the same words as one another? Would other people close to you also choose those words to describe you?

Person 1:

1. _____

2. _____

3. _____

Person 2:

1. _____

2. _____

3. _____

When you look around at the people in attendance, you notice some people who have always been critical of you sitting in the audience. These are people who do not necessarily appreciate you, but want to show their respects. Select two of them to also describe you in three words. They'll be honest, giving you credit where it is due, from their perspective. What would their words be? When you are writing this next group of answers, do not consider anything from the last question. Think about it independently, on its own.

Honest Critic 1:

1. _____

2. _____

3. _____

Honest Critic 2:

1. _____

2. _____

3. _____

Bringing it home

Ok, you now have three lists of descriptive words: one describing your role models, a second from people who love you, and a third from your critics. Consolidate them in the lines below and remove any duplicates. If you see an opportunity, feel free to combine two similar words into one new word that may better encompass both. You may wish to check out the list of *being* words in the appendix to help you consolidate words. This is a good time to start moving your description words (adjectives) to *being* words (nouns).

_____

_____

_____

_____

_____

Now, choosing from the words above, list the characteristics that you feel you already clearly *are* in your life.

_____

_____

_____

_____

_____

Then, choosing from the same set of words, list the characteristics that you feel you fall short of being, or are disappointed in yourself for *not* being.

_____

_____

_____

_____

_____

Now select the top 5 words from each of the last two lists and rank them. You may choose to rank them based on how many times those words showed up in your descriptions of your role models, consistency between what people who both appreciate you and critics would say about you at your funeral, your own affinity to the word which causes you to be inspired or committed to it, or any combination of those options. *These are your lists.* Just ensure that number 1 is your top choice for each, number 2 is your second choice, and so on. You may also choose to consolidate similar words. All words on this list should be nouns.

<table>
<tr><td>I Already Am:</td><td>I Desire to Be:</td></tr>
<tr><td>1._____</td><td>1._____</td></tr>
<tr><td>2._____</td><td>2._____</td></tr>
<tr><td>3._____</td><td>3._____</td></tr>
<tr><td>4._____</td><td>4._____</td></tr>
<tr><td>5._____</td><td>5._____</td></tr>
</table>

You should now have a list of *being* words that motivate and inspire you. The ultimate goal is for you to include in your declaration only the *being* words to which you are willing to commit. It is recommended that you add words cautiously, starting with 1-3 words, because each word will require significant effort as you use it to make changes to your automated meat-based survival suit, as we will discover later.

I am _____, _____, and

_____.

Speaking of your meat-based survival suit, this path was developed as a practical way to get you to commit to a statement of being. If you are a purist, you've probably noted that this process begins with a *having*: I *have* a role model, I *have* an opinion about my role models, I *have* friends and critics who have opinions. This is correct. And for the purist, there is a second path to take.

The Being Salad

Breaking the paradigm that causes us to *search* for our being (which necessitates it comes from our past somehow, or is going to be given to us from something that happens outside ourselves) is difficult to do. We can get too caught up in figuring out our being.

You are already always being. Hence, while you are waiting for the perfect day and time for *who you want to be* to magically unveil itself (good luck with that), you are moving through life as someone who you did not choose to be. Instead, your meat suit is deciding who you are, just like it always has, and is delaying your ability to be the master of yourself. The next technique goes around this limitation and is a powerful way to declare yourself independent from any biases you may have.

The Being Salad is simple: take a piece of paper and cut it into 35 small pieces. Go to the appendix and choose one word to write on each piece of paper. When you are finished, fold the slips in half, put them into a container of some sort, and then randomly pick between 1 and 3. Whatever is on the pieces of paper you pick out of the bucket is who you commit to *be* for the next period of time. You decide the timeframe to commit to these beings. In my experience, the minimum timeframe in which to elicit interesting results is about two weeks.

This exercise is meant to have the following results:

1. You get a chance to discover new ways of being.

2. You will discover the many different biases of your meat suit, biases that prevent you from being who you declared.

3. You will get to practice being, so when you ultimately choose your permanent beings, you will have practical experience in "being."

    I am _____, _____, and

    _____.

Congratulations! You have completed the first section of the Alignment Commitment: you have declared your*self*. We will explore the implications of this declaration in Part 3: Mountains and Bogeymen. In that section, you will learn how to use your declaration of being as a tool to maintain integrity with yourself. We will also review the types of issues you can expect to encounter once you start using your declaration of being in your everyday life. The second part of the Alignment Commitment, addressed below, is the creation of your Purpose.

Creating your Purpose

"He who has a why to live for can bear almost any how."
—FRIEDRICH NIETZSCHE

Now that you have completed the first part of the Alignment Commitment—the "being"—you must now add the "why", which is the purpose portion of your commitment. It is this purpose that directs your resources (time, energy, money) in one direction rather than another. Declaring your being is relatively easy, even if implementing your being can be difficult; whereas, the purpose part is the hardest to determine. It is also the portion of the Alignment Commitment that research has shown to have the most impact on health and well-being.

Why do you need a why?

Basically, your purpose statement—which we describe with "so that" statements—is your *why* for getting up in the morning. Research shows we have a non-conscious need to have a reason to do things[50]. Basically, the brain loves to ask and have answered the question "Why?". Though we know the answer to this question is important to us as human beings, we don't know why the *why* is so important. How do we know the answer to the question *why* is so important? Because of the benefits we have observed from decades of research.

As far back as 50 years ago, scientists have observed the positive benefits of having purpose and meaning. Research has shown people with purpose having higher life satisfaction scores[51], and older people who reported a higher sense of purpose had lower levels of the stress hormone cortisol in their systems[52], a lower chance of becoming disabled[53] or getting Alzheimer's disease[54], and better social connections. It was unclear, though, if purpose arose from having things like better social connections, instead of the other way around. In other words, if you have low stress, high life satisfaction, or good social connections, would your purpose be somehow revealed to you, or at least give you a higher sense of purpose because you already have these things. In science, they call this type of evidence *correlation*, which is different from *causation*. While the research from 50 years ago showed these things were associated, they did not say which caused the other or if maybe something else—some other factor not measured—caused both of them. Scientists ran a new experiment in which they looked at people who were all suffering from either breast cancer or colorectal cancer[55]. Randomly dividing them into two groups, one group received standard cancer treatments while the other received the standard cancer treatment plus specific training in finding purpose/meaning in their lives. The latter is known as MMI (Meaning Making Intervention).

The study group was chosen specifically because of their life-threatening diagnosis, which obviously caused psychological distress. This psychological distress is associated with reduced self-esteem and sense of self-efficacy (belief in control over one's own destiny). This experiment removed the possibility that purpose and meaning are the result of having a better life situation to start with. Would adding meaning and purpose to the patients' lives make a difference? Would it improve self-esteem and/or self-efficacy? Surprisingly, the group who went through the MMI program showed increases in both self-esteem and self-efficacy.

Interestingly, the patients who took the MMI program were far more likely to seek out support compared to the control group, which also could have helped their overall improvement. Hands down, this showed that having your own "why" makes a difference. It suggests that having a "so that" in your life significantly impacts your health and well-being. Hence, there are clear benefits to creating a purpose that adds meaning to your life—i.e., a purpose and meaning to life mattered. One point for purpose in life!

Now that we know how important your "so that" is, let's define it and make clear what we are talking about:

Purpose (your "so that"): a stable and generalized intention to accomplish something that is at once personally meaningful and at the same time leads to productive engagement with some aspect of the world beyond the self.[56]

Developing your "so that" statement

> "Ultimately, man should not ask what the meaning of his life is, but rather must recognize that it is he who is asked. In a word, each man is questioned by life; and he can only answer to life by answering for his own life; to life he can only respond by being responsible."
>
> —VIKTOR FRANKL

The "so that" portion of your statement needs to be personal and personally-motivating. Though your "so that" may change throughout your life, I hope to support you in finding something that will not only capture the essence of your life, but will endure. I call this a "SPICY Purpose," where SPICY stands for Stable, Personally Meaningful, Inspirational, Communal, and Y (Why).

Creating a SPICY Purpose

Stable

Writing a purpose statement should not be a project made up of countless individual, smaller steps. It should be a single stable intention for one's life. It is counterproductive to make your "so that" specific, or immediately measurable, or timebound. The "so that" is like a sailor who sets a course in a general direction (e.g., "northerly"), rather than an alternate direction like "easterly" or "westerly." Moving in a stable general direction, you can adapt based on the situations you face without needing to change your course. Stability of your purpose is important for building a life you love.

As you move through life according to your Alignment Commitment, you will build relationships and apply yourself to developing certain skills, which take time and energy. You will have successes and failures, and each will add to your experience, allowing you to develop some level of mastery, some reputation, or some movement towards making your mark on the world. In fact, if you are reading this book, chances are that you have already developed some of these things (reputation, relationships, and some level of mastery over something).

Research shows that we prefer to do things that we are good at, and for most of us our meat suit hates change, so creating a purpose statement that is stable will speak to our meat suit. But this can be both a benefit and a prison depending on your perspective.

Benefits of Stability

We love to do things that we are good at. I have an aunt who is a nurse and even when she is exhausted by her job, she is always happy to field health questions. Her mastery of a particular skillset through knowledge and experience allows her to provide a recognizable value to those she loves, and that makes her feel good. It provides purpose in her life. Furthermore, that same career experience has provided her with memories, friends, and life stories that make up her history, a history she is proud of. But all stability does not lead to these feelings of satisfaction, and even this type of stability can have a downside.

Prison of Stability

When we are young, we may not have mastery over our meat suit, and this can lead us to make decisions based on survival. I know many people who have taken life paths based on parental pressure, financial fear, or societal dogma. These paths often have the benefits of stability, but can also lead to us waking up one day and realizing we are living someone else's life—or are just tired or bored. We are no longer on a path that an independent self would continue to choose, but we no longer feel able to make an independent choice—too much is dependent upon our continuing on this stable path. Sometimes this shows up as a midlife or quarter-life crisis; sometimes we say someone has golden handcuffs; and at other times retirement rolls around and the purpose-built life we were leading is simply gone. Stability becomes a trap that prevents living a life we love and opens us up to regrets.

The Flaw in this Story

I used to have a wonderful doctor that I really appreciated. I would literally travel halfway around the world to have my annual physical with him instead of finding a new doctor closer to where I lived. One day, he informed me he would be changing jobs and that I needed to find a new doctor. He had had enough of being a primary care doctor who helped one person at a time. He decided he wanted to develop software to help doctors better manage their patient care. He felt he could make a much bigger impact by making a change. This change did not affect his underlying "so that": the desire to improve people's lives. He would continue doing so, just in a very different way.

This story underlines how your purpose statement needs to be more than a project, a title, or career path. Asking a "why" such that your "so that" is general enough to be stable in your life will ensure you are able to move forward and keep your life SPICY—independent of your feelings towards, or what happens with any particular project.

Personally Meaningful

Meaning is just one condition of having purpose in life. Meaning and purpose are not synonymous. You can find meaning in watching the sun rise, but you are unlikely to find purpose in it. A SPICY purpose statement will be personally meaningful. Or maybe it will be your meaning that will trigger the purpose. Later, I will present a path for you to choose a "so that" statement that will originate from the places in your life to which you are already applying meaning. But before we do that, let's consider what is meant by personally meaningful.

As much as our being can be created independent of our meat suit and its history, our "so that" is created based on meanings that are generated based on our meat suit, its knowledge and history. It is the purpose part of our declaration that recognizes and honors the connection between our consciousness and our physical world—including our meat suit.

That being said, there is a difference between something that is personally meaningful to you, and something that has meaning based on what your parents, social groups, cultural heritage, or education have instilled in you. You will find that lots of things have meaning to you. And the things that have meaning due to your parents or your cultural upbringing may also have meaning for you personally, but not necessarily. Also, though lots of things will have meaning for you, your method of prioritizing those things with meaning may not be aligned with your own personal preferences. So, in order to make your purpose statement SPICY, you need to evaluate the things in your life that have meaning and sort out the ones that have the most personal meaning to you, and then prioritize them based on your own personal preference. Read on to discover two examples two examples of what is meant by personally meaningful.

I am originally from a suburb of Detroit—Motor City! It used to be that if you lived in or near Detroit and wanted financial security, you worked in the automotive industry that gives that city its reputation. Both my grandfathers, my father, and most of my aunts and uncles work or worked for automotive companies. Based on this shared history, nearly all of my family members value things such as which car you drive (always a GM, Ford, or Chrysler), where and what your job is (i.e., at which automaker or supplier), and how much influence you wield in the auto industry. Job security is also important, and success is measured by the size of your home, whether you have a vacation home on a lake, the number of "toys" parked in your garage, and the schools your children attend. This construct of meaning created by that particular social structure tends to dictate most people's path in life. But I know two men who are different.

Many jobs in Detroit are still found based on who you know. Since the whole family was in the automotive industry, my Uncle Pete had a golden ticket into a big automotive company in the 1970s. But the life this career path offered did not align with his own life priorities, nor did it provide the type of meaning he wanted to create for himself. For him, doing physical work outdoors with the sun on his face, having the flexibility to spend time with his kids, and controlling his destiny gave him more meaning than anything he could do at a big company. So, in spite of all the social and family pressure to play the game everyone else was playing, my Uncle Pete set out on his own to create and run a landscaping company. Almost 50 years later, his meaningful path has led him to a very different life than the rest of his family. A SPICY life; a life he loves.

My friend Stanley also grew up in the Detroit area, in nearly the exact same situation as Uncle Pete. Stanley loved international travel, cultural exploration, and living abroad. In my experience, because Detroiters laid down such deep roots after Henry Ford introduced the idea of the five-dollar-a-day wage, when thinking about anything "international" locals may react skeptically, thinking of foreign workers stealing their jobs, or even being simply disinterested in the idea of international travel. Stanley's decision to explore the world beyond Detroit was not a rejection of his background, but instead was more of a personal revolution. Stanley has been working and traveling abroad for almost 20 years, and his friends and family agree he lives a SPICY life. He tells me he would not have it any other way: he lives a life he loves.

Inspirational

To ensure that your SPICY purpose is one that will actually make you get off your butt and spring into action, it needs to be inspirational. Your "so that" needs to keep your meat suit sufficiently mentally stimulated to continue along the path of execution. Because the Purpose Statement honors the connection between you, and the material world, it also needs to be worded in such a way that you are also able to inspire others to action. An inspirational "so that" will nourish you, push you out of your comfort zone and engage others onto your path.

Nourishing

A properly chosen SPICY purpose statement will provide you with physical, emotional, and spiritual energy based on both the idea and its execution. You will need no convincing that your stated purpose is worth the time, energy, and even pain it demands at times. Of course, no "so that" will always provide nourishment, but choosing a "so that" that drains you is a waste of your life and can be unhealthy.

A SPICY purpose evokes a fundamental desire to pursue your commitment through good times and bad times. Sustained action is required and it is helpful to have a purpose statement that is somewhat easy to talk your meat suit into during difficult times. But the critical thing about the purpose statement is that you are willing to commit to it. A commitment creates an obligation; in this case, one that is meant to restrict your freedoms of action including thoughts and behaviors. It is this self-imposed restriction that allows you to separate and differentiate between your own conscious choice, and choices being made by the meat-based survival suit as it reacts to the world around it. Your conscious commitment and execution of that commitment is your path to freedom.

Aspirational—not realistic or achievable

SPICY purpose statements don't need to be realistic or achievable, neither of which necessarily motivate or inspire. In 1950, it was not realistic to go to the moon. In 1980, it was not realistic to easily be in North America and simultaneously communicate with people in Asia, Europe, Africa, and the Middle East for close to zero cost. In 1990, it was not realistic to sit in your living room, decide to read a book, buy that book from the comfort of your living room, and begin reading it within 5 minutes. In 2000, it was not realistic to run a global company with hundreds of employees from your home office. In today's world, people are making the unrealistic *realistic* every day. Being realistic limits one's potential and the potential you can bring to the world: it is a *past first* way of approaching the future. As you create your "so that," create it future first.

Avoid creating your purpose by starting from only what you are good at. Though this is a common way to find purpose, this approach can be very limiting. It uses the fact that you are good at things you practice as a proxy for contentment or even passion. It assumes the reason you practice is because you enjoy it or it inspires you, which is not necessarily accurate.

We have a natural bias for enjoying things we are good at, and not enjoying things we are not good at. This is because things we are good at are easier, giving us a shot of dopamine when we succeed. But if we create our purpose based on this positive sensation, we are basing it on a bias. It is possible to be inspired by the unknown; we can be inspired by a challenge and the chance to grow; we can be inspired by something completely outside our comfort zone. And this bigger picture thing that is beyond what we know or are good at can inspire us and drive our purpose in life going forward.

Before I graduated from high school, I wrote out a bucket list—the 10 things I wanted to do before I died. Only five years later, I was surprised to see I had done nearly everything on the list. So, I created another list: one filled with bigger and bolder ideas—and then I did everything on that list within a few more years. By the time I was 35 years old, I had completed five lists. The results I achieved may appear impressive, but they actually say little about my capabilities—and a lot about my small-mindedness. What I thought were big and bold plans were not as significant as I expected. Each time, I failed to dream big enough because I had no idea what big really was.

Community

I have seen a lot of purpose statements. Some say things like "so that I can be a millionaire," or "so that I can be famous and have a million followers," or "so that I can be beautiful." These purpose statements may be stable, personally meaningful, and even inspiring to the people writing them, but they lack an important detail: providing value to others outside of self; that is, community.

By our definition from earlier in this section, a purpose statement must *productively engage with some aspect of the world beyond the self.* Why? Because without community, success becomes lonely, disappointing, and even depressing. No one wants to be a millionaire or beautiful while being stuck alone on a desert island. And popularity that comes at the expense of a real, true, and intimate community can be as lonely as solitary confinement.

Your purpose statement becomes truly SPICY only when it goes beyond you and explicitly includes benefit to others. Let's look at the evidence showing the importance of discovering the social part of your purpose statement.

You may be familiar with Dr. Harry Harlow's experiments on baby rhesus monkeys during the 1950s[57]. Dr. Harlow divided a sample of monkeys into two groups: one group was given nutrients needed to survive from a "mother" monkey doll made out of cold metal; the other group got the same nutrients, but from a softer, fluffy "mother" monkey doll. The outcomes surprised the researchers at the time. Monkeys who were getting proper nutrients but no affection from the mother showed behaviors reflective of poor mental well-being. They were emotionally unstable, lacked stress resilience, and exhibited problem behavioral throughout life. Yet these results should not have been all that surprising: rhesus monkeys and humans are very closely related species, with many biological similarities.

Other studies also show that meaningful social connection is key to human survival. In the Harvard Mastery of Stress Study, a prospective study done over the course of 35 years, 126 randomly selected, healthy men were asked about their relationship with their parents when they were in their 20s. By middle age, of those who had a negative perception of their parental relationship, 100% had been diagnosed with a significant disease, such as coronary artery disease or high blood pressure. Fewer than 50% of the subjects reporting warm relationships showed signs of disease[58].

Furthermore, a meta review of 148 studies[59] looking at the quality and quantity of support of more than 308,000 people—in other words, their positive connection to community—showed the importance of community. The review showed that a lower perception of being loved and supported resulted in a massive increase in premature death and disease from all causes, including unnecessary risk-taking and reckless behavior. Conversely, those who had the perception of being loved and supported had lower death rates from all causes.

The evidence is clear: humans are wired to be social. One of the best ways to develop these strong social connections that benefit your own health is to find ways to benefit others. It is not all about you: we do better when we have others to care for. Your purpose statement will only be SPICY when it includes others and provides some benefit outside yourself to society or the world at large.

"Y" = WHY

Your purpose statement must address the question *"Why?" Why am I here? Why do I get out of bed in the morning? Why do I keep going in life?* It needs to answer that question for you on both good days and bad days. It needs to answer that question for you when others let you down, when things don't go your way, when you suffer a setback, when the world seems against you, or when you are ready to give up. The answer to the question *"Why?"* will ultimately sustain you when your meat suit is telling you to retreat.

You can go through your SPICY checklist up to this point and have a nice statement that seems stable, has personal meaning, is inspiring, and includes other people, but in the end when the rubber meets the road, as they say, your purpose statement needs to stand the test of time. You may need to revisit your purpose statement from time to time, reconsidering, adapting, strengthening it to endure through the tough times. You need to mold your meat suit to your will and not allow the reverse to happen. A SPICY purpose statement will recognize that *why* is only a tool to support the intimate partnership between you and your meat suit. In the end, it is you who gets to take the credit or blame for the outcomes of your life. This is your life—doing this will allow you to live a SPICY life, a life you love.

The Purpose Statement in action

Now that you have a checklist for ensuring that your purpose statement is SPICY, let's look at a brilliant example of a complete Alignment Commitment—one that includes both the *I am declaration* and the *so that statement*.

David Blaine is the type of magician who likes to push the boundaries of possibility. He has done spectacular stunts from being buried alive for a

Re-examining Past, Present and Future

week, to hanging above London in a glass box for a month without food. He holds the world record for holding his breath underwater for 17 minutes (no, that is not a misprint—he accomplished this on the Oprah Winfrey show). In a TED Talk, Blaine discussed his journey to accomplishing this feat, including the pain and suffering he endured. At the end of the talk, he tears up, saying:

> *"As a magician, I want to show things to people that seem impossible. It's pretty simple, it takes practice, training, and experimenting while pushing past the pain to be the best I can be."*[60]

Looking through the lens of an Alignment Commitment, Blaine's motivation and process fit beautifully into the format we have been discussing:

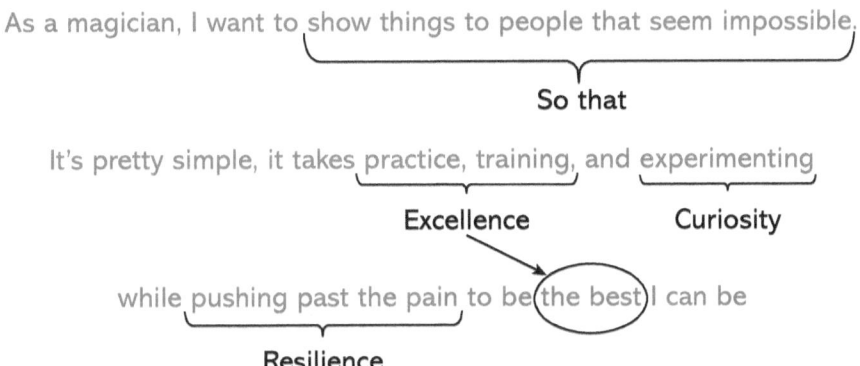

And can be rewritten like this:

> I am *Excellence, Curiosity, and Resilience* so that *I can show things to people that seem impossible.*

David's declaration of being is "Excellence, Curiosity, and Resilience." His "so that" is to show things to people that seem impossible. Blaine's purpose is SPICY—it's stable, personally meaningful (as indicated by his emotional response), inspires him, and is about others—and it definitely answers his *why*. This Alignment is what allows him to endure to do the physical, mental, and emotional work to achieve his chosen purpose in life.

His purpose statement is vague, but also specific. It opens doors to so many possibilities, but also closes doors to others.

David Blaine's Alignment Commitment has been powerfully declared and is being lived with integrity. The outcome is a very SPICY life; one he would not have any other way: a life he loves.

Creating your personal Purpose Statement

The goal of this exercise is to guide your discovery of a purpose statement that suits you. As for the declaration of being, there are two routes to accomplish this. The first route is longer, and requires careful thinking. The second route is much faster, but can be equally (or more) profound. Choose the route that you find most suiting.

SPICY Path #1: The reflective route

We are going to start with activities that you enjoy in multiple domains in your life, and then work to see if we can distill somethings out of those lists that can lead you to a SPICY Purpose Statement. Though the questions are numbered 1 to 5, do not feel you need to complete one question before moving onto the next, and do not hesitate to go back to a previous question and add to or change your answer. This is a developmental journey, not a set process. Hence, iteration is both likely and necessary, and therefore highly encouraged! For best results, embark on the journey yourself *after* reading through all the questions and reviewing the examples to help you understand how each step leads into the next.

1. What **activities** do you most enjoy doing in each of the below domains? Why? What do you get out of them—socially, emotionally, spiritually, etc.? These should be the things that give you energy and animate you, the things you never regret doing.
    1. Career
    2. Family
    3. Community
    4. Self

Example:

Career: *I enjoy when I can raise up new managers or employees to a higher level and help them achieve their goals and advance in their career. (Many times, we achieve this by pushing them out of their comfort zones.)*

Family: *I love teaching my son new things or new perspectives. Any time I can surprise him with a new way of looking at the world that he finds interesting or exciting makes me happy.*

Community: *I enjoy bringing people together for things like barbecues, or providing something extra that gives people an opportunity to connect and enjoy time together. I also like to pass on my knowledge and information about different topics that I master.*

Self: *I like doing things that cause me to learn and push me out of my comfort zone, especially in the company of others. This can be taking a trip to climb the tallest mountain in Africa, or taking on a project that I believe in but that everyone else thinks is going to fail, or researching a way of looking at the world differently than others that results in new paradigms or understanding. I also enjoy my reputation for being and thinking differently than others, especially when others find what I offer interesting and are motivated to act for themselves.*

2. What do these things have in common? Are there **patterns**, and if so what are they?

Example:

Teaching or passing on knowledge

Motivating people to do interesting things

Bringing people together

Going out of comfort zones

3. What are the **outcomes** of the actions and patterns of actions you described above? How would others describe what you bring to the table?
   1. Career
   2. Family
   3. Community

Example:

Career: My bosses say that I bring a passion and a drive to take on difficult projects and find ways to see them through.

Family: My wife sees that I have an amazing level of patience with my son, and that I have a way to support him in modifying his perspectives on things that help him. She sees my son really loves and connects with me, so something I am doing must be right. I see a challenge when I need to find a way to show him a new beneficial perspective. She also thinks I talk too much and hold very strong opinions, which can be annoying. My parents and family think I am crazy and have no idea how I am able to live a life so different than they could have imagined for me or anyone.

Community: The people around me think I am interesting; they see I have a never-ending willingness to share my ideas. They agree I have strong opinions, but see I am well-educated and can help them accomplish their goals if they can convince me to put the time and energy into a project. They know I will follow through with a commitment if I make one. They see me as someone thinking differently, but who also makes my crazy ideas reality.

4. What do these things have in common? Are there **patterns**, and if so, what are they?

Example:

Going outside comfort zones

Strong opinions

Sharing and passing on knowledge

Executing on projects

5. Consolidate the lists of common things and patterns from above so you have them in one place:

Example:

Bringing people together

Going outside comfort zones

Sharing and passing on knowledge

Motivating people to do interesting things

Strong opinions

Executing on projects

6. Prioritize the items on the last list. Feel free to write something about your prioritization that may help you in later steps. Be open and honest with yourself—you can always destroy the piece of paper or Word file later. This should be a very personal analysis, so don't worry about droning on; just write whatever comes to your mind and feel free to add to it later as you think more about it. Take your time. For many people, this is not a process that will be completed in an hour or day.

The below example shows how to think and write about the items on your list:

1. *Sharing and passing of knowledge: This is really the thing I love to do. If I did not need to worry about money, I would only do this. I love both learning and sharing, but no one pays you to learn, and teaching is so underpaid that I would not want to subject my family to such a change in lifestyle. And teaching in traditional schools seems more like a prison for the teacher's*

mind than an institution for educating people. people. Plus, I don't have a degree in education. I am just a curious person.

2. *Motivating people to do interesting things: I hate to see people miss out on life, or their dreams. I always want to push people to do what they love, especially if it pushes them outside their comfort zone. I love to hear their stories of adventure and see the excitement in their faces as they tell those stories. There is a part of me that needs other people to do interesting things so I can be surrounded by interesting people.*

3. *Going outside my comfort zone: This is more about not missing out on life. I really want to avoid coming to the end of my life and thinking I should have done this or that, but I didn't because I was scared. I guess my fear of regret is there to overcome my fear of taking action today. I also assume other people fear missing out on life, or I fear it for them—I am not sure which it is.*

4. *Executing on projects: This is simple, I like to get things done. Executing just supports the first three things above. Maybe this can be construed by others as excellence. Need to check if it came out in my "I am" portion.*

5. *Bringing people together: Yes, I like to bring people together to execute on things. It is not a goal for me separate from the first three things on the list. Without those three things, I would not be so motivated to bring people together for the sake of it.*

6. *Strong opinions: The fact is that I have strong opinions. Anything I do is impacted by this part of me—my passion manifesting. Speaking of which, I need to make sure Passion is somewhere in my declaration of being as who I already am.*

Further notes to self: *Maybe my need to teach is all about helping people go where they want to go in life. I guess I think* *if they knew the right stuff, they would feel it was easier to do what they wanted to do instead of procrastinating. Maybe I assume what they miss is knowledge, and if I can only provide it then I can help them.*

Additional note 2: *Though I go out of my comfort zone to avoid regret, there is a significant part of me that does it in hopes of inspiring others. I want to show "if I can do it, you can do it because I am no better than you." I know people think I have strong opinions and maybe they think I am arrogant or that I think I am better than them, but I do not feel that way inside, I really think that anyone can do anything I can or have done.*

7. Review what you have written and create a handful of **"so that"** statements using these concepts. Don't worry about getting the right one—you may have two or three different ones, or different versions. None of these steps are easy, but this one is one of the most difficult. It may help to re-state your declaration of being:

   I am _____

   So that, _____

   _____

   So that, _____

   _____

   So that, _____

   _____

   So that, _____

   _____

Example:

I am Passion, Inspiration, Excellence, and Curiosity

So that I can teach things to people to help them do the things they want and avoid regret.

So that I can help myself and others go out of our comfort zones and live the lives we want.

So that I can create the possibility for myself and others to live lives we love.

Note that none of the purpose statements account for all of the things on the list. If passion and excellence are in the *I am* statement, then there's no need to include it in the purpose statement. Those things will be part of the foundation of this person's approach to the execution of the purpose statement, since those things come directly from who they *are*. Also notice that there was a recognition in the second two examples that teaching was only a means to accomplish the number 2 and 3 items. This meant that pushing people out of their comfort zones (2) and living a life wanted or loved (3) were the real drivers of purpose. It also could have been that the person has such an aversion to teaching, due to the notes from the journal, they figured it would not be motivating to include it in the purpose statement.

8. Now make sure your purpose statements are SPICY by checking them against the rubric:

    1. **Stable:** Which statement, statements or parts of statements are worded in a way that is general enough so that they will not need to be changed? Which are headed in the direction you might want to keep for your whole life?

Example:

*So that **I can teach** things to people to help them **do the things they want** and **avoid regret**.*

*So that I can **help myself and others go out of our comfort zones and live the lives we want**.*

So that I can create the possibility for myself and others to **live lives we love**.

2. **Personally Meaningful:** Which statement, statements or parts of statements are worded in a way that captures the things that are personally meaningful to you? Which stand out as something you would want to be blamed or given credit for creating in your life, or in the world?

Example:

So that I can teach things to people to **help them do the things they want** and avoid regret.

So that I can **help myself and others go out of our comfort zones and live the lives we want**.

So that I can create the **possibility for myself and others to live lives we love**.

3. **Inspirational:** Which statement, statements or parts of statements are worded in a way that would spiritually, emotionally, and mentally nourish, and capture something that is aspirational for you? Remember, it is not necessarily something you are good at or know how to do yet, but it needs to motivate and inspire you to action, and if you were to tell others this statement, it might just motivate them as well.

Example:

So that I can teach things to people to help them do the things they want and avoid regret.

So that I can **help myself and others go out of our comfort zones and live the lives we want**.

So that I can create the possibility for myself and others to **live lives we love**.

4. **Community:** Which statement, statements or parts of statements are worded in a way that include community? Remember, though it is your purpose statement, it is as much about others as it is about you.

Example:

*So that I can teach things to people to **help them** do the things they want and avoid regret.*

*So that I can **help myself and others** go out of our comfort zones and live the lives we want.*

*So that I can **create the possibility for myself and others** to live lives we love.*

5. **Y (answers your "Why?"):** Which statement, statements or parts of statements are worded in a way that would make you feel proud to be coined its creator? Something that, if others pinned on you at your funeral, you would be proud to take both the blame and credit for the outcomes? Something that could drive you to get out of bed in the morning, even through tough times. Furthermore, check which statement, statements, or parts of statements are worded such that, when you execute your "I am" declaration, it will best express yourself.

Example:

So that I can teach things to people to help them do the things they want and avoid regret.

*So that I can **help myself and others go out of our comfort zones and live the lives we want**.*

*So that I can **create the possibility for myself and others to live lives we love**.*

6. Now go back over your selections and see if you can splice

together a purpose statement that captures the SPICY essence of what you have written.

Example:
So that I can help myself and others go out of our comfort zones and live lives we love.

Spicy Path #2: The viral route:

This route to creating a SPICY purpose statement is dependent upon you having already powerfully declared your being. The viral route transforms this powerful declaration of being into the thing you wish to generate in the world for others. If you have declared "I am generosity and passion," then your *so that* would be: "so that others can have the possibility of generosity and passion in their lives." In other words, you are "X" so that "you can give the possibility of "X" to others."

This route has a benefit of being naturally independent from any type of *having*. You need nothing particular to make the purpose of your life adding the possibility of passion, or generosity, or love to the world. When you have a purpose that is independent of having, it tends to be applicable anywhere and anytime, independent of your situation.

Write out your Alignment Commitment with the *so that* created along this viral route. Then answer the questions below to make sure it is SPICY.

I am _____,

so that _____.

Stable: *Is your purpose statement written in a way where you could see yourself committing to this in your life for a long period of time without feeling the need to change it?*

Personally Meaningful: *Does this purpose statement, as written, talk to you personally? Is it something that comes from and is valued by you free of any goals to impress others or resist them?*

Inspirational: *Is your purpose statement written such that it will nourish you mentally, emotionally and spiritually when you think about it, and as you see the outcomes being generated or not generated in your life?*

Community: *Does your purpose statement, as written, include others?*

Y (answers your "Why?"): *Is this purpose statement providing you a reason to get out of bed in the morning? Will it sustain you through rough times? Can you feel it in your gut as something that you want to stand for in your life?*

If you answered yes to all the questions above, then you have a SPICY purpose statement. Congratulations! But remember, there is not a "right answer" to this question—there is only *your* answer.

The Alignment Commitment

At this stage, you should be clear about the reason to develop an Alignment Commitment and have completed your own. I recommend you write it down here and memorize it. You may wish to write it in places you won't forget, like in the screen saver on your computer, or as the background of your phone, or on a whiteboard in your office—someplace you will be reminded of it often.

I am _____,

so that _____

_____

_____

_____.

PART 3: MOUNTAINS AND BOGEYMEN

PURPLE IS NOT A REAL COLOR

"We must look at the lens through we see the world, as well as the world we see, and that the lens itself shapes how we interpret the world."

—STEPHEN R. COVEY

Congratulations for reaching this part of the book. It has been a long journey through both a lot of science and self-reflection to come to the point where you can put your Alignment Commitment into practice. Now we need to ensure this commitment does not get put on a shelf somewhere to collect dust.

This part highlights the things that will get in your way as you begin to execute a life based on your declaration, and reveal your Alignment Commitment itself as a tool in maintaining commitment.

Most of us know we have biases, even if it is uncomfortable to recognize them. Of course, we see biases in other people, often thinking them to be worse than our own. Our own biases are so difficult to see because they are literally the lens through which we view the world. Biases begin from the sensors our bodies use to collect data about the world, are confirmed by the way we process that information, and then are compounded by the filters we use to turn that data into something useful. Our bodily sensors are depicted by the darkened ring labeled "Meat Suit" in figure 8. This is our mechanism to interact with and filter information from the world. It does not have the goal of objectivity: instead it filters information in a way that is evolutionarily advantageous for us. Truth and reality are unimportant for this filter; instead it focuses on ease of information use for the purpose of survival. It is a critical part of our meat-based survival suit. It is also the foundation of our biases and the part that places barriers in our way to moving powerfully forward in our lives.

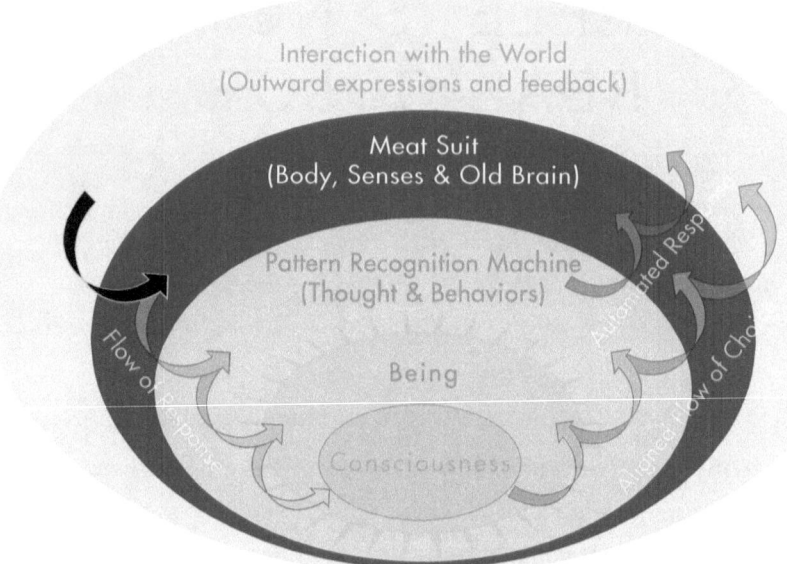

Figure 8: Our model of self from part 1 (meat-suit)

For example, when I say, as in the heading for this section, purple is not a "real" color, I mean that there is no such thing as a photon with a wavelength that we see as purple. Photons can have a wavelength that we see as red, or green, or blue, but the color purple is literally a product of our brain, created when an object reflects both red and blue photons into our eyes. Purple is an example of how our senses alter our perception of the real world.

This ring of senses and initial processing is not only subconscious, which is how we talk about most of our biases, but it is literally a physical inability to see the real world. Humans have two types of photoreceptors and three types of cones that together allow us to see red, green, and blue. Our eyes, by definition, can only process light in the visible range, using only the information available to our brains. Our brain does not even receive data from the majority of the frequency spectrum available, including ultraviolet and infrared perspectives. The mantis shrimp, in comparison, has between 12 and 16 photoreceptors and can see light on the spectrum, from ultraviolet to infrared and including polarized light, allowing it to differentiate between normal cells and cancer cells[61]. (What an interesting superpower to have.) This stomatopod can see a more "realistic" version of the world than humans can.

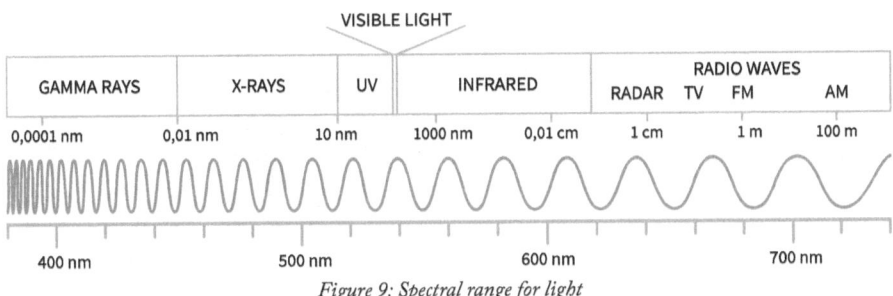

Figure 9: Spectral range for light

Our human perceptual limitation is not confined to our eyes. Our senses of sound, taste, touch, and smell also use only small portions of the information that the real world has to offer—giving us a fraction of the real picture of the world around us.

Creating reality

Once we receive the limited information that our senses are capable of detecting, it gets sent to our brain for initial processing, where reality is further filtered and altered. Figures, 10, 11, and 12 are illustrations of optical illusions that result from the ways our brains automatically process the information we receive via our senses.

Figures [10], [11], and [12], from left to right: The Kanizsa triangle illusion , The 3-prong optical illusion, The line illusion (Lines are identical in length)

This shorthand processing allows our brains to process the massive amount of data we receive from the world, making it digestible and enabling us to make rapid judgments, many of which ensure our very survival. Without this auto-data compression and the limit to our sensory input, our brains would need to be 1,000 or 1,000,000 times larger than they are now. Presently, the human brain is roughly 2% of our body's mass and uses 20% of our energy. Imagine the food bill for maintaining a brain 1,000 times bigger than the one we have now – yikes!

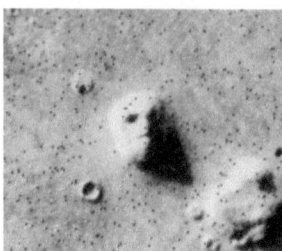  

Figures [13], [14], and [15], from left to right: Face on Mars, Dog in clouds, Elephant Rock New Zealand.

We have further filters to help us comprehend even more complex signals in the world—those of social interactions and meaning. Figures 13, 14, and 15 show the extent of our biases in terms of automatic pattern recognition. Our brains take the things we know, create cookie-cutter filters to spot them, and then apply them automatically. We are pattern recognition machines, always scanning the world for known patterns, which turns out to be very useful for survival. Imagine hunting for a gazelle on the plains of Africa: having very quick pattern recognition of either a gazelle (your meal), or a lion (your threat) would be a definite advantage. This automatic pattern filtration system allows us to recognize known things many times faster than we are consciously aware. But it also means our brain is wired for a certain amount of "false positives," where we would see the shape of a lion in something that is not really a lion, or recognize a stick as a snake, or yes, even see the face of a man in the moon. False positives are better for survival than having a pattern recognition machine that misses 10% of real threats but avoids false positives. It is also better than a pattern recognition mechanism that spots 100% of threats with no false positives but requires 20 seconds more processing time. Though our automatic brain, in

Purple Is Not a Real Color

combination with our senses, causes these biases, it was the most efficient way to keep us alive in the world of hunters and gatherers.

Beyond lions, snakes and bears

This automatic pattern recognition goes beyond simple geometry and animal recognition, also applying to the internal thoughts and behaviors we confront as we interact with the world and other people. As shown in figure 16, the next and final filter in the model is the one closest to our being and consciousness.

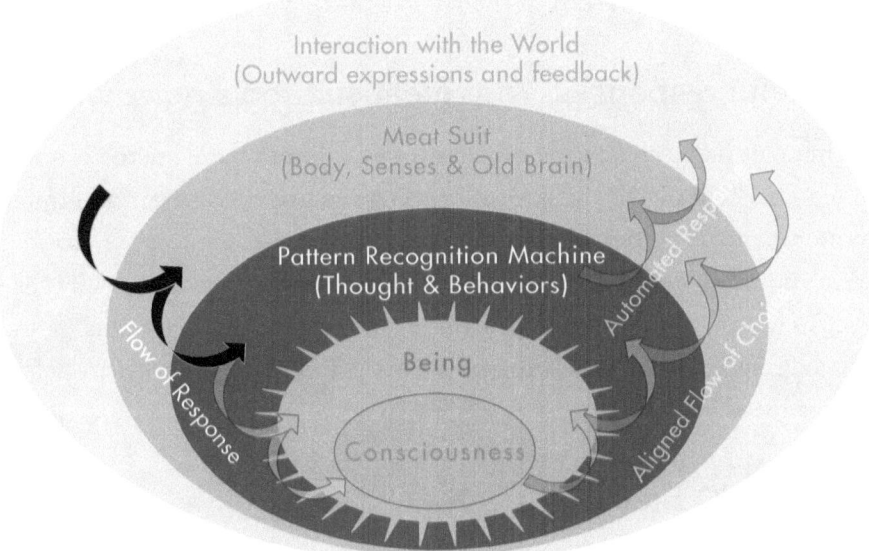

Figure 16: The mode of Self from part 1 (pattern recognition machine)

This final filter finds patterns and applies abstract meaning to those patterns. This level of filtration occurs after basic processing, compressing, and data reduction. The final step in our filtration system includes both learned and inherent thoughts that are used to give meaning to action like those of Franz Stigler, when he decided the damaged B-17 was more like a parachute than an enemy aircraft. John did the same when he applied a filter allowing him to equate his job with being a good father and husband, and Jackie did the same when she connected a sense of worthiness to her ability to have a family.

This final step in the information filtration process makes us not just pattern recognition machines, but meaning-making machines. Because this machinery is so close to our consciousness and being, its mechanisms have a heavy influence over our thoughts, emotions, and decision-making processes, giving them the ability to cause us the most trouble. Thankfully, we have the most ability to control and change this machinery, despite it being a very sneaky and stubborn machine to change.

There are two important parts of this machinery to recognize: the portion that gets triggered and the portion that responds. You leverage control over both parts, so let's look at them and how they impact your life.

Unhelpful responses: Your meat suit tools gone wrong

All humans have inherent biases built into our brain; these are the primary things that will get in the way of keeping integrity with your alignment commitment. Together with learned biases, these inherent biases are your brain's coercion and propaganda machine working to overcome your conscious control. Psychologists call these "cognitive thinking errors"[62] and knowing about them can help you identify and circumvent them before they can lead you astray.

The STUPID Brain

The umbrella term *STUPID BRAIN* will help you remember some of the most common forms of cognitive thinking errors that can create negative impacts on your relationships, career, personal health, and of course, will get in the way of you maintaining your alignment commitment.

>   **S**hould-ing
>   **T**ragedy Seeker
>   **U**nholy Martyr
>   **P**essimistic Forecasting
>   **I**ndecent Labeling
>   **D**eceptive Emotions

Black-and-White thinking

Right mongering

All about me

Idiot Oracle

Negative Nelly

This list is not exhaustive (I describe even more below), but it will help you catch the ones creating the biggest barriers to your forward momentum and get control over them. Identifying them will allow you to move towards your declared being, and your SPICY commitment.

Should-ing

Statements about what you or others "should" do are one of the most common distortions caused by your brain. These are especially damaging as they tend to be unreasonable, even though our brain lies to us to convince us that they are perfectly reasonable. Examples include: I *should* be more perfect, my wife *should* be more understanding, my children *should* be better behaved, the world *should* be more accepting of others. Human beings *should* all over the place: on themselves, on each other, on things and the world. Meanwhile, should statements are nearly always deficient, discounting the background, context, desires, expectations and even real capabilities of ourselves and others.

In turn, our brains' beloved *should* statements create an internal expectation that our views, perspectives, and paradigms *should* rule the world and everyone and everything in it—which nearly always leads to negativity.

Should statements can be one of the most common ways we hand over our power of being to the control of the world, or others, or even to your survival meat suit. So, to maintain alignment with your SPICY commitment, stop "Should-ing on people." And while you are at it, stop "Should-ing" on yourself too.

Tragedy Seeker

This brain distortion causes us to over-emphasize or exaggerate the importance of things or their meanings. As our brain is wired unevenly, with about five-times more circuitry for sensing threat than reward, this brain mechanism is usually negative. Some people have brains that have been wired to be very reactive to negative events and can see any small thing as a possible catastrophe. It is important to note that it is not that you are seeking tragedy, but your brain has been wired to be a tragedy-seeker. Anyone who has been accused of this type of negative or alarmist thinking knows how uncomfortable it is. You don't want to see tragedies or potential tragedies, but your STUPID BRAIN keeps presenting them to you.

The following Zen parable is a great example of this[63]:

> Once upon the time, there was an old farmer who had worked his crops for many years. One day, his horse ran away. Upon hearing the news, his neighbors came to visit.
>
> "Such bad luck!" they said sympathetically.
>
> "Maybe," the farmer replied.
>
> The next morning, the horse returned, bringing with it three other wild horses.
>
> "How wonderful!" the neighbors exclaimed.
>
> "Maybe," replied the old man.
>
> The following day, his son tried to ride one of the untamed horses, was thrown, and broke his leg. The neighbors again came to offer their sympathy on his misfortune.
>
> "Maybe," answered the farmer.
>
> The day after, military officials came to the village to draft young men into the army. Seeing that the son's leg was broken, they passed him by. The neighbors congratulated the farmer on how well things had turned out.
>
> "Maybe," said the farmer.

The neighbors see tragedy where the farmer, by looking through a lens more consistent with the view of a non-deterministic future, sees—and accepts—uncertainty. By taking this non-judgmental approach, he maintains control over his thoughts, emotions, and behaviors. The farmer has a paradigm and skillset that allows him to have a higher Alignment Quotient compared to his neighbors. The skillset of the farmer is unlikely to be one he was born with, but one that he cultivated by conscious and effortful control over his STUPID meat brain.

Unholy Martyr

This STUPID BRAIN fallacy shows up when a person gets caught in the belief that by continuing to sacrifice themselves in one form or another, they will someday get a just reward. This trick of your STUPID BRAIN may masquerade as a commitment to *being*, but instead is deeply and strongly connected to *having*—having a reward in the future that will provide self-esteem by valuing the martyr's "doing" (their work and sacrifice). It is a STUPID BRAIN trick that can be quite sinister in many ways.

A martyr's self-worth and identity are tied to their sacrifice, making the sacrifice something like an addiction. As more time passes, the risk of the reward not materializing increases as those who are dependent upon the martyr begin to resent the emotional controls the martyr maintains over them.

In the case of the dependent being an organization (like your company, church, or any club or charity), the martyr is bound to be disappointed as people change, ideas change, and time passes, rendering the "sacrifice" of the martyr less and less valuable, recognized, or respected. This expected outcome can result in disappointment, frustration, anger, and even depression when the awaited reward does not materialize.

Beyond the martyr's own suffering, this STUPID BRAIN fallacy can allow or encourage others, whether a person, group, or organization, to become dependent upon the martyr. Once dependent, it can prevent them from finding their own way, following their own passion, developing their own self-discipline, building a sustainable structure, or simply taking responsibility for their life.

Pessimistic Forecasting

Your STUPID BRAIN is highly skilled at taking one small and insignificant failure as an indication of something more general and untrue about yourself and then using it to negatively forecast your future. Once that happens, the internal monologue from your STUPID BRAIN only serves to demotivate you from further action—action necessary for maintaining your Alignment Commitment.

Some examples of pessimistic forecasting include:

1. After going on a first date and not getting asked for a second date, using this experience to conclude you will never find a life partner.

2. Going on a job interview and not being offered the job, then deciding this means you will never get a job.

3. Taking one piano lesson and from that lesson doubting you could ever be good at playing the piano.

This improperly destroys your self-confidence and motivation. But make no mistake, this is no more or less than your STUPID BRAIN talking crap. Being able to catch your STUPID BRAIN in the act of pulling this stunt is important to allow you to live a SPICY life you love while minimizing regrets.

Indecent Labeling

Your STUPID BRAIN is brilliant at labeling people and things and putting them in neat and tidy boxes. Boxes that, upon further investigation, are mislabeled. This STUPID BRAIN mechanism attempts to hijack your relationships to people, places, activities, events, and even yourself by applying the label to a whole person or event instead of the single instance that they deserve to be applied to. It is the mechanism by which you label your new friend unreliable when they show up 10 minutes late for the movie. It is the mechanism by which you label your life partner uncaring when they forget your anniversary. It is the mechanism by which you label yourself a failure when you don't do as well as you'd hoped on your last project or school test.

Furthermore, this STUPID BRAIN mechanism can be insidious when it comes to your powerful declaration of being. When you catch yourself out of alignment with your declaration, if you allow your STUPID BRAIN to label you based on your failure instead of you retaking control and recommitting to your declaration, then you are functionally allowing this STUPID BRAIN mechanism to define who you are. Remember, you are not your past, so don't allow this STUPID BRAIN mechanism to hold you back from powerfully being.

When it comes to maintaining your SPICY commitment, these indecent labels only serve to maintain negative, painful, and wrong emotions that will make it harder for you to live a life you love.

Deceptive Emotions

This is one of the most difficult STUPID BRAIN tricks to accept in the moment, but one of the most important to find and squash if you want to maintain alignment. The other STUPID BRAIN distortions reveal types of thought. Many people may find it easier to realize and accept that you are not your thoughts but instead only have thoughts. Recognizing this STUPID BRAIN trick requires you to remember that you are not your emotions, but instead, only have emotions. Hence, emotions are a piece of information that your meat-based survival machine uses to convey information. The reality that emotions exist is a fact, but they themselves are not factual—just because you feel it does not make it true.

For example, at one time or another in our lives, we have all undoubtedly broken a promise of some sort. Upon becoming aware of that broken word, it is normal to experience the emotional feeling of guilt. The emotion is generated by your brain and can be helpful to remind you of a commitment or motivate you to keep pursuing a commitment. Emotions can be a useful tool if you control and use them for your conscious purposes. A problem arises when your STUPID BRAIN grabs hold of the emotion and then uses it to convince you that *you* are bad and wrong. You might be experiencing a *real* emotion (guilt), but that does not factually make you a bad person.

With this STUPID BRAIN trick, your emotions are employed as a weapon against your commitments, working to pull you away from being who you declared. If you let them, they can stop or slow forward momentum on your SPICY purpose, or even divert you from your Alignment Commitment.

Black-and-White Thinking

This STUPID BRAIN distortion shows up when we allow our brain to over-commit to some paradigm about a person or situation, and adopt extreme mental positions. Everything becomes either fantastic or awful. People, things, or events are either perfect or a total failure. You are either with me or against me. It is my way or the highway. When our STUPID BRAIN is in this state, it prevents us from being able to see the "gray" in situations. Our STUPID BRAIN closes us off from considering others' opinions, which closes us off to the diversity of the world and the various ideas and perspectives that can allow learning and growth.

Alignment to your declaration will require continuous learning and growth. This cognitive distortion cuts you off from information and perspectives that may open access to additional thought and behavioral tools that better help your expression of alignment. Knowing it exists may help you catch it and force your brain to consider the gray, so you have the best chance possible to life the SPICY life that you chose.

Right-Mongering

This STUPID BRAIN distortion is most common among perfectionists. It shows up as a deep-seated need to always be right, accurate, and correct, and an obsession with proving this to be so. In today's world of social media and polarized politics, it can be seen in people who have a constant need to prove others wrong and get into prolonged, relationship-damaging social media fights.

People struggling with this bias will find themselves unable to allow others to have separate and different opinions, views, or models of the world that are distinct, or even opposite to their own. The STUPID BRAIN hates hearing a differing opinion that they believe is "wrong," especially when it is not very well expressed or argued and compels the person holding it to educate, debate, or even argue with the other.

A poem in Dale Carnegie's *How to Win Friends and Influence People* gets at this exact issue:

> Here lies the body of William Jay,
> Who died maintaining his right of way –

> He was right, dead right, as he sped along
> But he's just as dead as if he were wrong.

Living a SPICY life you love is never about being right. It is about living a life you love which includes other people—other people who will think differently, behave differently, and believe differently than you. If you allow your STUPID BRAIN to use this temptation to steer you from your commitment, it will certainly oblige. But in the end, it will be you missing out.

All about Me

This happens when your STUPID BRAIN tries to convince you that others' bad moods, attitudes, or reactions are all due to you. Think about the boss who is having a bad day, and the employee who believes it must be something they did that caused the boss's reactions. Or the girlfriend who had a bad day at school or work and the boyfriend who starts to think that she no longer loves him.

When your STUPID BRAIN works to convince you that it is all about you, you begin to modify who you are based on false information. You change your focus away from your SPICY purpose and on to rumination over stupidly wrong information about your relationships and interactions with the world. Knowing about this fallacy of information flow through your meat brain's pattern recognition machine can give you pause before reacting—so you can respond in a way that is aligned with your declaration.

Idiot Oracle

Every STUPID BRAIN jumps to wrong conclusions about what other people think based on very limited or even no information. This bias shows up everywhere and has to do with our brain's tendency to "mentalize." An easy example illustrating this skillset or dangerous bias at play is the game of poker. In poker, being able to gather clues that allow you to predict what the other player is going to do next is an advantage. So, you intently focus on their facial expressions and body language, looking for patterns that will tell you something about the cards they hold. Being right in this case is the difference between winning and losing. Beginning and even intermediate players are easily fooled or just plain wrong in their determinations—and lose accordingly, especially when up against superior players. They read that hair twirl as a player having a good hand instead of the nerves of not knowing what to do. They see that smirk as evidence the player has a good hand, when in fact they were just bluffing. Both of those improper conclusions would cause them to lose.

Very much like the poker player, when it comes to situations and people in our lives, we tend to grab on to little cues we see and create stories about other people's thinking: stories we are convinced are true even when they may not be. We use these incorrect stories to come to conclusions about what other people think. Then, we take actions based on this wrongheaded thinking about their thinking and end up damaging a relationship, worrying unnecessarily, or making decisions that lead us away from our Alignment Commitment.

Negative Nelly

This STUPID BRAIN trick tends to surface when a person is already down in the dumps. You can tell them the good things about themselves or their situation, and they disqualify them all for one reason or another. It is not that they say you are saying untrue things, it is just that they attribute the positive evidence you bring to other factors and therefore negate them. For example, you might point out to a person who says "No one cares about me," that "you have a child who adores you and needs you." They respond with, "Sure, but he is becoming a teenager and his friends are becoming more important so soon he will not have any time for me or care about me anymore." This example shows how terrible this distortion can be as it allows the person to continue in their negative and damaging thought pattern despite the evidence showing a contrary argument. It is insidious and can keep a person away from their SPICY commitment for much longer than is necessary.

A negative nelly is different from a pessimistic forecaster, as a pessimistic forecaster takes one negative event and generalizes it to mean something about the whole future of their life. One negative event is allowed to pervade their hope and motivation about their future. A negative nelly takes a positive event or even a whole series of positive things and finds a way to turn them negative in order to maintain a negative view. It is as though a negative nelly has a magic wand and goes through their life waving it at all good things to make them *look* negative—even if anyone else would see them as positive.

Your meat suit strings: SAFETY

After reading that list, you may recognize your own STUPID BRAIN's actions and behaviors. These internal thoughts and behaviors are like the actions of a marionette dancing along. But like a real marionette, your STUPID BRAIN moves only when a string is pulled. Strings can be pulled by other people, by situations, circumstances, your own meat brain—or heck, you can even pull your own meat suit strings. We will talk about this later, but they are your strings, so why not use them to drive your meat suit around in your own consciously chosen way?

Science has identified a list of six strings that trigger the STUPID BRAIN dance that can be expressed by the acronym SAFETY. This work is detailed in a book I co-authored, published by the Academy of Brain-Based Leadership, called *Psychological SAFETY: The key to happy, high-performing people and teams*. What follows is a basic description of each trigger so you can have an understanding and framework that will allow you to you to recognize your own strings and how they trigger action by your meat suit.

Security is triggered by the brain's need for predictability. It is all about the C's in the brain's environment. The brain likes consistency, commitment, clarity, and certainty, and dislikes change. This string is pulled anytime things are unclear or uncertain. It can be pulled in a positive way, for example when we desire to watch murder mysteries or thrillers—it is the uncertainty of what is coming next that we enjoy. However, most of the time, we hate uncertainty and inconsistency. We avoid inconsistent people, we prefer to know the results of our school exams or medical tests, and waiting can feel like a terrible ordeal. Most of our investigative processes when buying a house, or a car, or a washing machine, for instance, center around finding certainty in the goodness of our choices. The need for security is a strong string that can initiate a cascade of STUPID BRAIN actions.

Autonomy is triggered by a sense of threat to control over one's environment (whether the control is real or not). A sensation of having choices within any given situation is rewarding to the brain, and—let's face it—few of us like to be told what to do, which is why it is seen by your brain as a threat. So, it should not be surprising that a STUPID BRAIN will respond harshly to autonomy being lost.

Fairness is triggered by the desire for the exchanges that occur within our environment to be fair—to us and to others. Fair exchanges are intrinsically rewarding, independent of other factors. When something is seen as unfair, the brain deals with it using the same networks as those involved with disgust. When we are on the receiving end of an exchange we deem to be unfair, the whole STUPID BRAIN is engaged: it starts doing everything from "Should-ing" to being a Negative Nelly, and it can spark an angry and unhealthy drive towards revenge at any cost.

Esteem is triggered by how we view ourselves, how we compare ourselves with others, and our opinions of how we think others view us. Another word used to describe esteem is status. Our brain is constantly searching to understand if we are better or worse than others, and when our esteem is under threat, our body and mind can have very strong and negative reactions driving our STUPID BRAIN into action. Furthermore, those who are hyper-sensitive to esteem can risk manipulation by others in all kinds of decisions, from house-buying to job titles, and can even be driven into unethical or illegal behaviors as they seek to maintain their perceived status inside their social group.

Trust is triggered by our brain's deep-rooted need to belong to a known group, clan, or clique. When we meet new people or people who are different from us, our brain tends to automatically treat them as a potential threat. In fact, our brain has a different set of neural circuits for dealing with strangers than for those within our community. This parallel brain circuitry drives our STUPID BRAIN to initiate an automatic behavioral script that treats these other people as if they are not human.

With any of these triggers above, your STUPID BRAIN will react like a puppet controlled by whomever or whatever pulls that string. And yes, your friends pull your strings as well as your enemies—your family pulls them, your boss pulls them, your co-workers pull them, the media pulls them, and society overall pulls them. The string can work in contradictory directions, also. Your STUPID BRAIN will respond in one way to a positive trigger, and another way to a negative trigger. Make no mistake, whether you like the direction of the trigger or not, you are still being controlled. Parents of toddlers use these triggers all the time, usually in the positive direction in order to get their toddler to eat, or change clothes, or clean up after themselves. Parents become the puppet masters of the toddlers via a reward which can be anything from esteem ("Wow, you are such a big boy for picking up your toys!"), to fairness ("You can play with your toys for five more minutes if you agree to sit down and eat dinner without complaining"). When we are adults, the triggers are the same and used in the same way. Whenever you make a big purchasing decision, whether to buy a house, a car, a vacation, technology upgrades, or even kids' toys, a multi-faceted effort to pull your strings, in the form of advertising and sales pitches, is in place. And because our brain has more circuitry dedicated to finding the threats than the rewards, our STUPID BRAIN tends to automatically respond to the negative much more often and strongly than the positive.

The last trigger in the Y is you.

You are unique and have ingrained beliefs based on your life experiences, any of which can trigger you. But make no mistake, they are nothing more than a string over your head, that you put there, and that anyone can use to make you dance at their whim. The SAFETY strings are common to every human, and awareness of them is the first step in getting your control back. But the "Y" is composed of strings *you* put there, and then forgot about. Let's briefly look at how this happened.

Dealing with You

This is not to say that there are no patterns or meaning to things; it is just that we are the ones who fabricate many of them. Some patterns exist whether we are there to evaluate them or not (for example mathematics concepts like the golden ratio), while some patterns we know to be false (that cloud is not really a rabbit), and others exist because we say so (Burger King has better hamburgers than McDonalds). Many of these patterns that we call beliefs or opinions exist because we inadvertently trained our brain to see things in a particular way. So, even though the color purple does not exist in nature, that does not change or negate my belief or opinion that purple is the best color. Whether I am aware of it or not, I might think purple is the best color because as a child I happily played in fields of purple flowers. In this case, the positive emotional experience stuck in my brain and transferred to the color of the flowers. Decades later, that positive experience shows up in my opinion about colors.

Many of our filters are similarly traceable. I am Catholic because I was raised Catholic and my beliefs are oriented around the Catholic faith—they have been habitualized. I am also aware that had I been born in Saudi Arabia or Cambodia or in the state of Utah, that it is likely my basic belief structure would be Muslim or Buddhist or Mormon, respectively. And the same goes with many of our other seemingly immovable beliefs and opinions: it is me who gets to declare the Starbucks Pumpkin Spice Latte good or bad.

Our biases that fit into this category are obviously learned preferences. Scientists have shown this to happen through "neuroplasticity": the brain's ability to reorganize itself by forming new neuronal connections. Sometimes, it is our consciousness that causes the wiring of these learned mechanisms; other times, it is a non-conscious reaction to something that we allow to go on and be wired into our brain. Some of these are harmless while others get in the way of who we declare ourselves to be and what we commit to do.

The story of David and his learned beliefs and opinions is an example of how learned preferences can be detrimental to maintaining alignment.

David is a young man from a difficult part of town. He grew up in a revenge culture, where if someone wrongs you (triggers your esteem), you do something to them in retaliation. To let something go is to show weakness (His You trigger from the SAFETY acronym). Escalation can occur and someone might be severely injured or killed. David ends up winning one of these wars of revenge, but he also lands in jail.

While in jail, David is introduced to a mindfulness class where he learns about compassion. At the end, he commits to being the possibility of peace in the world. This is a very powerful commitment to make, especially for someone with David's background. It does not take a very creative imagination to comprehend how both his STUPID BRAIN's triggers and his habitual belief system will conflict with his declaration and commitment as soon as he goes back into his home community. He will need to choose not to listen to the automatic and extreme internal reaction his body and mind sends him in order to maintain integrity with his commitment.

Anytime David faces a situation where his esteem is triggered, his body will tense up, his breathing rate will increase along with his heart rate, and he may feel heat on his face and neck. David's STUPID BRAIN will deliver a constant stream of thoughts that will serve to escalate his physiological reaction, which will feed back on itself. Together, David's STUPID BRAIN and body will work to overwhelm his consciousness and drive him to habitual action. David will need to ignore all of the signals if he wants to maintain his commitment to peace. What will make it even more difficult, which we will discuss later, is that his social structure and community will likely work against his declaration as well. This adds to to the challenge and makes it appear and feel like he has a massive mountain between where he is and the possibility for success in his declaration and commitment.

In order to succeed, David is going to need to be aware of his esteem trigger and is going to need to rewire his brain away from his belief that letting things go is weakness. Furthermore, he may need to develop a new paradigm of the actions of others that allows him to manage his STUPID BRAIN. He may also need to carefully select a new social group that can help encourage him towards his Alignment Commitment instead of undercutting it. David will need to build his Alignment Quotient in order to consciously reconstruct his life to allow him to maintain alignment and live a SPICY life of his choosing, instead of being nothing more than a puppet created and controlled by his environment. We will talk more about this process in Part 4.

So what's the point?

As you read through these lists and David's story, you may have noticed or related to how many of these things show up for you in your life. In order to build your Alignment Quotient, you must become aware of each of the circles in the model we have been discussing. The "you" which is conscious must become aware that all the information it receives for making decisions comes through these filters. Each filter alters the information in ways that are discoverable through observation. Success in achieving your Declaration and SPICY statement depend on you catching your brain attempting to put mountains and bogeymen in your way. Once you see them, you can move the mountains and kill the bogeymen. This is what is required in order to accomplish some autonomy from your brain and is critical to building your Alignment Quotient.

What is self-awareness?

Self-awareness is not something you can acquire overnight; it is not a goal to be achieved by crossing a fictional finish line, or by earning a certificate from some online course. Self-awareness is a journey of discovery of oneself that includes awareness of how our body and mind react to the world and how those interactions influence our decisions. Complete self-awareness is only an ideal, though, because the world and the situations we face are always changing; hence, we get to discover the new ways our body and minds react throughout our lives. You will only become aware of yourself in context: as an old person, a person in love, a handicapped person, a poor person, or a person in any other state when you actually experience it. Anything else you do is a best guess and would likely be wrong. Therefore, being self-aware is a mix of two factors: first, a body of self-knowledge (understanding the way your body and mind react through thoughts, feeling, and emotions as well as understanding your beliefs and biases) and second, a state of observation of self.

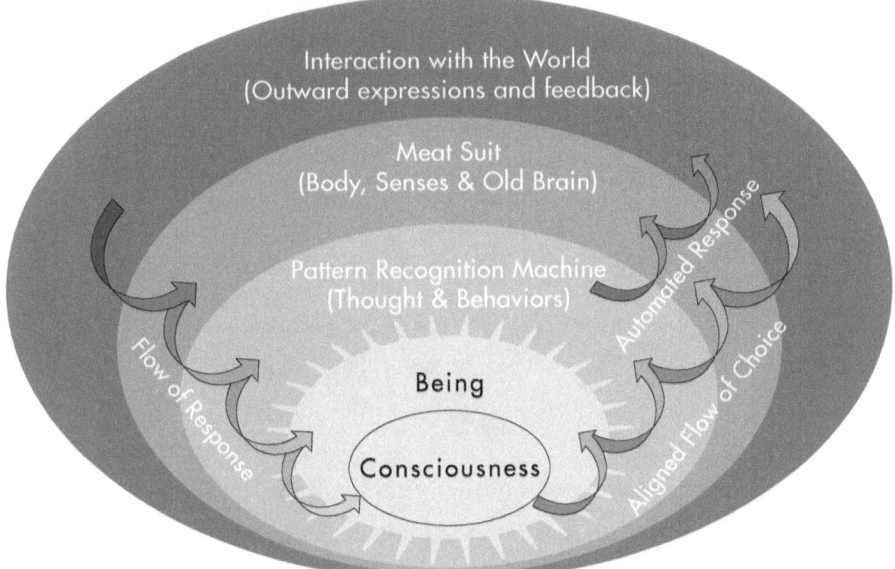

By understanding how your body and mind work through this model you will develop a body of Self-knowledge

Neuroscience shows that people who are more self-aware have some larger brain parts, including the prefrontal cortex, the insula, and the somatosensory cortex. As you become more self-aware, these regions of your brain grow and become more connected; in other words, you drive the change in your meat-brain so it can automatically help you become more self-aware. (Yes, you can use your meat-brain to help you habituate self-awareness.)

Most important are the life outcomes possible through better self-awareness. The more self-aware one becomes, the more capable one is of making decisions freely: decisions of one's own volition where rewards are earned by the "you" with eyes wide open, instead of being a puppet controlled by your meat suit's reactions to the world. Though you are unable to eliminate most of your biases, because they come as standard equipment on your meat suit, you can learn and build your ability to ignore some and rewire others—effectively disabling them.

This process of self-awareness might seem difficult, as our whole world of information meets our conscious mind in a form meant to deceive us. How do we bypass this false picture? Unfortunately, science does not have an answer, but our ancestors, including famous philosophers and leaders, had methods that can be used as a guide. I will lay out a way of thinking, which includes breathing new life into overused words like Integrity and Mantra that will serve as a foundation for a powerful method to support self-awareness along your path.

Integrity: The Key to Alignment

> *"If you have integrity, nothing else matters, and if you don't have integrity, nothing else matters…"*
>
> —ALAN K. SIMPSON

Integrity is a highly sought-after human characteristic: business owners look for it in their managers, managers look for it in their employees, others look for it in their friends and lovers. It is so highly revered that when I searched for "integrity courses," Google provided millions of results. But integrity is also poorly defined and understood—nearly everyone claims they have it, while having no way to measure or prove it. The word Integrity once had a clear meaning around which people could build a personal, pseudo-scientific inquiry. Over time, the word has taken on a fuzzy aura, making it seem impossible and even confusing to implement in today's world.

Integrity[64] comes from the Latin *integer*, meaning something like whole, or complete, or sound, or pure, or honest, and which was originally applied to undivided numbers (e.g., 1, 2, 3) rather than fractions (e.g., ¼, ½, 10 ¼). While the original meaning did not have any ethical connotation, that changed in 16th-century England when the word took on its current moralistic meaning: "adherence to moral and ethical principles" and "soundness of moral character."[65]

The inherent lack of clarity in the concept of morality has obscured some of the value of integrity's original definition. You see, morality is a collection of principles and beliefs that a group of people agree to live by.

One group's morals are not necessarily another's. Differences do not need to be dramatic to provoke violent clashes even within groups, as we have observed in the Catholic and Protestant divide of the 16th century, as well as in the current Shia and Sunni split within Islam.

Layering morality over the definition of integrity would seem to be an obvious evolution. Most humans, in most circumstances, seem to share a set of common beliefs and principles which in turn can give false hope that all humans can be united in their views. But in practice, it is only under special circumstances, and for limited amounts of time, that we fully align. Still, we yearn for those rare moments; we like harmony, which provides certainty in an uncertain world. Aspiring to align everyone's morals feels like a worthy goal because it removes the uncertainty that comes with diversity.

Unfortunately, this desire for certainty through homogenous morals and ethics has turned the word "integrity" into a way of labeling others, a way to control through social pressure—a social weapon. We wield this weapon against one of humanity's most valuable attributes: diversity.

In England during the Tudor period, nurturing social diversity was not the goal. It was a time when freedom of movement was limited, and anyone who moved from town to town was strapped to a wagon and whipped until they bled, only to be returned to the town of their birth. This was a time when imposing your ideas on other people was standard practice. European powers were in the process of taking over the world and subjugating other cultures. Niccolò Machiavelli wrote his best-known work, *The Prince*, as a political treatise on how to manipulate your way into power, and then maintain it. The 16th-century concept of integrity did not take into account a world in which different moralities mixed peacefully and were considered equally valid. *My moral and ethical standards were right, and yours were wrong.*

Today's world is much different. Business is global and cultures have been intermingling with an exponentially increasing frequency thanks to cheap travel, increased incomes within developing countries, and the internet. The current definition of integrity is based on a world that no longer exists—the days of pushing our own morals, ideals, beliefs and perspectives onto others are disappearing. Interactions among cultures are driving balanced and mutual exchange and adaptation of morals, ideals and beliefs.

Rediscovering Integrity

If we lift the moral veil from our concept of integrity and turn to its original meaning, we see its relationship to wholeness and, relatedly, its connection to soundness, honesty, consistency, and stability. If a person with integrity is whole and complete, then it must mean that "who he is," "his words," and "his actions" are in alignment: they are consistent and stable. This is our working definition:

> *Integrity: Honoring yourself as your word (your promises and declarations). Being whole and complete.*

This definition of integrity, combined with your Alignment Commitment, removes any mythical meaning or vagueness from the word integrity. As such, having integrity does not mean you are a good person, or that you are ethical or good in any way, shape or form. If your declaration is your word, it means simply that you *are* who you said you would be.

This view of integrity provides a path for self-awareness, creating an internal measurement device for scientific inquiry into oneself. We discover where our STUPID BRAIN is preventing us from maintaining our commitments. And most importantly, we can also choose to act differently, to act powerfully in such a way where "I" am the decider and chief of my life.

How can *integrity of being* look to others when put into practice? Like being stubborn about the right things, at the right times, with the right people, in the right situations and circumstances, and in spite of your own STUPID BRAIN. This can look like being unreasonable or could look like taking a stand for something no matter the cost to your own personal status in the world. How might it look to you? Like setting your ego aside and overcoming your STUPID BRAIN in order to maintain a commitment to your declarations—whether people see it or not and despite any negative outcomes you may face.

With integrity guiding you, you can cut the strings that prevent you from living a life you choose. Integrity is an essential component of the Alignment Quotient. Without integrity, there can be no alignment.

> *"Until you make the unconscious conscious, it will direct your life and you will call it fate."*
>
> —CARL JUNG

Declaration of being as mantra

Mantra is how we operationalize the first part of our Alignment Commitment, our declaration of being. Originally a Sanskrit word derived from "man," *to think*, and "tra," *a designation of tools or instruments*, its literal translation is "instrument of thought." Mantras have been used for centuries as a way to focus the mind or even elicit altered states of consciousness.

Looking beyond its religious or spiritual connotations, we can take sports as an example of this tool's power. In any sports match where supporters want to energize their team, people commonly join together in making sounds: vocalizations that resonate through the stadium to increase excitement and pleasure at important moments in the game. Chant mantra is being used as an instrument to maintain alignment of your thoughts towards a particular state of being—in this case, at a sporting event. The experience can be very powerful, evoking a very different state of consciousness compared to what people experience in board meetings, or customer presentations, or discussions with your significant other about the decisions you are making together.

The mantra is not mystical, but instead simply a tool to help you align your thoughts with your being, and can come in many forms. At a sporting match, the time when everyone is chanting is a time that you are not focusing on what happened yesterday or will happen tomorrow. You are not focusing on anything good or bad happening in your life outside of that moment. You are focusing on *your intention* for the play happening in front of you, right now.

Mantras are everywhere, from the simple words we use to cheer ourselves on, like "I think I can, I think I can," to the communal songs of worker strikes and protests around the world. The power of the mantra to focus the mind and assist in maintaining a certain type of awareness or consciousness in the moment is unarguable.

Your declaration as a mantra

Your declaration of being, "I am _____," is a mantra you can use anytime, anywhere, always keeping you aligned from minute to minute. By keeping it in your mind, you have pre-selected a tool to verify your integrity and discover more and more about yourself. It is also a reference point for generating your behaviors in any situation.

By using your declaration of being as a mantra, and verifying your integrity with that mantra, you are sure to uncover biases that may have been in your way your whole life. This method works because you are already always *being*. In this moment you are *being* somebody. That is because *being* exists only in the present.

Using your declaration of being as a mantra allows you to verify your integrity with questions about who you are *being* right now. If you commit to be "passion," or "joy," or "generosity," you can stop in any instant and ask "Does my *being* square with my commitment right now?" The answer is either "yes" or "no." If the answer is "no," you can start doing something about it—not tomorrow, not next week, but right now.

For example, let's say I have made a declaration of being "I am passion." I ask myself:

1. Am I *being* "passion" right now?

2. Am I exuding passion in my thoughts, actions, and heart?

3. Am I acting as my role model for "*being* passion" would act right now?

If the answer is "yes" then fantastic! You are having integrity with your declaration of *being*. If your answer is "no" then, without judgment, you need to ask yourself more questions: Why am I not *being* my declared being right now? What is getting in my way? What is holding me back? What can I begin doing to have integrity with my committed declaration?

Using your declaration of being as a mantra is a powerful way to codify a method you already know and are familiar with so that it can be leveraged more effectively. Being able to catch your meat suit's automatic system, and then take control over it based on your own powerful declarations and choices is what allows you to live a SPICY life of your choosing.

Here's an example of this method in action.

In one of my corporate training classes, I had a student named Derek who had a young family. He had declared his being to be "generosity." It happened to be that the next weekend was Thanksgiving and he and his wife were headed to his in-laws' house. He really was not looking forward to this visit as his in-laws frequently criticized how he was raising his children. When he arrived, in fact, that is exactly what happened. As he found himself getting frustrated, he checked his being against his commitment and realized he was "being defensive." He was out of integrity with his declaration. He recognized that his brain was throwing "should statements" at him, saying "They should leave me alone," "They should respect my parenting style," and "They should consider the possibility that their way is wrong and mine is right." It was these *should statements* from his automatic habitual brain that were preventing him from *being* his declaration. He immediately stopped focusing on his brain's "should" and shifted to a generous perspective. He started to hear in their comments a wish to help, and care for his children. From this new mindset created through his being, his behaviors flowed differently. The conflict disappeared, their insistence dissolved, and the the whole event became more peaceful and pleasurable for everyone. He said the whole atmosphere changed, all because "I changed who I was being."

Resilience: An unintended benefit beyond self-awareness

Using your declaration of being as a tool in this way will help you maintain vigilance over the invisible strings that quietly lead you towards regret and motivate you to continue onwards. But this tool also goes further. As you are confronted with new or difficult situations in life that are sure to occur—whether through a career change, change in life status, or any number of issues that cause you to have a strong emotional response—you can reflect on your behaviors and ask, "How could I have behaved differently in that situation to be more aligned with my committed being?" or "How can I look at what is happening in my life right now so I can match my views with my declaration?" or "How could I look at the actions of others so that they do not trigger my STUPID BRAIN so much?"

As an example, a student may fail a series of tests and think negatively about their performance upon first receiving the results. The student can, immediately or later, revisit their brain's emotional response to the situation, compare it to their declaration and decide to change their perspective and look at the results as a way to challenge and better themselves. This process involves two parts: a) recognition of the brain's negative response, and b) reinterpretation of the situation whereby you have a perspective which is more closely aligned with your declaration. The reinterpretation process is you changing your brain's automatic thinking. This skillset is called "cognitive reappraisal," which scientists know to be a critical skill for resilience.

Cognitive reappraisal is defined as an emotion regulation strategy that involves changing the trajectory of an emotional response by reinterpreting the meaning of the emotional stimulus. It is a strategy for you to actively reprogram your STUPID BRAIN's unhelpful automatic messaging. When your brain and body are experiencing stress, anxiety or high emotions it is very easy for the conscious you to lose your way—like a boat going through a bad storm. Your Alignment Commitment is your reference point during these difficult times and acts very much like a lighthouse for a boat, letting you know where to turn. If you leverage your Alignment Commitment, you will have a powerful ally for mastering your meat suit, and that is the key to powerfully living a life you love.

> *"In a world full of mostly unconscious survival machines, those who are awake, have powerfully declared who they are, and have integrity with that declaration have fantastic power."*
>
> —ANONYMOUS

The power of journaling

Once you make your declaration, and then begin living into it, the journey of self-discovery begins as if you have a new pair of glasses on. When you first begin your journey, you may find it easiest to discover the places you lack integrity with your declaration. You may find hidden negative habits that profoundly affect your experience of life, you may discover streams of thoughts that bother you like a splinter in your foot while on a long hike, and you may discover new ways to deal with a body and mind that scream at you as though a bowling ball had been dropped on your big toe. As you uncover these things, your declaration will be your beacon no matter how dark times become. All you need to do is remember it is there, maintain your focus on it by using it as your mantra, turn the rudder of your boat in that direction, and then stubbornly keep it aimed there with integrity.

Alignment is a process of mindful self-reflection leading to self-discovery and self-awareness. It happens in the moment. As you start, you may want to take note of and record the barriers that you discover in a journal. Those barriers may come in many forms and may show up in your excuses, your thoughts, or your feelings. You may wish to keep this record on your phone or in a small notepad. I recommend that you review these things and look for patterns once a week or so.

When you are journaling, make sure not to focus only on failures. Yes, these failures are important as you begin to take conscious control over your behaviors and guide them towards your declaration, but finding and recognizing your successes are equally important. When you seek out and find the places you have integrity with your declaration, you begin to see the patterns you already have in place that are aligned with your declaration.

You begin to see where you are successfully reprogramming your meat suit or simply the places you have caught yourself and taken conscious control over your life. By creating a positive journal and record you begin to reinforce your commitment, because your brain loves success.

The science of journaling

The way your brain delivers information to you about the world, and your place in it, is through story. Those stories may be real and true, or they may be made up by your brain. And because of our intimate relationship with our brain, we tend to accept these stories as fact and live into them as if they are true. This can be a mistake that leads us far astray from our declarations and commitments. One of the scientifically validated benefits of journaling is that it helps to separate the "story," which is a creation of your brain, from the "you" that observes the story.

Illeism is an ancient rhetorical method for making this separation, whereby a person refers to themselves in the third person (she/he/they), rather than the first person (me or I). Illeism is a way to capture the experience of being and observing what is happening from outside one's body[66]. Even if you don't use the third person to write about yourself in your journal, this tool is activated when you read and reflect on your journal. "You" become empowered to objectively look back on the mélange of your observations from your body and mind and see them for what they are: stories that your brain creates and uses to manipulate you—not for any nefarious purpose, but because it is STUPID and all it knows is either simple survival or things you have trained it to do over time.

Journaling[67] empowers your consciousness to separate itself from the body and mind and beliefs and interpretations of the world. It allows you to see your perspectives as merely a story that your brain is telling you, rather than the absolute truth—just one of several different truths. And when you look back at those journals, you can review a record of the way your brain thinks—not you, but your brain.

My journal

Below are some of my personal journal entries, uncensored, from my own experience. At first I was reluctant to include them but I ultimately did so because I believe they can be helpful. I know from talking with people over the decades that I am not the only one who has had these experiences. And if you are going to drive towards a created and declared future, you may find yourself experiencing and learning similar lessons. I want you to know that you are neither crazy nor alone…you are simply dealing with being a human being who has a brain that, from time to time, is a *STUPID BRAIN*.

The journal passages below were written while I was on vacation with my family, when I decided I was going to change the declaration of being I had maintained for close to two decades. My previous declaration was Passion, Inspiration and Excellence, and my new declaration was Peace, Love, and Joy. My aim was to challenge myself to a new being, and this is a record of my experience. Welcome to my *STUPID BRAIN*.

Sunday. Today, I decided to test the being "Peace, Love, and Joy" …the first thing I noticed is how difficult this would be…I immediately started seeing the thoughts in my brain, which were completely out of integrity with my new declaration. I did not realize how much catastrophizing that I do as a standard way of thinking. I caught my son coughing…and immediately I started worrying if he had some serious problem as he has been playing in water more than ever, and I had heard of dry drowning in children. Now, he does not have a fever, and is in good spirits, but I was still worrying. In fact, I found myself constantly worrying. It seems that I always do this and very often…This is totally out of line with the beings of peace and joy….

Wednesday. Ok, so today I caught myself again, this time it was different…I caught myself complaining like crazy to my best friend about my wife. I never realized how many "should" statements I use about her. She "should" understand this about our son…or she "should" consider this or that about my needs and she doesn't. I was constantly "should-ing" all over her through the whole conversation…I realized that if I wanted my best friend to hate my wife and think she was a horrible and unempathetic person, I was well on my way…This behavior had nothing to do with my declared being of "love"…The worst part about it is that I did not catch myself while I was doing it, but only later at night when I was reflecting on my day. It is as if this is just a normal habitual thing I do when I am upset about something, and I don't even realize it. I am going to need to be more vigilant about this particular thing.

Monday. On vacation today, I did a workout with one of my friends. The workout was quite short but intense, one of those sets of things like lots of burpees and hanging for time followed by stretching. First, it is good to note that I realized I am out of shape – though not as bad as expected, however my stretching is horrible as I am about as flexible as a crowbar. What was interesting is that as I was doing the workout, and as it became harder and harder and the burn started to set in, I found myself talking with myself in a voice you would expect to hear from a military drill sergeant saying things like "Come on, PUSH", "Don't stop now!", "KEEP GOING!!" – which I guess many people who exercise will recognize as I do not believe I am alone in this type of self-talk. This is the talk of someone pushing past the pain to be consistent with "excellence"…However, as this was going on, I reflected on who my new declared being was "Peace, Love, and Joy"….and I realized how my little mental habits during exercise were completely out of integrity with my new declared being. I immediately started changing my approach to self-talk. I started reflecting on how nice it was to be able to exercise outside in the sun during summer with my friend and focusing on enjoying the experience. When I was stretching, I was thinking about how nice it was to feel the stretch and feeling the love of the activity, I was feeling at peace with the whole activity and the place I was. I was still pushing hard, but appreciating the experience rather than fighting against it…Surprisingly, I could feel the result in my whole body.

Friday. Last night was interesting. I was putting my son to bed after he had a fun night outside playing. He was very tired but also still a little wired up from the fun. I gave him his bottle and he was drinking it and then when he finished, he wanted some light play, meaning he wanted to hold my hand and throw it back and forth from side to side to show his power. Normally, I would find myself half-having fun and half-annoyed that he didn't want to sleep so I could get to bed. But tonight was different, I really felt peace, love, and joy through the whole process, which took about an hour when instead I had expected him to be asleep before he finished his bottle – which is his standard when he is so tired. I tested my usual excuse to leave by telling him that I needed to go wash his bottle – but he clearly and forcefully said "No" as he grabbed my hand and put it on his chest. He simply wanted to spend some time with me before falling asleep. The feeling of peace, love and joy was so prevalent that I stayed next to his crib enjoying the feeling well after he went to sleep. I had not felt peace like that in a long time. This year has been very difficult with the loss of a cherished family member, and many other difficulties. It felt like I was starting to recover and enjoy life. It was nothing less than wonderful.

Tuesday. Tonight, I had a strange episode that was sparked by a sense of déjà vu. I was sitting on the couch in our newly rented Airbnb playing with my son when I had something akin to a flashback. It was as if I had seen what was happening or going to happen exactly in this place, facing this direction, with my son and it was a very bad thing. I do not remember the rest of the vision that came from that moment, but I do remember the feeling that followed whatever happened – and it was bad, death, doom. After that moment of recognition, I felt like I was living in a horror movie that was about to happen. It was as if I had either seen the future for a brief second, or seen into another dimension, or had a quick peek at God's plan – one in which my son was about to potentially die from some illness. I cannot explain it to anyone because they would not listen to me, or worse, they would think I am being ridiculous or even worse, it would unnecessarily worry them also and I would ruin everyone's night. I cannot explain it to myself – it was just a combination of a feeling and belief – completely unjustified, there is no evidence, but that does not change the feeling and mental-emotional sense of doom I was experiencing. I do still remember my declaration of peace, love, and joy – but, this sense of doom is overwhelming any logical power that I can muster. The feeling I am having did not come from a logical place and seems impossible to be undone by any logical process. It took me most of the night, but I did find a way to create a competing feeling, belief, sensation of peace…

Follow up to Tuesdays journal. I was not, at first, able to eliminate the other feeling, it slowly dissipated over 2 days with about 80% of it gone by the next morning, but I was able to choose and have a competing reality of peace and love available. To create this I did what many endurance athletes do when they are experiencing pain, I created a counter story that spoke the same language as the competing story. I threw logic out the window and built a story that made sense to my brain telling my brain – "if doom is about to happen, and there is nothing I can do about it, then I need to make sure that those around me that I love experience this last period of peace as true peace and love and joy."…This is not any more logical than the original déjà vu moment that sparked the feeling, but it spoke to that part of my brain that was convinced about the first story…I was still in a bit of distress, but I was able to get a hold of my behaviors, and though I noticed, others were not aware I was struggling with this event. As more time went by with nothing bad happening, I was able to show my brain the evidence that suggested maybe it was wrong. Slowly, I was able to get myself out of this situation where my brain hijacked my mind by flooding my awareness with so much data via a tremendous amount of negative thoughts, sensations, beliefs, and feelings. Even if I am me, and I am distinct from my body and brain, as long as I have a living and breathing and thinking physical body, the I is connected at the deepest levels to it, and its messages are heard, and have impact on me, the perspectives I am shown, and therefore the decisions I make. It will always be up to the me to observe, to maintain the strategic view, and fight the internal battles to stay on course. It is not easy, but it is what it means to be human – which is a wonderful thing.

• • •

I hope my journal provides an example of how the brain can work against and with you with the stories it weaves together. When I was experiencing life in real time, it was "my life"; it was real to me, and I made decisions about what to do in the engulfed presence of brain-created stories and reactions made from a mix of my thoughts, feelings, and emotions. But when I re-read the journals, I am able to separate and distinguish the stories and reactions my brain created from the actual results. The craziness and prevalence of my STUPID BRAIN's reactions and stories was laid bare.

> *"He who controls others may be powerful, but he who has mastered himself is mightier still"*
> —LAO TZU

Getting started

By this time, you have created your Alignment Commitment and you understand how to use it to discover your biases. But knowing and doing are very different things. The tools below will help support your path forward in going beyond awareness and planning, and towards actual implementation in your life. These tools can be found at www.thealignmentquotient.com.

Tool 1: Random Being Check

You are already and always *being*, and this being is easily discoverable by yourself—if only you were to look. But most people do not look. In general, whenever we add or change a habit, whether it's a new exercise routine, diet, or quitting smoking, we are more likely to succeed with support. With this in mind, we have built a tool to help you discover who you are being through a gentle, random reminder. This tool uses your mobile phone number to send you text messages at random intervals throughout the day. The tool delivers two simple questions: "Who are you *being* right now?" and "What is getting in your way of fully *being* your commitment?"

This tool is designed to help you overcome the "confirmation bias" that can show up in a couple of ways. The first way is through positivity bias, or by only looking when you are being your declaration and not looking when you are out of integrity. The second is when a person has a negative bias and only looks when they are out of integrity. The random reminders will allow you to catch yourself at times not chosen by your own subconscious brain, giving you the opportunity to discover yourself in a more wholistic way. When the reminder text arrives, we recommend stopping and thinking about who you are being at that moment, and if possible, making a note in your phone or notebook that you can use for tracking patterns or journaling when you have time. If you catch yourself being out of integrity, no need to ruminate about why you are not being who you committed to be through your declaration; you can immediately use this reminder to adjust who you are being in that moment. By starting, even in small ways, to practice your declared being in these random moments, you will empower your consciousness and begin the process of realigning your survival meat suit towards your own declaration.

Later, you can return to your notes and journal about your thoughts and any patterns you discover. And don't forget to also record the good things. Where you discover your STUPID BRAIN at work, you may decide to note some specific things you are planning to do the next time you confront it. While reflecting on your notes and what you discovered about your being, it is important to observe the way you analyze the information. You need to look at your mind's way of justifying who you were being when it was inconsistent with your commitment. Your brain is going to have brilliant ways of coming up with logical explanations for why you were who you were. But make no mistake, these excuses are meant to keep your consciousness under the control of your physical body, your STUPID BRAIN, and its automatic responses. Remember that it is *you* who declared and committed to that being, and only you can maintain that commitment.

Matt's declaration of Generosity

Matt's case is a perfect example of how this tool works in everyday life. Matt's declaration was generosity, and that one little declaration changed everything when he had reminders. By using the Random Being Check tool every day from the time he wakes up until the time he goes to bed, including on weekends, Matt has discovered some profound things about who he is and has been able to make important strides in changing his meat suit to be aligned with his powerful declaration.

At work

Text reminders arrived while Matt was in meetings, or talking with factory employees, or dealing with suppliers. Often the text reminders inspired Matt to make slight adjustments to things like his tone of voice, or cause him to unfold his arms, or work on his tactfulness in a discussion. Though these were small adjustments, they significantly impacted the perception that other people had of dealing with Matt. He seemed more approachable and understanding.

At other times, the text messages arrived at times of high stress. These times challenged Matt because being generosity was not easy during times when his body and mind felt like they were fighting for survival. But he did decide that he needed to be generous with himself and not put so much pressure on himself to be perfect. He was always going to do the best job possible, but he found that he was beating himself up during these stressful times and that was not helpful for him or his team.

Matt found that when he was beating up on himself, he would transfer some of that punishment to his team. He had always felt that he would never put on his team what he would not put on himself—but that unfortunately gave him permission to beat up his team when he was beating up himself. Even when he was not putting the same pressure on his team through direct action, the fact that he was beating himself up would oblige his team to take notice and as a result they would become stressed. He knew his team was full of competent and motivated perfectionists like himself, so there was no benefit to putting them under additional pressure. By being generous with himself, he could be generous with his team and relieve the unnecessary stress and pressure on them as well.

Matt's team did not perform better or worse on paper, but what did happen is that they all worked in an environment that was more enjoyable and less stressful. Matt's declaration of generosity and alignment with that commitment improved the overall climate of their workplace—and over the longer term, likely prevented burnout and negative health implications.

Though it was easier to see all of the places he was failing, Matt also took notice of the times he was thinking and behaving consistently with his declaration. He began to notice how he freely gave time to coach anyone who came into his office. He started taking credit for the fact that he supported every charity that employees presented to him, whether donating to a cancer run, or buying candy bars from his employees' kids who were raising money for school. He started to realize that, in many ways, he was a generous person already.

At home

When texts arrived after work, Matt might be eating dinner, watching TV, or helping his daughter with her homework. Much like the texts that arrived at work, these texts would remind him to watch little things like the tone of his voice, facial expressions, or ways of speaking. But they also reminded him to be thankful for the work his wife was doing, and to be empathetic when his daughter needed to have the same math problem explained for the fifth time, or to remember that being generous can mean putting off watching that TV program or sports match in order to listen. Though these things may have seemed insignificant, Matt started to really feel more generous and the little things impacted his family life in a much more positive way than he would have expected.

Social events

One area where the random text reminders were most helpful for Matt was at social events. Matt was always a big talker. As a gregarious person, he loved to tell stories and boast. But this meant he could also suck the air out of a room. Matt's wife had complained about this, telling him he might want to let other people speak from time to time, but he had always ignored this advice. Once he had committed to being generosity, he realized that he may wish to be generous by listening to others at parties and social events. He knew his stories were interesting and funny, and he always had new ones, but thought that maybe he could give some space to others. When a text arrived, it would cause him to listen to himself and consider if he had been taking up an outsized amount of the conversational space, and if his answer was "Yes," he'd find a way to get others to talk. He worked on numerous methods to gracefully steer the conversation away from himself by looking at the patterns in his exchanges. It was very challenging work for him, but over time he became quite successful at it.

At first, his friends were a bit taken back. They asked his wife what had happened. They were shocked that he seemed to be interested in them and wondered if he was thinking of running for political office or something. As far as his friends were concerned, he had made surprising and massive changes. To Matt, he was still struggling along, but doing his best to be aligned with his declaration.

Accidental Pavlovian benefit

Through the Random Being Checks, Matt discovered how his meat suit could be leveraged to help him, rather than hurt him. There are only two questions that could be in the text: "Who are you *being* right now?" and "What is getting in your way of fully *being* your commitment?" At first, Matt would look at his phone and read the texts and think about the questions. Over time, whenever his phone would vibrate or buzz, he would automatically ask those two questions to himself. This had the effect of turning every single notification on his phone into an opportunity to check to see if he was being aligned with his declaration or not. It was as if the phone vibration or ring was a reminder to check who he was. He had trained his meat suit, with the help of his phone, to act as an automatic reminder.

Tool 2: Micro-Feedback

The second tool allows you to gather micro-feedback from your social environment. Improvement towards a goal is impossible without feedback. And though feedback from your social environment is never perfect, it can still be useful if used correctly. The goal of this tool is for you to have access to information that will enable you to leverage how you are coming across to others, so you can retrospectively estimate whether or not you have integrity with your declaration or not.

This tool can be applicable to your whole Alignment Commitment or just parts of it. You create a list of 3-5 questions, and the tool creates a unique link that you can email to a select group of people to gather feedback from. When they respond to the link, the system compiles their feedback into a report for your review.

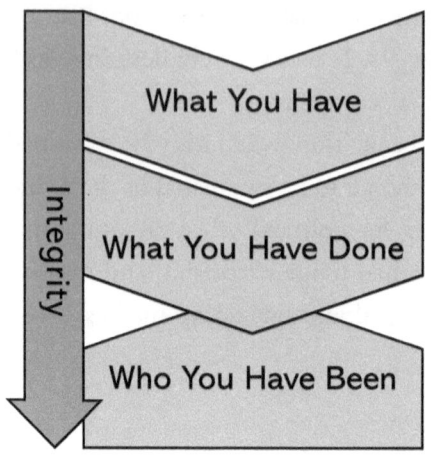

Who do you select?

The first consideration is who to request feedback from. The goal is to gather feedback that will allow you to uncover evidence regarding maintaining integrity with your Alignment Commitment. So, who you ask depends on your situation. If you are asking questions about your declaration of being, be sure to ask people who you have interacted with since your declaration. They should be people you interact with often. You may choose a mix of people who you expect would have noticed a change, maybe because your interactions with them have changed, as well as people who may not have noticed anything different. If you are asking questions about your SPICY purpose, then ask people who are involved with, or aware of whatever project you are working on.

Don't avoid asking people who are critical of you. I don't mean blatant emotional enemies who will simply be hateful and use your request as an opportunity to injure you, rather people who you know don't agree with you, or people who seem overly critical of you. Their feedback can be highly constructive if they are willing to be open and honest and once you understand how to use that honest feedback from critics. Sometimes the feedback you receive from honest adversaries is more useful to your development than that from your friends, who may have a positive bias towards you, or may want to give you feedback that makes you feel good.

Asking being questions

The appendix dictionary proposes a few questions for each of the 35 ways of being. These questions are to be used as a starting place. You are free to use them as is, but you can also create your own. You may notice that for each being word, there is a mix of questions that can include a question about how others perceive you, a question about how others experience you, and an open-ended question that allows them to give you some advice on how to improve on that being. Together, these questions are meant to triangulate whether or not you have integrity with your being. It is not a good idea to depend on one question. For example, you may find that your friends rate you high on two questions, but then you see tons of advice on how to improve. This could mean your friends don't want to hurt your feelings by rating you low on the first two questions, but instead let you know you have work to do through their advice.

The "7 or fewer" rule

When you begin working on maintaining integrity with your declared being, you will come across many challenges. Each word that is added to your declaration of being will add another area of biases to discover. For some people, they will only really be able to focus on one being, and this will be a mountain to climb in itself. This person will only need 1-3 questions to get feedback, seeking advice on how to better have integrity with a particular being. Other people who have chosen two being words that they believe they already embody plus one from the list of beings they desire to integrate into who they are, will find it much easier to make change. For these people, they can get all the feedback they require from 7 questions: 2 sliding scale questions for each being, and one open-ended advice question that could be asked generally for all beings, or specifically for the one they believe they most need to work on. Make only one question open-ended, to minimize the cognitive burden that open-ended feedback imposes on those you are requesting feedback from. The process should only take people a few minutes to complete. By framing your request for feedback generously in your email, and you follow the 7 or fewer rule, you will be able to ask for feedback every few weeks or so. This will allow you to track trends over time as you learn to fully express your declaration.

Here is an example from the dictionary of being words in the appendix of the types of questions you can ask.

Optimism

Social Feedback Question Suggestions

How much do you agree with the following statements?

1. My positive outlook does not seem to be affected by naysayers. I can always argue for a positive way of looking at a future, no matter the circumstances.

    a. Strongly agree b. Agree c. Slightly agree d. Neither agree nor disagree e. Slightly disagree f. Disagree g. Strongly disagree

2. I do not get stuck in past circumstances. If there's a light at the end of the tunnel, I will spot it and make it my purpose to get to it.

    a. Strongly agree b. Agree c. Slightly agree d. Neither agree nor disagree e. Slightly disagree f. Disagree g. Strongly disagree

3. Open-ended question
    What can I do to inspire more optimism around me?

Out of Integrity

Not Trusting

Introverted

Fearing Judgement

Bragging

Here are some additional open-ended questions you may consider instead of the ones selected regarding a particular being.

1. What would you like to see me add to my life to be more complete?

2. What do you think gets in my way of reaching my full potential?

3. Which of my behaviors do you believe are most damaging to me reaching my potential?

4. Describe me using 3 words. Why did you choose these?

These questions may provoke all kinds of useful feedback that can guide you along your path of integrity with either your being, or creating, improving or executing on your SPICY purpose. The feedback to these questions can be very informative, if you know how to read it and use it.

How to read your results

One important skill you will need to develop is how to read feedback from your social community. As the saying goes, when someone points a finger at you, they have three fingers pointing right back at themselves. Because we are all looking at each other through a series of filters and biases, I can never tell you anything factual about yourself beyond your height, skin color, weight, etc. Anything I tell you about who you *are* is only me reporting the way I experience you. Do not ask for feedback in the hopes it will be positive, but instead look for integrity with your declaration. Feedback that tells you that you have integrity with your declaration can come in positive or negative form—both can show integrity, which is what you want to verify. Here are some examples:

The meaning of passion as we have defined it for this book is:

> *Passion: a being that exudes intense desire or enthusiasm*
> *Being Passionate. A way of Being that moves beyond purpose, stays unreasonable and requires no justification.*

According to this definition, someone might say you are "overwhelming," while someone else will say you are "full of energy." Both feedback items fit a description of a person who is Passion—even if one seems to reflect a negative experience while the other reflects a positive experience.

Another example is excellence, which we define as:

> *Excellence: being outstanding or extremely good.*
> *Being Excellent. A way of Being that propels one to a level of mastery, to accomplish one's task for every reason possible, not just the perceived reasons as stated by others.*

One person may give a description of this person as a "task master," or "drill sergeant," where a second person would say they "always get things done on time." Both are expressions of excellence through different biased lenses; both examples show that the person has integrity with their declaration. You may not like the judgment that others have of you, but our goal is to discover where you are out of integrity, not what other people like about you.

Once the feedback is collected, you can assemble it on a page, Excel sheet, a white board, writing your declared beings across the top. Then see if you can categorize the feedback you receive into each of these beings. You may already have some general feedback through periodic performance reports that you received at work, or other feedback that you have received over time from your friends, family or colleagues. You may wish to revisit that feedback and see what is there and add or consider it to the overall body of feedback you receive through this tool. Taken together, you can begin to analyze and digest what they are saying. Here is an example of feedback that was collected over time:

Passion	Curiosity	Inspiration	Excellence
Stubborn	Creative	Creative	Creative
Emotional	Flexible	Emotional	Stubborn
Hard Working	Open	Hard Working	Hard Working
Caring	Learner	Caring	Learner
Energetic	Deep Thinking	Energetic	Caring
		Inclusive	Energetic
		Inspriring	Striving
			Manipulator
			Deep Thinking
			Pushy

Notice that there are both positive descriptions and negative descriptions that are consistent with the declared being. Passion showed up to some people as *stubbornness*, and to others as *energetic*. Excellence showed up as both *pushy* and *manipulator*, while also showing up as *caring* and *striving*. None of this feedback should be ruminated over. Feedback is meant to reveal your level of integrity with your declaration and to find places that are holding you back from being fully aligned.

With this goal in mind, notice there was feedback that did not fit into any of these being categories. The person who received this feedback determined it did not belong anywhere in the list of declared beings—these are areas where integrity is lost.

How did they make this determination? When others give feedback that their experience of this person is as, for example, a braggart, he or she needs to evaluate for themselves. Is this description rooted in a meat suit compulsion that is leading to being out of integrity with their declaration; or is it due to a chosen behavior initiated by inspiration that had the result of other people experiencing the person as a braggart? Or maybe the fact of this person being successful in holding integrity with excellence has triggered others to be jealous and consider them a braggart. Just because people gave feedback saying this person was a braggart does not make it true, it only makes true that some others have that experience of the person's behaviors.

In this case, the person reflected on their actions and observed themselves and decided these were automatic, habitual, and unseen compulsions from the survival meat suit. The person could clearly see that not trusting others was out of integrity with being inspiration, curiosity, or excellence. Introverted, not as a personality characteristic, but as a form of being was rooted in them guarding themselves in an un-natural way, which is, again, not inspiration, curiosity or excellence. Fear of judgment and bragging are the same. These were areas that could be improved and rather than being upset, the person was able to be thankful for the feedback helping to uncover the places where their own choice was being subverted. Furthermore, the person can create more specific questions to use with the micro-feedback tool. Future follow-up questions might be:

1. In the last weeks, how much would you agree with the statement, I have shown significant humility in my interactions with others?
   Use scale from Strongly Agree to Strongly Disagree

2. In the last weeks, how often have I given credit to others compared to giving credit to myself?
   Never, Rarely, Sometimes, Often, Most of the time

3. What advice would you give me to help me elevate others rather than myself?

Notice the first question asks about others' specific experience of this person. The second question asks about the instances of a specific behavior, and the third asks specific advice about actions and behaviors that could be put in place. None of the questions brought up bragging per se, but instead focused on what the person was putting in place to replace bragging. We will get into the reasoning behind this approach in Part 4 when we discuss the Pink Flying Elephant effect.

Conclusion

In Part 3, we have looked at how your body and brain create a flawed and biased picture of reality. We have reviewed the ways our STUPID BRAIN generates propaganda in order to convince us of a worldview that may be disconnected from our conscious choices, and lead us away from a life of our choosing that we love. We have refreshed our view on integrity so that it is useful in the context of living a life of our choosing. We have understood how our declaration of being, the first part of our Alignment Commitment, can be used as a mantra. We have discussed and shown how using our declaration of being as a mantra, along with integrity, enables self-discovery and allows our Alignment Commitment to act as a reference to guide us through difficult times. We have reviewed and explored the value of journaling. And finally, we have reviewed two tools available through our website thealignmentquotient.com that can support your pursuit of your Alignment Quotient.

In Part 4, we will look into the reality of living a life aligned with your Alignment Commitment, including the strengths and issues of social feedback, the problems that arise with aging, the issues one faces when reality disagrees with your commitment as you put your SPICY purpose into action, and how to begin putting your Alignment Commitment in action in every part of your life. All of this so that you can live a life you love while minimizing regrets!

PART 4: WRESTLING WITH ALLIGATORS

THE EXPERIENCE OF BEING ALIGNED WITH INTEGRITY

"All things are subject to interpretation. Whichever interpretation prevails at a given time is a function of power and not truth."
—FRIEDRICH NIETZSCHE

As you begin this journey of living an aligned life with integrity according to your Alignment Commitment, you will find it may feel like wrestling with alligators at times. The alligators did not appear out of nowhere; they were always there—you were just unable to see them. They were lurking around, waiting to strike when you were weak and in a position to regret your life.

Living an aligned life will allow you to find them and wrestle them when you are strongest and can either overcome them, or avoid them in the future. In Part 4, we will review our new life paradigm. Much of this section is learned through the experience, though also backed up by science. Our most important topic is how perception and beliefs interact with reality while living this new aligned paradigm.

Seeing only what you are focused on

The experience of life when you have alignment with your being can be dramatically different than the experience of life out of alignment. This is because your brain has limited capacity to focus. Its capacity is akin to sucking juice through a small straw, or viewing the world through a hole the size of two of your thumbnails at arm's distance[68].

Due to this limitation, when you have full integrity with your declaration, your brain tends to allow more of that stuff that makes up your Alignment Commitment through your attentional straw. This is not a unique phenomenon: when a person buys a sports car, they tend to see more sports cars on the road. If you adopt a dog, you tend to see more dogs than you previously noticed. Those who are pregnant or have a pregnant significant other notice a lot more pregnant people, as though everyone around them became pregnant at the same time. It is not that those things or people were not there before, it was only that your attentional straw was already filled with other things—hence, you were functionally blind to them. It was only when you put the sports car, the dog, or pregnancy in your attentional focus that you gave yourself the capacity to see them.

When you are focusing on your declared being and SPICY purpose, you may start to see it show up in lots of places. For example, if you choose creativity for your declared being, you will tend to see all the examples of people being creative, and you will notice all the times people were interested in your creative ideas. You may also notice all the places people are not creative and reject your creative ideas.

This is a normal occurrence and should be expected. When you create your Alignment Commitment and then begin living your life with integrity towards that commitment, your view of the world becomes filled with the things connected to your focus. This has a great benefit as it is part of the process of retraining your meat suit, which, over time allows your subconscious to be leveraged to keep you on track automatically. This phenomenon can help you to get your STUPID BRAIN working with you on your journey towards creating a live you love, instead of working against you.

Don't fight against not being, just be

As you begin to see your being—and the lack of your being—at a higher frequency than before, you need to keep in mind what I call the Pink Flying Elephant Effect. There's a silly game which illustrates well how easy it is to control other's thoughts. Start by telling someone you can make them think about the craziest of things and that they are powerless to stop you. They will say that you won't be able to: they are convinced of their ability to remain impervious to your mind control. You respond by saying "Fine. Just don't think about pink flying elephants." They will immediately realize they have lost, as the first thing that comes to mind is a pink flying elephant. The more focus they put into not thinking about it, the more prominent it is in their thoughts.

Applying this principle to your being and alignment, when you see the spaces and areas your being is *not*, the most successful way forward is to simply put it there. Fighting against the *not-your-being* is the best way to negate your own alignment. You have a limited diameter straw, and you don't want to take up valuable attentional space with "not your being and SPICY purpose," as that defeats the point. Imagine a corn seed in a field becoming angry that there is a place in the field without a corn seed, and then, as a result of that anger, does not grow. That seed has robbed itself of the ability to create more seeds that later can be planted in the unplanted places. Be who you have chosen to be, where you are, how you can and do not worry or focus on the "not being."

There is a lot of scientific evidence that those who remain focused on the positive live longer, happier, healthier lives with better relationships. In this case, positive does not necessarily mean "optimistic," but that something is present, rather than absent. By focusing on what is, and not what is not in regard to your Alignment Commitment, you will have more overall success in building your Alignment Quotient with the added advantage of becoming a more optimistic person and therefore reaping all the associated benefits to your health and wellness.

Failures in alignment—clean up your mess

Focusing on adding in your *declared being* where it is not, doesn't imply that you should ignore your failings. Failure from time to time is a guaranteed and normal part of the process. When you have these failures of alignment, an important step is acknowledging them. Sometimes they are internal perceptions and other times they are outward expressions, but whenever they have real impact on the world, they create a mess that you should clean up.

The messes can be emotional, like being rude to your spouse when they have an idea about something to do together that you don't like, or literal, like missing the garbage can when throwing a candy wrapper away. Since these things are relatively small, they can be easy to ignore and move on from. But they also have a real impact, so stopping to acknowledge them and then doing something about it can be of great benefit to you and those around you.

You will also find yourself making large failures in alignment. These failures can cause significant conflicts, like intense arguments that you allow to go on longer than is healthy, or breaking a trust that causes harm.

We tell the world who we really are when the chips are down or when people are not looking. Making repairs when you are out of alignment will send a powerful message to your meat suit and your social group no matter if it is small or large. The message being, I am who I am, and where I make messes by not being aligned, I will fix them because that is who I am.

This is not about ruminating over every failure. It's about apologizing to your spouse for balking at their idea or bending over to pick up the candy wrapper. These actions are examples of you taking responsibility for your lack of alignment and then actively taking steps to put your life back into alignment with yourself and with the experience others have of you. This is what it takes to put your being in place where it was not, and is another critical key to maintaining alignment and powerfully living a SPICY life of your choosing while minimizing regrets.

Patrick's Rule: Being with what is so

My friend Patrick has a saying: *You must be with what is so.* I call this "Patrick's Rule" because it is a wonderful guide for living a life you love with integrity while recognizing that there is a reality beyond our STUPID BRAIN's perception. Patrick lived his younger years as a very active person, riding his bike tens of miles every day. He designed mazes and puzzles for fun and created abstract art using mathematical equations. He seemed to have unlimited energy, vigor and enthusiasm for life. In his early 40s, Patrick had a heart attack which changed his life forever. The doctors caught the heart attack in time to do a surgical bypass. Expecting to bypass one or two arteries, they ended up bypassing five. Patrick slowly recovered from his surgery, but was soon diagnosed with diabetes, followed by a brain tumor. Patrick's wife was devastated and ended their relationship. Now, Patrick was not only very ill, but also alone.

Patrick's problem was not one of perception: it was a real, life or death situation. There was no alternative perception for Patrick to adopt that would bring back his health or his lost relationship. He had to "be with what was so."

Patrick was very clear when explaining to me how all of this made him feel: Horrible. Every one of his STUPID BRAIN mechanisms was at work. "This should not be happening to me," he told himself. "The universe is against me. I am unlovable and will be lonely forever and die alone." His physical capabilities and his ability to experience a normal life were hijacked, not by his brain, but by a reality he could not control.

It has been more than a decade since Patrick's diagnosis and divorce. Unfortunately, his health situation did not improve. Patrick is very well-versed in being and integrity and has openly shared the details of his life today in two very different stories.

In Patrick's first story, he often has days when he cannot get up from the couch. He cannot sleep laying down in a bed because he cannot breathe. He cannot work, and rarely has the energy to go outside. He is almost totally dependent upon other people to survive. Some days, Patrick is seriously depressed about this story.

Then, there is a second story he tells. Patrick got remarried, to a wonderful woman. As I write this, they just celebrated their ten-year anniversary. At their celebration, Patrick told her that when they met, he was in bad shape but had promised to fight to give them ten years together.

Now that it was ten wonderful years later, he was happy to say he had kept his word. He went on, saying that even though his health is much worse than before and his mind not as sharp, he would fight for ten more years together, if his wife would still have him. She responded with tears, "Yes."

Accepting what is so and focusing on what is possible

There is a part of Patrick's life that is real and unavoidable, and there is a part that is changeable. Patrick still loves his life; Patrick still maintains his commitment of being the possibility of peace love and joy in the world. Patrick loves and is loved dearly. Patrick's purpose is to spread peace, love, and joy to everyone he interacts with. His declaration of being and his purpose are the same, and he is fully able to control both as long as he breathes. His Alignment Commitment is fully under his control even if his body is not, and even if his brain is screaming at him. He still has power and freedom in that one domain, the domain of his chosen being and purpose.

That being said, Patrick must accept what is so. He has to accept that he no longer has control over his body in many instances. He has days where he is upset, and sometimes he gives himself the freedom to just allow that upset to be what is so. Just because he has declared himself to be peace, love and joy does not mean he is a slave to his declaration. Sometimes, his emotions are so overwhelming he just allows them to be. He knows they are not him; they are just what his brain is doing right now.

Patrick has two ways of looking at things. First, he is aware of what is happening, and he knows whatever he is experiencing cannot go on indefinitely; it can only be unveiled when he gets there. For him, knowing it will pass and that there will be something else after prevents him from succumbing to the deepest and darkest places his brain wants to take him. Second, he knows it could always be worse. He uses his negative brain to remind himself that the situation could be even worse than it already is. He sees this, in a way, as a positive way of thinking. He tells the story about driving himself to the hospital while having a heart attack and thinking at least he was not in the middle of nowhere, far from a hospital, and at least he had a reliable car, because it would have been much worse if that had not been the case.

Patrick does not avoid reality; he embraces it. Whatever he is experiencing right now, whether that is physical pain or emotional pain, he understands this is an unavoidable reality, and that reality could always be worse and no matter what it will pass and something else will come after. With this way of being with what is so, he maintains as much control over himself as is possible. This is the essence of Patrick's Rule: Be with what is so.

You are not always going to control everything with your consciousness; you can only control what is within your power. Many times, we cannot control external factors or situations, but sometimes we also cannot control internal situations. At those times, like Patrick, we have to accept what is so and just be present with it. He understands he still has control over certain things and focuses on what he can impact. At that point, he knows he must choose a direction—a direction based on conscious choice—and declare it Then he simply has to take action: putting him in integrity with his declaration[69].

Reality and Deception

Though Patrick's Rule of being with what is so is immensely valuable, it is not completely devoid of flaws. Because of the prevalence of bias—ours, others', and society's—we must constantly review our position and observe outcomes and learn from them. There are numerous instances in which our engagement with our social environments cause problems with our attempts to maintain integrity with our declarations. Here are four:

1. When people are unable to see us for who we are;
2. When we neglect others' feedback;
3. When both our internal ideas and our social feedback match but are wrong; and
4. When social feedback pressures us to maintain poor habits.

Dan's misunderstood declaration of generosity

Dan loved his children more than life itself. He grew up during the Great Depression, when the generosity of some allowed others to survive dark times. This period left a deep impression on him. Dan always declared he would be generosity so that he could bring people together and experience joy. When he had kids, he wanted to make sure they appreciated all they had; he wanted to show them how to enjoy life and love people independent of what they had. For this reason, unlike other parents in the 1950s and 1960s, he and his wife intentionally did not give their children all they could afford. This meant his children did not have the newest toys, his family did not always upgrade the household appliances whenever something new came out, and it meant radio was their sole technology for far longer than the other families who were buying color televisions.

Dan also observed that TVs were preventing families from getting together, keeping people in their houses staring at a box and isolating them from the community. Community was important to Dan, so the children invited friends for family dinner, and he made sure the family spent time at soup kitchens on the weekends. He modeled community participation by serving on the school council, and in local government, which took time away from his family.

Dan's ideas were considered extreme. Thankfully, his wife supported his ideas, even when the children complained and her social circle suggested she push him to become more modern. To be sure, Dan's children did not see him as generous. Rather, they viewed him as a strict Luddite and a money miser. But Dan was always there for his children and his community. As it happened, because he did not upgrade everything so often, he had money to save and invest. This meant he could provide financial support for his children and community when they needed help. Though his peers gave him a hard time for being such a square, Dan was known as someone who would give you the shirt off his back if you really needed it. Throughout his life, he helped many people in his community.

Dan's children went through their teen years and early adulthood thinking their dad was old-fashioned and out of touch, but as they became older and started building their own families, they saw that he was always there for them, doing things that were quite progressive at the time, like babysitting his grandchildren and helping his daughter with household chores when she was pregnant. As they aged, Dan did not change, but the opinions his children had about who Dan was did change. As offspring often do, Dan's children appreciated their father only later in life, even adopting many of his practices, including spending time with their children at soup kitchens, participating in the local community, and avoiding excess. What Dan created through his being and purpose turned into a multi-generational family tradition. You could say integrity with being can enable that being to "go viral"— not overnight, but over generations.

In this case, Dan had stuck to who he was in spite of the pressure and feedback from society. One of the great things about being is that for every hundred ways of not having integrity with who you are, there are a hundred ways to have integrity. We tend to judge based on some retrospective reflection of what may have been perfect, but when going forward into that unknown of life right in front of your face, perfect is the enemy of good progress. And if the desire to be perfect, or the fear of not choosing the most efficient way to be who you are and live your purpose prevents you from having integrity at all, then you have only defeated yourself.

Claus's self-deception

Claus was raised in a very Christian family. He learned about Jesus before he learned his numbers. His family went to church every weekend and Claus attended a Catholic school where he had an hour of religious instruction, five days a week. When Claus was young, he considered becoming a priest because he wanted to help people just like Jesus did. Claus was a very sensitive child and could not stand it when kids on the playground would pick on weaker kids. As Claus grew, he started to see himself as a "protector of the weak," and his Alignment Commitment evolved into "I am compassion and a defender so that people can love each other and live in peace."

For many years, Claus believed he was living with integrity, even when he was asked to leave his (non-Catholic) Christian Bible studies group because he showed unwillingness to consider others' ideas during discussions. He believed this even as he was constantly arguing with those who held different political, social, or policy views. Claus would get feedback from others that he seemed closed-minded, that he seemed unable to really connect and identify with others' ideas when they were different than his own, that he seemed to be a bit of an intellectual bully. From Claus's perspective, he was constantly frustrated at how ignorant others around him were, even when he was attending a top university with some of the most intelligent, learned, and diverse people in the country.

Claus held firmly to his ideas and ways of being until he did a study abroad in Europe. He noticed how differently everyone in Europe seemed to think compared to him. Eventually, he met someone who was willing to argue these topics as passionately as he was, but from a very different perspective. This new friend told him to his face that he was a pure bully and had no compassion for anyone. He told him that his ideas simply served to divide people and would only lead to fighting because they had no respect and gave no space or consideration for anything or anyone that was different. Claus both loved and hated these conversations: they were intellectually challenging, but they questioned his sense of who he was and what he stood for in the world. If this new connection was right, it would mean that Claus had been wrong about everything in his life: all his assumptions about his being were wrong, and he was doing the opposite of his stated purpose.

Claus decided to run some tests. He spent time asking his new friends questions to dig deeper into other people's thoughts without responding. Many times, this process uncovered the commonalities between Claus's ideas and the others—the same people who he would normally fight with. He found these tests were causing him to feel more compassionate, and leading others to seeing him as more compassionate. His relationships and conversations were far more peaceful, and people who thought very differently from him still were interested to hang out with him, to travel and enjoy the scenery with him, to have a nice dinner and drink with him. Prior to this, who Claus was being was disagreeable and argumentative with an insatiable need to be right. None of this was consistent with his declaration and was causing the opposite of peace in the world. Claus had been deceiving himself for more than twenty years. He realized he needed to change something or commit to a new being and purpose. He realized he was the problem, and to be consistent with who he had been being all his life, his mission statement should really have been "I am argumentative so that I can prove to others I am right." And that thought repulsed him.

Eventually Claus began to understand that by listening with curiosity, and honestly and generously asking questions, he could discover other people. He had not been able to learn this before because of his inconsistent methodology. He also learned that the answers to his questions from others allowed him to appreciate and care for the other person. This created a peaceful and compassionate environment between them. He started to realize that stating his being as "defender" was about fighting for his own ideas, which had nothing to do with his purpose of having peace in the world. He remembered that his original intention was to be like Jesus and live with compassion. However, his approach was destroying any possibility of compassion between himself and anyone else who thought differently than him. Before his paradigm shift, Claus could only have compassion for those who fit his bias of deserving compassion: in other words, those who were destitute, or being physically or psychologically beaten down or abused. He was never able to really have compassion for those who found themselves in more common but still difficult situations, which closed him off to pretty much everyone around him. Claus had not only turned all these people away, but also slapped them in the face through entire conversations in which he spent time proving that his own points of view were right while theirs were misguided or wrong-minded. Claus had been living his bias, not his declaration of being.

This type of issue plagues many of us. Our thin straw of focus means we see what we want to see—including what we see about ourselves. Self-deception is the one area that social feedback can help resolve if we are willing to ask the questions to people who are willing to give us an honest answer. But relying on social feedback has some risks as well, and one of them is when our social group is just as deceived as we are.

The "She's a witch!" effect

The name of this section is inspired by a scene in *Monty Python and the Holy Grail* in which a village of people in the Middle Ages wants to condemn a woman as a witch and tries several ridiculous arguments to convince the lord of the land to burn her. In the end, the villagers—and the lord—succumb to an illogical but socially acceptable group bias that the woman was indeed a witch. The important thing to remember about the human condition is that we are all running on autopilot most of the time, meaning our biases are in charge when we are not paying attention, and even much of the time we are paying attention.

The story of Janice and Silvia is an example of the "She's a witch!" effect from the real world:

Janice was a manager of a large factory department and was great at what she did. She prided herself on being fair yet firm. Her Alignment Commitment was "I am passion, resilience, and fairness so that I can inspire my family, friends, and the world to achieve whatever they desire with integrity." Janice had five managers who reported to her, each with their own teams. It was April when Janice noticed that one of her managers, Silvia, was calling in sick more than normal. Janice wondered if Silvia was simply prolonging her winter holiday and neglecting her work, but did not say anything.

One morning, Silvia called in again, saying she needed three additional days off. The team had major customer visits planned, and Silvia was a key person they would need to meet. Janice called a management team meeting to plan a course forward through the week without Silvia. The meeting started with a focus on Silvia's inopportune absence, and how maybe she was not as committed to the success of the team as others. Some questioned her "illness," and still others wondered if she was looking for another job. Janice had intended to focus the meeting on how to fill the gap made by Silvia's absence, but found herself listening intently to her managers' thoughts, as they seemed to reinforce her own ideas about Silvia. Janice worried that Silvia would set a lower standard for her whole team if she was allowed to get away with this type of behavior.

Janice imagined how she would confront Silvia on her return to work. She spent hours finding creative ways to "punish" Silvia; for instance, by giving her really awful tasks, transferring some of her team to other teams to assure she would be short-staffed, withholding any pay raise or bonus, or even by suggesting that the team stop inviting her to lunch.

When Silvia came back, she sheepishly walked into Janice's office and asked if they could speak in private. Janice agreed, bracing herself for the "good excuse" that was coming. Silvia apologized for missing work, and then started telling a story. She and her husband had been trying to have kids for years, and a few months earlier, in December, they had finally saved the $15,000 it would cost to get medical support for getting pregnant. In December and January they had been going through the medical testing. She had been taking hormone shots and finally was able to get eggs implanted, which is why she took so many days off during that time. She was so excited in February to find out she was pregnant. They had gone to the doctor for the first trimester ultrasound a couple days before the meeting they were having in Janice's office. As Silvia continued, her voice began to crack and she started to cry. The ultrasound had discovered the baby had died and she would need to have surgery or her life would be in danger. Silvia was now sobbing, and Janice was both shocked and speechless until she managed to say "Is there anything I can do?" Silvia looked up at her and said that she was happy to be back at work because she enjoyed her job so much and she enjoyed working with Janice and the team, and being at work helped her to avoid rumination on what she had gone through.

Later that day, Janice reflected on what happened and acknowledged that her whole purpose in life was to inspire others to achieve whatever they desired with integrity. She saw that was what Silvia was doing, yet Janice's own blindness around resilience and passion shut her off to the reason for her being who she declared she was. In fact, she felt bad because had she demonstrated integrity with her declared being of resilience, she would have simply focused on being resilient in the face of losing Silvia for the customer meeting. Had she maintained integrity around resilience, she would not have listened to the team complain and justify her own incorrect feelings about Silvia. Rather, she would have inspired them to be resilient as well. In this case, it was not only Janice's bias that had pulled her out of integrity, but it was the bias of her community that had helped her along to justify that bias.

Social pressure can justify a bias that we already have, but it can also be a set of chains holding us to habits we know are unhelpful or unhealthy.

Obligatory interdependence: Stay negative, Jeremy!

Humans are particularly social animals, characterized by something called "obligatory interdependence." This means that we depend on one another in uncountable ways, ranging from the obvious (our lives are impacted by the people who grow our food, process our gasoline, ensure that fresh water flows from our faucets, and make our cell phone connections work) to the less obvious (our social connections can influence who we have coffee with in the morning, whether we smoke or not, which clubs we join, which books we read or TV programs we watch, which social media platforms we use, what we eat and drink, and what activities we do in our free time). The reason the latter type of interdependency is not obvious is because we may not immediately think it is our social networks that are holding us to these patterns. But anyone who has tried to quit smoking will know the feeling of loss that comes with not being able to take smoke breaks with friends or colleagues. Anyone who has stopped drinking alcohol knows the questioning from friends, and maybe even the alienation, that comes with making that change. The social pressure that comes from being part of a community or group with a certain culture can cause all kinds of issues when you make a change to who you are.

Jeremy was an engineer, and engineers are trained to be critical thinkers and problem solvers. He is highly trained to see problems and evaluate different options to fix them. From a career perspective, this makes him a risk-analyzer and world-modeler at a mathematical level who can break down any issue into component parts and review what could go wrong. From there, he can then set a path forward with the lowest risk possible and the highest chance for success. This skillset allows Jeremy's straw of attention to draw in specific information that allows him to use his filters to see every possible problem: problems that he can then solve. When Jeremy got his MBA, he started to spend more time with salespeople and entrepreneurs and business leaders who, on one hand, appreciated his ability to think critically, but on the other hand, could not stand what they saw as a negativity in his assessments of their plans. For Jeremy, problems were neutral things to be solved. But for salespeople, problems are barriers to getting a deal done, and a threat to commissions. Jeremy noticed his new colleagues had a marked positivity bias that they used to fend off naysayers.

The issue with the cultural divide extended deeper than simple issues with management. The people who loved to talk with Jeremy were the lower-level folk. Why? Because Jeremy was always able to see problems. He became the sounding board for many of the complaints in and about the company. In this new environment, Jeremy was the only one looking at how to solve the problems, and, sometimes, the problems were not real or important, which meant Jeremy needed to focus mental energy on all these things by himself, which was very lonely and stressful.

Some of the people who had been complaining to Jeremy then said that they thought *Jeremy* was overly stressed and worried too much about the issues in the company. They had never expected any of them to really be solved! Jeremy realized then that maybe these people just had been using him to vent and the problems may not have been so serious. Or, they may not have ever really cared about them. Once Jeremy realized this was happening, he set out to modify the way he looked at the situation. He decided to "be positive." This change in being led to a series of changes in behavior, from the way he thought to the way he behaved.

These changes were jarring to those around him. The people who had come to complain to him were no longer satisfied with his reactions. Jeremy had trained them to see him as the person to complain to, and now he had broken that unspoken agreement with his change. He did not realize the change he was making would so dramatically impact his social environment. The people wanted to hold him to who he was before.

Our declaration of our being is partially driven by an unspoken exchange between us and the people we interact with. We create a hidden pact between us saying "I can depend on you to *be* this and you can depend on me to *be* that." If this pact is broken, it can be unsettling and we may fight to get it back. These unspoken contracts can be some of the largest challenges that we face when making a change to who we are.

It is for this reason, I suggest you make an active declaration and write it down in a prominent place. Then, find ways to remind yourself about it. Of course, you can declare it and keep it to yourself, but it can be useful to declare it to others, especially when we know this may mean a renegotiation of those unspoken contracts in important relationships.

Leveraging your meat brain: Creating your community

In some cases when you make these new Alignment Commitments, it may mean losing friends. For example, someone may declare who they are is freedom, and the behavioral change that follows might be giving up alcohol, or gambling, or going out and partying as much. These behavioral changes may mean other people see the unspoken contracts that make up that relationship as broken and may decide to go their separate ways.

Your new Alignment Commitment means you will need to make new social contracts, which may lead to a new social group. This new social group may or may not include those people you had previously included. Many times, people are surprised at how accepting others are of those changes. Many times, the changes you make benefit both yourself and those you love, but sometimes, especially with unhealthy habits like smoking, drugs, or negativity, you will lose people in your life. From the perspective of your whole life, this may not end up being a significant loss, but in the short term it can certainly feel dramatic. Your STUPID BRAIN may make you feel like you are being punished for making important changes in your life. Your STUPID BRAIN will use this rejection as evidence that you are making a mistake with your new commitment. When you embark on being powerfully aligned with your commitment, you need to be aware that your body will react to these changes in your social environment.

In order to comfort and soothe your STUPID BRAIN, you need to be aware that you will have a new social group on the other side, and that your loss will be compensated with other gains—gains that will support you on your journey to live a life you love.

The other piece of knowledge that may soothe your meat brain is knowing that though some people may never come back into your life, others who were lost might come back later. Those who do come back will likely recognize the strength and courage you demonstrated by going forward on the path you chose. Some may even admit to you that your actions inspired them to make changes in their lives (this is not uncommon). Not giving in to your STUPID BRAIN is the only way to inspire others with your powerfully chosen SPICY life.

Leveraging your body: Creating helpful stories

Because the unhelpful stories we tell about ourselves often *seem* totally adequate, they can be difficult to identify and rewrite. Your fear of dying due to a long fall from a high place *seems* totally justifiable—after all, if you fall off a mountain or are in a plane crash, you are very likely to die. From the perspective of your STUPID BRAIN, it is better to err on the side of caution to avoid any chance of death. But when that story comes into conflict with your Alignment Commitment, it becomes problematic. For example, if you are committed to becoming an aerobatics pilot, or if you wanted to check off the box on your bucket list called "skydive once before I die", or if you had a commitment to stay close to your family, but they live overseas—in all three cases you will deliberately and regularly get into airplanes (and sometimes jump out of them).

These unhelpful stories go beyond reflecting simple fears. They can be personal stories, or communal stories. They are unhelpful when they hold you back from moving forward with your powerfully declared Alignment Commitment. Here are some examples:

> Alignment Commitment
> **I am compassionate so that I can soothe the pain of people in need.**
>> *Unhelpful story #1*
>> People who live in poverty are dirty and have dangerous diseases that can hurt me or my family.

Unhelpful Story #2
LGBT communities are destroyers of society.
Unhelpful Story #3
Asylum seekers are invading our country.
Unhelpful Story #4
My cousin is a lazy deadbeat and deserves whatever he gets.

Alignment Commitment
I am ambition, passion, and inspiration so that I can enable abundance in the world.
Unhelpful story #1
Money is the root of all evil and rich people are going to hell.
Unhelpful Story #2
Lawyers, politicians, and businesspeople are all corrupt, only out for themselves.
Unhelpful Story #3
I could do much better in life if other people did not get in my way.

The body-mind connection unveiled

I spent years working with bio-measurement devices at universities and large companies to show people how their stress, which is largely created by these stories we hold, shows up in their bodies as they confront different situations. The goal was to have a quantifiable measure of stress, and to provide evidence that people can pay attention to their sensations as a way to become more self-aware. This work included wiring up thousands of people—from 20 to 60 years old, with titles ranging from student to business executive to homemaker—with medical grade heart rate monitors and recording their data as they went through codified experiences.

We measured heart rate, breathing rate, and heart rate variability. Most people are familiar with heart rate, which is typically measured as the average number of beats in a minute. Your heart rate as measured by a typical heart rate monitor counts the number of beats in a set period—maybe ten seconds, maybe 30 seconds—and then divides the number of beats by the time it was counted over. So, maybe the monitor counts 12 beats in ten seconds. Ten seconds is 1/6th of a minute, so 12/(1/6) = 72 BPM (beats per minute). But because heart rate is an average, it hides the detail of what goes on with your heart. As your heart beats, the time between beats can vary a lot. A heart rate variability calculation uncovers this variation which can be more than 0.1 second.

You may think that 0.1 second is nothing important, but when compounded over a few minutes, it can uncover that your heart was beating at an actual rate of between 50 BPM and up to 85 BPM within that three-minute period, with an average of 69 BPM. So, your average heart rate is covering up the fact that something more is happening.

Researchers have known for a long time that heart rate variability is an indicator of stress levels, which can be either physical, emotional, or both. Basically, your heart rate variability drops as your heart responds to stress. Think about it like this: as your body or mind becomes more stressed, your heart becomes more militant and starts to beat like a military march, without a lot of variation between beats. This is important as your heart is one of the organs controlled by your autonomic nervous system, which also controls your breathing, your kidney and liver functions (blood cleaning), your digestion, the hormones that control blood sugar levels such as cortisol, and even your reproductive system.

When your body is responding to stress, it makes use of a very old mechanism that was likely intended to maximize your ability to survive a predator attack. When a predator attacks, your autonomic nervous system responds by shutting down all blood cleaning, digestion, and reproduction, and both increases your breathing rate and heart rate and reduces your heart rate variability. It also releases the hormone cortisol into your blood. These mechanisms cause system increases in the oxygen and sugar supply in your blood while shutting down many of the processes that tend to use that sugar. This gives your muscles a burst of energy and a survival advantage. At the same time, you have the sensation of your heart racing. Your focus and vigilance is on high alert, particularly in finding threats as the higher brain gets less blood supply while the lower brain gets more. This same mechanism for fighting off a predator is activated in any social interaction that your body and mind perceive as a threat.

Over the years of doing these measurements and then coaching people based on them, it became obvious that the majority of stress was caused by the stories that people told themselves. Yes, the stories you tell yourself about situations in your life activate these same meat-based survival mechanisms for fending off predators. For example, the difference between the stress measured in heart rate variability of a person giving a speech varied substantially between a person who held beliefs such as "I am horrible at giving speeches and am going to look like an idiot" and a person who believed " I have valuable insights I will be passing to the audience and feel confident I can deliver those insights in an interesting way." Make no mistake, I have watched many speeches over the years, and whether the person believed they were going to pass valuable insights to the audience or not was not at all correlated to my perception of their delivery of interesting insights or value. That being said, the story they told themselves did make a difference in their experience of giving the speech and did make a difference in the stress their body displayed via heart rate and heart rate variability.

The stories extend beyond speeches. I have seen students react to stories they tell themselves about traveling alone to pursue their passions, about the experience or fears of a chosen career path, about being vulnerable and allowing others to help them, about making mistakes, about doing something that puts them at odds with the expectations from their social circles, and many more. All of these stories were self-limiting and few of them were justified. Each story activated physiological processes that activated their STUPID BRAIN. From there, the STUPID BRAIN propaganda held them back, diverted their time and energy, and stunted relationships. Our stories are a powerful trigger for the STUPID BRAIN and the life derailing propaganda it delivers. The only way to overcome them is to see them, confront them, and eventually replace them.

Replacing unhealthy stories

Recognizing these stories is only step one. The next step is developing a *new* story or paradigm that can counteract and replace the previous unhelpful one. Imagine each story fills a cup on a particular topic. Each topic has a limited number of cups. If you fill those cups with stories that are helpful to your conscious desire to maintain your Alignment Commitment, then there will be no space for the other unhelpful stories—they will spill over and dissolve away. As part of your commitment to alignment, you must discover your stories, identify the unhelpful ones, and replace them with stories that aid you in alignment. Here are some examples of replacement stories for the examples we gave before: replacement stories that are aligned with a declared Alignment Commitment.

> Alignment Commitment
> **I am compassionate so that I can soothe the pain of people in need.**
>
> *Unhelpful story #1*
> People who live in poverty are dirty and have dangerous diseases that can hurt me or my family.
> *Replacement Story*
> *Since dirty and diseased people are rejected by others, they are the ones most in need of compassion and soothing.*
>
> *Unhelpful Story #2*
> LGBT communities are destroyers of society.
> *Replacement Story*
> *LGBT folks are people who are suffering as much as any other people and are in need of my compassion as much as anyone else.*
>
> *Unhelpful Story #3*
> Asylum seekers are invading our country.
> *Replacement Story*
> *Those poor people. Maybe compassion requires curiosity to find out more about why they are coming here since I feel so strongly about certain groups.*

Unhelpful Story #4
My cousin is a lazy deadbeat and deserves whatever he gets.
Replacement Story
He is family, and someone needs to do something, or else he could end up dead.

Alignment Commitment
I am ambition, passion, and inspiration so that I can enable abundance in the world.

Unhelpful story #1
Money is the root of all evil and rich people are going to hell.
Replacement Story
Those who have money and resources are better placed to transmit abundance to the world, especially if they are truly creating value.

Unhelpful Story #2
Lawyers, politicians, and businesspeople are all corrupt, only out for themselves.
Replacement Story
People with knowledge, power and influence can be powerful allies if I can inspire them to join me on my SPICY purpose.

Unhelpful Story #3
I could do much better in life if other people did not get in my way.
Replacement Story
Navigating the world and other people is part of the process of learning to enable abundance and doing it successfully will surely inspire others!

Living your SPICY Purpose

How does this all fit together? You have a declared being which you are using as a mantra and you have a SPICY purpose statement that together create your Alignment Commitment. You know there is a reality that you have to deal with, and there is a lot to this integrity of being. After all this knowledge, and all this work, what can you actually do to begin living your SPICY life?

In fact, now that you know all this stuff, the actions that will build your Alignment Quotient require *doing* things. You need to put what has been learned into practice in order to truly build the skillset that allows you to gain the ability to declare and maintain integrity between who you declare (being and purpose) and your thoughts, emotions, behaviors, and actions in spite of the situation or circumstances. So, we are going to break down four ways you can begin building your Alignment Quotient and moving towards a life you love.

The first of these four ways is an internally focused perception of your external situation. The second way is small external actions which do not make structural changes to your life, but just add some SPICY-ness to it. The third way requires resources, including your time, and will require you to begin actively building a new tribe to complement or replace your other tribes—I call this the "SPICY Passion Projects" route. The fourth way is a dramatic shift which may require significant structural changes to your life.

These techniques can be applied in any order, rather than sequentially, depending on your individual circumstance and motivation. The most important thing is to actually get started.

Way #1: I Spy with my little eye a SPICY Perspective

Over years of talking with people, I have been impressed by how they have been driven to dramatic change in their lives. These people were driven by the feeling that their current situation was bad: maybe their spouse was terrible or their life was being wasted. When revisiting those conversations years later, those same people had found that their situations were not really so bad, that their purpose in life was right where they were, and their lives were really filled with meaning. They all said they had been "going through a phase." Their phase almost cost them everything they had, and they were lucky to have family and friends who stuck by their sides and helped them through that phase. But what was going on? What was happening that caused this "phase"?

In all of these cases, these "phases" seemed to look something like an existential crisis, or depression, or anxiety, or all of them—none of which are uncommon. If you have ever gone through an existential crisis, or if you are going through one at the time you are reading this book, then you will notice how your STUPID BRAIN is screaming at you. Though this type of screaming seems different than normal STUPID BRAIN stuff that wants to keep you where you are, this STUPID BRAIN screaming seems to be driving you to change—change your spouse, change your living situation, change your routines, change your social groups, change your career.

As you know, your STUPID BRAIN is always thinking of survival. And these situations are no different. This drive to change is usually about running away from a threat and towards a perceived reward. In this case, the threat may be an awareness of your own death and how it is going to happen, or the threat can be boredom, or the threat can be caused by a fear of missing out, or the threat can be caused by a sense of unfairness inside your community or your family situation or at your company. It can be triggered by a big thing, like a key person in your life who supported you passing away, or a series of small things, like little social habits that over time became things that others depended on you for and therefore led you to feel trapped. In all cases, your STUPID BRAIN is still driving you towards survival. This may be helpful but may also be leading you to a disastrous outcome, including serious physiological reactions like panic attacks, a racing heart, or generalized anxiety.

But before you make the leap away from your perceived danger, you can use your newly created Alignment Commitment and look at your situation with new eyes. Your STUPID BRAIN will likely cause you to focus on all the threats: the spouse who traps you, the school that is unreasonable, the friends who are loud and overbearing with too many problems, the job that is an underpaid bore. But there is always more to a situation than your STUPID BRAIN allows you to see. So, this first way is a practice of looking for your SPICY purpose inside of your current life framework.

Think of the child's game, "I Spy." If you are not familiar with this game, the rules are that one person says "I spy with my little eye something beginning with ...," and then they name the first letter of the name of something they have just seen. The other players then look to see if they can spy the same thing. In this case, you are the only player. Where can you spy your own SPICY purpose already showing up around you? Where are you already actively engaged with your SPICY purpose, but did not see it, or did not see it in that way?

For some people, this game may seem difficult at first. You may need to bend your neck, squint your eyes, and reconsider many things in order to see it. You did not get into an existential crisis by making the good things easy to see, you got there by making them hard to see. So, you will need to really look hard. When you find them, write them down and celebrate them! Here are some examples that people have told me over the years.

1. A bored and disengaged executive whose SPICY purpose included helping others thrive, felt trapped by golden handcuffs in an old industrial company. He saw that he was mentoring young people to advance in their careers—in other words, helping them thrive. He also realized that the majority of his company's shares were held by retirement funds, meaning his work was helping old people thrive in their retirement. His SPICY purpose was all around him.

2. A disenchanted homemaker whose SPICY purpose included experiencing and transmitting culture to her family, felt trapped in a small uncultured town by sick children and the career demands of her workaholic husband. She saw that she was already in charge of different events at her kids' school and the church, which included preserving the local cultural heritage. Sure, this was not the dramatic version of the life she thought she wished for, but it was something she did not appreciate before she looked.

3. A lonely retiree whose SPICY purpose was to enjoy his late years with people he loved felt lost because his family was far and his friends had mostly died. He realized that his work with his church had created a new family who he cared for deeply, and who really appreciated him for his humor and generosity.

A great first step is to play "I Spy" and see what you can find, and then celebrate a level of alignment that you had built in without seeing it. Alignment is about being who you choose in spite of the situations, but in this case, you are already being aligned with your SPICY commitment in spite of the situation that is driving your STUPID BRAIN crazy.

Way #2: Little SPICY treasures

The next fun way to move towards your SPICY purpose and declaration of being is to add what I call "little SPICY treasures" into your day. These are little acts that don't cost much in terms of time or resources but are hyper-aligned with your declaration. They can be added at any point of your day in any way you choose. They can be planned or done in the moment. These little acts can be tremendously rewarding and inspiring and will give your meat suit a nice reward for that alignment in the form of dopamine.

These acts are very much like the little acts of kindness that you may hear about in motivational stories, but these are aligned with a declaration that you made. The little acts of kindness are focused on one type of being—"kindness"—but you can also do an act of passion, or an act of excellence, or a little act that covers any of the beings defined in the appendix. You can also do an act that is aligned towards your SPICY purpose, like a little way to help someone out, or make someone smile, or encourage someone in a positive direction. Here are some examples to give you a sense of the distinction.

I am excellence so I can inspire others to be their best.

Little SPICY Treasure possibilities:

1. See some trash on the ground: pick it up and throw it away.

2. See a co-worker helping a colleague: take the opportunity to say *thank you* to them, letting them know you saw their action and approve.

3. See your spouse had a rough day and give them a hug: let them know you appreciate all the work he or she does.

These little SPICY treasures take very little mental or emotional energy, and almost no time or resources. Some of these things will be done with or to others, but others will be done alone with no social reward simply because that is who you are. They are small things that will begin aligning your habits and behaviors to your chosen declaration, and that will become powerful change agents as they begin to add up and create a future world that is is more closely connected to your Alignment Commitment.

Wonderful example of how Little SPICY treasures work

I spent my teen years in a small town called Pinckney, Michigan. At the time, Pinckney had two gas stations, and a man named Ernie worked at one of them. Ernie had a mental handicap, which meant he thought and talked slower than most others. He lived downtown and rode to work on a lavishly decorated bicycle covered in pinwheels and colorful streamers that glistened in the wind. When I first met Ernie as a kid, I did not know what to make of him. I guess I thought he was a little creepy because he was obviously different from me: he was much older than me, but acted younger; he spoke and moved in a strange way; he even smiled strangely.

Ernie always greeted people with a smile and welcoming eyes. He wanted to make every child waiting in the car happy and always had a lollipop to give. Ernie was the most kind, most thoughtful, most gentle, and most socially aware person I have ever met.

Even if Ernie knew nothing about the concepts I discuss in this book, Ernie gave little treasures that were hyper-consistent with who he was to everyone he met—his Alignment Quotient was naturally very strong. In the process, he set an example that made everyone want to be a better person. Families went to that gas station over the other one in town just to have Ernie fill their tank with gas.

Ernie had more impact on the culture of the community than did most of the people defined as community leaders. None of the small things Ernie did took any great amount of resources since Ernie did not have many resources himself. He was not wealthy, he was not gifted with great intellect, nor did he have the time or energy to donate to some big charity project. But Ernie did have his little treasures: a smile, a kind word, a gentile disposition, and a treat for every kid who came by the gas station.

A few years ago, Ernie died. The comments left online strongly suggest that Ernie, the man pumping gas, had a huge impact on the local people and culture. I know he had a huge impact on my personal view of people with a mental handicap and I will never forget him. But make no mistake: everything Ernie accomplished that made such a difference for the people in his community, he accomplished through little things, little treasures that were aligned with who he was.

Way #3: The SPICY Passion Project

The third way to put into action your declaration is by creating a SPICY Passion Project. This way will take time, energy, potentially money, and will likely cause you to create a new clan or group. SPICY Passion Projects are a wonderful way to begin declaring a future and then being the one who makes it reality.

SPICY Passion projects can be created in a special way that causes you to learn and grow towards your Alignment Commitment. They can feel quite different from a traditional project: they will nearly always push you out of your comfort zone.

You can begin by simply making a list of things that are missing in your community, or work, or family. Things that, in your opinion, if they were added, would be an improvement for everyone. This starts as a brainstorming exercise where you write out all your ideas without judgment. And I mean, no judgment. There will be plenty of time to sort ideas later. At the end of this brainstorming session, you should have between 5 and 10 things that you see as missing from your community, work, or family.

Once you have a list, ask yourself the question, "If I was responsible for creating this in the world, would this idea be consistent with my SPICY purpose statement?" Spend a few minutes thinking about each item and cut your list down to 2-5 ideas. Then, ask yourself, "Does this idea motivate and inspire me to action?" If the answer is yes, you might just have a SPICY Passion Project in the making. I will not go into the details about how to create a spicy passion project here, but you can get support on your path with the resources that can be found at www.thealignmentquotient.com.

SPICY Passion Projects are one of the training courses we offer which provide you tools and support to make them reality.

SPICY Passion Projects have several necessary components: 1. A social group to support (Passion Projects are never done alone), 2. Measurable, real-world outcomes, and 3. A time scale (Not a timeline, but a deadline). It has both a beginning and an end and creates some new outcome. This is how you practice future first.

To give a sense of what a SPICY Passion Project can be and the types of things that can be accomplished, here is an example:

The Squirt Gun Project

When I first started practicing my Alignment Commitment, starting with my declaration of Passion, Inspiration, and Excellence, I took on a project specifically to explore my being inside my mission. This project was to help a charity called Trail's Edge Camp, started by C. S. Mott Children's Hospital at the University of Michigan in Ann Arbor, and created for children in the hospital's ventilator department. Each year, the children come together to play and laugh and enjoy being around other kids with similar conditions. Camp is a wonderful experience for both children and volunteers. For many of the kids, this is a rare chance to be in nature rather than in doctors' offices or at home. It's also a welcome break for parents and caretakers. My first year visiting the camp was so inspiring that I decided it would be a great place to test my mission.

You can imagine that "just being a kid" is more challenging for these kids than others. All of these kids are restricted in their activities by a machine that must be connected to them at all times to keep them breathing. The machine batteries must be charged and maintained, and the machines themselves beep constantly, announcing that they have to be checked or the connections cleaned many times per day. The kids are under supervision by a medical professional 24 hours per day. But Trail's Edge has done everything possible to make sure the kids really get to be kids, doing things like going up in a specially built tree house, swimming, riding horses, shooting cross bows, throwing water balloons, and having squirt gun wars.

The squirt gun battles were a highlight for the kids. To make them safe for the campers, each and every ventilator had to be shielded with plastic. Some of the kids in wheelchairs were quadriplegic and steered their chairs with their chin or tongue. For those kids, an electronic squirt gun was attached to their chair with zip ties. The child would steer the chair into a firing position and the partner would pull the trigger for them. The kids had a blast! But I felt something was missing. I myself *love* water fights and thought the kids should have the chance to squirt their own guns. And that's when the idea for my SPICY Passion Project was born.

By the time I had decided to do this project, camp was about ten weeks away. I am a mechanical engineer, and figured I had the skills and the network to build these guns. I also had a good job and so planned to finance it myself—which turned out to be my first failure.

I bought a few electronic squirt guns and took them apart, looking for the one with the best space to integrate a circuit board. I also went through my contacts to see which friend with an electrical engineering degree would be most willing to help me. I called one and said "Hey, I am working to build a voice-activated squirt gun for some handicapped kids at camp, will you design me a voice-activated switch circuit?"—which turned out to be my second failure. My friend said "Yes," and within a week, I had a nice design.

Next, I ordered a slew of components from Radio Shack and spent my nights assembling. Four weeks later I had the first circuit board. My first test was a *disaster*. I couldn't figure out why nothing worked right. I only had six weeks left. I scrapped my friend's design and bought an off-the-shelf voice activated switch. Another three weeks went by as I waited for more boards to arrive and built another prototype. Test 2 was also a failure. Now I had three weeks left and no squirt guns.

I went back to the original design that my friend provided and worked to fix it, running more tests and using different settings on each board, but nothing worked. I now had only two weeks left, and reluctantly started to accept that my project was going to be a failure. I was distraught over the thought of letting these kids down.

In my depressed state, I called one of my friends and told him of my failure. I explained that these kids only have this opportunity once per year and the rest of the time, life can be drab and full of medical procedures and that maybe they won't get another chance to have this experience since their medical conditions were so precarious. I was almost in tears as I expressed my mission on this project.

My friend thought for a minute and asked, "You mean you just want a sound-activated squirt gun for these kids?"

I said, "Yes! And I am going to fail because I am an idiot and I am going to let these kids down."

"I wish you would have told me," he said. "I thought you were trying to start your own business. I have a friend who used to sell these. I think he discontinued them but might have some in his warehouse—I'm sure he'd donate them to this cause."

I was shocked! Within a week, we had 20 voice-activated squirt guns. The company was very happy to get rid of them for such a good cause and the kids had a blast. The project ended up a success, but more than anything I learned a valuable lesson about myself and my mission statement. Had you asked me at any time in my project if I was being "Passion, Inspiration, and Excellence" I would have said "Yes." I was passionate about the project, and I was being excellence in my pursuit of building the machines: I was being the engineer and project manager that I was trained to be and the excellence I exuded followed the lines of my training. So what had gone wrong?

First, I kept my passion and my inspiration to myself until the very end. I was passionate and inspired, but I did not exude these beings; I did not express them such that the underlying mission could pull from the resources of the world and flourish. When I finally did express them outwardly, the results were astounding. Second, excellence had, in my mind, been about doing all the work myself and making it "right." Excellence showed up as a type of perfection that was totally unhelpful. Had I truly understood excellence, I would have allowed it to show itself in a result that came out of a community rather than only out of myself. My way of understanding and being excellence was dictated by a subconscious need to be given credit, or to control every aspect of my project deliverable, or to avoid bothering others before I understood exactly what I needed from them.

Thankfully, by doing this project, I was able to grow more fully into both my understanding of inspiration and excellence, which ended up being a critical lesson that allowed me to have integrity with my mission and build my Alignment Quotient.

These particular failures were only possible to learn from because I was so passionate about the hard goal (delivering voice-activated squirt guns to kids at camp), the limitation of time that was imposed (10 weeks), and the communities involved which kept me motivated and inspired me to take action. The success of the project was accomplished through the community, but it was the chance for me to fail that taught me more about what it meant to be aligned with my declaration.

Carryover benefits of my SPICY Passion Project

The learning that I gained on the squirt gun project came out at work as well. Soon after completing this project, I was tasked with building a technical center in China for a large multi-national company. This was not only a significant career opportunity, but also came with a substantial pay and positional raise. During this assignment I continued to maintain my declared being. I never told anyone of my mission, but at the end of the project, my Swedish boss—who was thousands of kilometers away—wrote me an email that said the following:

> *"You have a seldom-seen drive and passion for the impossible, to accomplish things within budget, time and quality and you create an aura of enthusiasm around you."*

When I read this, I see my declaration of being: "Passion, Excellence, and Inspiration." Had I not taken on my SPICY Passion Project and almost failed, I am not sure I would have been able to be successful on my professional project.

Way #4: A SPICY Life Revolution

The decision to make a SPICY life revolution is an amazing one. People who follow their passions and take the leap against conventional routes through life inspire us and certainly live lives they love. From Jane Goodall to Elon Musk to Richard Branson and more, we have heard stories of fame and success that go against conventional wisdom. But a SPICY life revolution is not about monetary success or popularity—it is about a full self-expression with your Alignment Commitment that, in your estimation, can only be accomplished with dramatic change.

> *Self-expression: when you powerfully assert your declaration and SPICY purpose into the world with integrity.*

No one can tell you when or how to make a SPICY life revolution. The decision is very personal and unique to you. There are no standard rules here. This move is not for everyone, and making a SPICY life revolution is not better or worse than any of the other ways described which allow you to be fully self-expressed in your declaration. It is merely another way to do it.

Here are a few SPICY life revolutionaries:

Ted: the executive turned entrepreneur

Ted is an engineer who has always had issues with the way corporations treat people. He hates the spreadsheet culture that he feels blindly follows financial numbers. He has watched problems that could have been foreseen and resolved end with unnecessary closings of factories with jobs lost and all the societal pain that goes along with those poor management decisions. He has watched while corporate executives break laws and take corrupt actions that enrich themselves in the short term and hurt society over the long term. One day, he had had enough and decided he needed to create his own company, where he could build a business that allowed him to do a job, earn money, benefit society and work with people in a way consistent with who he was.

It has been almost a decade since Ted made that decision to make a SPICY life revolution. He has a thriving business that includes helping companies fix their underlying problems so they can stay competitive and profitable. He has a team of people that surround him that have the same ideology and level of passion that he does, with everyone working towards the same goal. His hiring practices enable good people to earn a good and fair wage and he treats his employees and their families like they are highly valued. The path to his success was not easy, but Ted is very proud of what he has accomplished, and most importantly he is living a life that is fully self-expressed.

Kendra: the homemaker freeing herself from the American dream

Kendra is a homemaker who always wanted to be a mother. She and her husband lived the American dream in a house on their own property, but over time, Kendra became frustrated with the sense that she and her husband were only working to make ends meet. They were slaving away to pay off their house, cars, and all the other material stuff they thought they needed. Their evenings and weekends seemed to be spent cutting grass, or cleaning or fixing something around the house. This life felt like it was missing something; she felt trapped in a life without purpose.

After discussion and exploration, they made a joint decision to make a dramatic lifestyle change. They sold their house and changed to an RV lifestyle, traveling and living in their mobile home. Now, she is able to spend more time with her family and community. She has been able to do things like donate a kid's playground to the local park. And she is able to see the country with her kids and see things they would never have been able to see before. Kendra feels she finally has a life filled with purpose where she gets to fully express herself—a life she says is her best life!

Greg: the entrepreneur awakening

Greg has been a tech entrepreneur most of his career. He has written and directed movies; he built a company that made award-winning video games; and he secured multiple revolutionary patents for interactive video. Thanks to his work, he was a globally recognized innovator and highly sought-after speaker. By any measure, Greg was a successful tech entrepreneur—including having his company ranked in the Deloitte's Technology Fast 500. But as any entrepreneur knows, over time, who you are becomes intimately intertwined with your business. Between customers to sell and manage, being on display at marketing events, caring for hundreds of employees, and fighting to keep things moving forward, Greg had become Mr. Interactive Technology.

One year, Greg went on a trip to Egypt and had an experience that changed his life. He does not like to characterize it as a religious experience, but it surely was an awakening. This awakening changed the way he viewed the world and himself in the world, and he realized that he was not living a life that was in alignment with who he was. Over the years that followed, Greg worked slowly to bring his life into alignment. Greg has maintained his entrepreneurial spirit but has assured balance by spending time between cutting edge technology work and helping guide others on their journey to hear and listen to their inner voice.

As part of coming into alignment, he has created an internal "sovereignty" that prevents him from becoming his companies. He has also moved a part of his life into building a company called SpiritQuest Tours that provides opportunities for people to visit places that "ignite the soul." Greg is living his best life, a life he loves and as part of that life is helping others live lives they love.

I hope these four ways of executing your Alignment Commitment in your life can guide you to beginning the journey of living a life you love.

Managing impermanence (creating meaning as we age)

"Society grows great when old men plant trees whose shade they know they shall never sit in"
—GREEK PROVERB

Most of our lives are built based on the understanding that we have a bright future full of potential. As we age though, we tend to become more aware of our mortality, and the future may seem to hold less and less potential. Even if the data suggest that young people are not finding meaning and purpose in life, it seems as though it would be easier to find that mission or purpose when there is a full life ahead. And the data shows that the older we become, the less we are willing to build meaning and purpose. As we age, and especially after we become senior citizens, the probability of death at any future year increases. However, our lack of energy for the future and any belief we have that our best years and most impactful years of our lives are behind us is not based on a thorough understanding, recollection, and awareness of the death statistics themselves. Rather, it is based on a belief that begins to move into our constant awareness and depress our energy, excitement, and vigor far before our final days arrive.

Nancy's prison

Nancy lost her husband of more than 40 years when she was in her early 60s. At that time, she felt like her life was over—a common, normal, and natural reaction. However, she never seemed to recover. She took some normal actions, like planning for her own death, which included writing her will, buying her funeral plot, and doing other things that she felt she needed to do to prepare for her own death.

But then she went further. She seemed to give up on life and become anxious about death always being at her door. She would say things like, "I am not going to be around for much longer, so what does it matter." She would get upset when her friends died and openly ask why she was still here. She avoided traveling and eventually began to leave the house less and less often. Her comfort zone shrank. She still did things like go to church, get her hair done, and go shopping, but she stopped building relationships with new people or exploring the world.

She was waiting for death and assuming she did not have much time left. But the fact is that she lived 25 years after her husband died. Twenty-five years that could have been spent differently; that could have been spent building a new life, exploring the world, and doing different things. She had 25 years to make a new reality, but she gave up.

Little did she know that she did make a difference for some people—by showing them what *not* to do. She showed them that, if they ever found themselves thinking along those lines, wondering when their time would come, that they needed to stop and focus on what they were going to do with whatever time they had left.

Data show that older people who have meaning and purpose live longer, healthier lives. They have less injury, less incapacitation, less incidence of dementia and similar degenerative disorders. They also tend to have more friends and are more socially connected, which makes a big difference on measures of life satisfaction. But when people focus on death only because they are 60 or 70 or 80 or even 90, they fill that attentional straw with something that they can do nothing about, and their focus becomes preparing for death instead of living life. Which, no matter your age, makes no logical sense.

Death is imminent—but every minute can be SPICY

Death is imminent for us all, but the fact that we are doomed is the exact reason to live with passion, energy, excitement, and vigor every single day. As we age, many people lose this passion, but let's be clear: this is more about a belief than a reality. And the proof lies with those who find out they have a terminal illness early in life. Some of these younger people tend to have and build far more purpose, energy, and vigor into their lives than 99% of the people in the world.

As you may remember from my Squirt Gun Project, I spent some summers volunteering for Trail's Edge Camp, which is run by the University of Michigan's C. S. Mott Children's Hospital. It was named Trail's Edge because when the camp was started, the technology and medicine that was keeping ventilator-dependent kids alive was revolutionary—it was at the edge of any previously traveled paths.

The first year I attended camp, I just came as a visitor. I thought I was not ready to deal with the emotional trauma that I anticipated having as a result of the experience. These were kids who had diseases so profound that many of them steered their wheelchairs by using their tongue. They depended on medical professionals and caretakers most of their day. I would get anxious every time I heard the beeping that indicated one of the mobile ventilators was not working properly. My first day of my first week at camp was very emotionally difficult.

But then something happened. I fell in love with the kids! Yes, these were children with really terrible diseases. Some of them could even break bones if picked up incorrectly. But there was so much real and profound joy in hanging out with them. The kids were full of energy, excitement, and life itself! It turns out that I was more preoccupied with their diseases than they were. They were here to play and have fun, and I was being the stick in the mud.

After that realization, camp turned into one of the most meaningful experiences of my life. We played, laughed, joked, and enjoyed life at such a level of vigor that I have not experienced any time previously or since. Every year they mourn and celebrate the lives of the kids from previous years at camp who have died over the last year. Every year there are tears of sorrow and joy—these kids live every day as fully as possible because they don't know if they will be there tomorrow, or if their friends will be there tomorrow. The threat of an end to the future for these kids does not depress them, or stop them, or even slow them down. They are aware of the preciousness of every day and have a full understanding of the concept of impermanence that many of us, young or old, lack.

Most healthy young people lack the understanding of impermanence. Old people underestimate the amount of time they may have left in this world and the impact that they can still have. For young people, the future is now and death far away. However, the fact is that people die at all ages; there is no magic age at which no one dies. But realizing that we never know how much time we have left, and that the only real certainties in life are that change and death, are important elements of maintaining awareness. So, what are you waiting for!?

In this chapter, we have provided guidance on living a SPICY life you love today, in the real world. We talked about some of the issues you may come across, from a heightened awareness of anything associated with your Alignment Commitment, to a warning to ensure you are putting things that are not there in place instead of fighting against what is not there. We have talked about cleaning up messes you make when you are out of integrity, and we have talked about dealing with reality. We have talked about the issues with social feedback. We have talked about the ways you can begin to implement your Alignment Quotient into your everyday life, including examples, and we have talked about dealing with the fact we are all going to die and how that is no excuse not to get going. With this, you are ready to go out and start building a SPICY life you love.

Conclusion

> *"Today you are You, that is truer than true. There is no one alive who is Youer than You."*
>
> —DR. SEUSS

You now have a complete path for powerfully creating and living a SPICY life you love while minimizing regrets. By choosing alignment, and making an Alignment Commitment, you choose a level of freedom that can never be taken away from you without your permission. This does not guarantee a life free from pain, disappointment, anxiety, or failure. Any path that promises that is simply a lie. Life in its entirety, as something full and complete, includes both pleasure and pain, good times and bad times.

Many people sleepwalk through life. Then at the end of their life, when things don't work out, they blame society, they blame their situation, they blame their parents. Some people blame their own meat suit, because that is what they listened to and what led them where they are. Strangely, when they have success, they take credit for it themselves—but make no mistake, it is the meat suit that is still in control and giving itself credit for success while laying blame for failure elsewhere.

What an amazing life to live when you are aligned such that you can both take full credit for the success and responsibility for the failures. By choosing alignment, you will choose to step outside your comfort zone when it matters most—just as Franz Stigler did when he saved those Americans in that B-17 bomber. In Stigler's later years, he would say that of all the things he had accomplished both during the war and after, making the decisions he made on that day to be aligned with who he was, was the most important accomplishment of his life. Will you be able to say the same? Or will you have excuses and others to blame for your life outcomes?

As Dr. Seuss says, "There is no one alive that is Youer than you." The declaration of being and SPICY purpose statement that make up your Alignment Commitment are a powerful tool to ensure that you remain true to your unique self. This tool is especially important in a world that can draw you towards a level of conformity that only leads to missed opportunities and regret. I hope for you that you will choose to take this path, claim your freedom, and use your power. I wish you the best on your journey to create and live a SPICY life you love.

AUTHOR'S NOTE: HOW I SEE IT

I am not a fan of depression. However, as a person with hypomania, I experience "depression lite" as a normal part of my life. Hypomania is a disorder that causes cyclical highs and lows. It was once explained to me as mini-bi-polar disorder. A bi-polar person sees himself as a god one day, and a piece of garbage not worth the air he breathes the next. A person with hypomania sees himself as god's gift to software one day, and an idiot who can't do anything right the next.

When I was younger, hypomania had disastrous impacts on my life, and I did many dumb things as a teen. When I was up, the world was great. I could be quite gregarious. I flirted with a lot of girls, I was hyper curious, and I had creative ideas across many areas of study. I seemed to have unlimited energy and positivity and could go for days on little sleep. However, when I went down, my brain told me I was stupid, I chided myself for wasting so much time on dumb things that will never work, I felt like a loser who couldn't stick to anything or do anything important, I cut down anything I had just created or built, and I viewed myself as incompetent, lazy, and even stupid. Sometimes, as many people with depression know, the self-talk could be much worse than anything I wrote above.

As I aged, I learned to manage my depression. I say "manage," because I tried to get rid of my up and down cycles once and it was a mistake. I found that when I was more "even" and had eliminated my ups and downs, I had no personality, life had no flavor or spice—it was bland, like eating mushy flavorless oatmeal for every meal; every day with no change and no interest.

After this failed experiment, I decided that managing the ups and downs was better than simply eliminating them. So the next experiment was how to manage my hypomania, which caused me to investigate depression itself.

What I found was that both sides of my hypomania were very useful to me. Someone once told me that hypomania is one of the best mental disorders to have—it's like a superpower. In my up periods, I have the positivity and energy to attack new problems and the creative mindset and arrogance to come up with novel solutions. And I pursue them in spite of what anyone might say. This happens to be one of the key reasons that my career has been so diverse and has allowed me to be a part of, and successful in, so many interesting projects. I wore this professional distinction as a badge of honor long before I understood I had hypomania.

It is true that people looked at me as arrogant when I was in the up part of the cycle—but when I was in the down cycle, I saw myself as a piece of garbage. I would rip apart the project that I was so positive about the previous day. Sometimes I would throw away half of what I did; other times I would throw away everything and start all over.

When I was in a down period, people rarely saw me. I would find ways and excuses to separate myself from people, whether by spending more time in my cubicle working (or acting like I was working), staying home and watching TV alone, or just ignoring phone calls and e-mails. So, my professional reputation tended to revolve around the way I appeared during my up time. But truth be told, I spend the same amount of time or even more in the down periods. The people who spent time with me more often (family and close friends) tended to see me during the down times as well as the up times, and so they saw the whole cycle. To them, I was known as the person who would find ten of the last two problems. This sounds like a very bad characteristic, but I found interesting research that changed my perception of depression and depressed people.

I took a strange test in university. This test had only 10 questions, but they were very odd questions. They asked things like "guess a range, in kilometers, of the distance between Salt Lake City Utah, and Beijing, China going eastbound," or "guess a range of the speed in centimeters per minute of the fastest snail in the world." Respondents are supposed to answer such that there is a 90% chance that the real answer lies within their selected range. To get a 90% chance you cannot select a range like 1km to 1,000,000km between Beijing and Salt Lake City, or 1cm/min – 1,000,000cm/min for the snail, because those ranges would have a 100% certainty that the real number is between. This limitation forces you to pick numbers like 1,000km to 3,500km between Salt Lake City and Beijing, or 10cm to 25cm/min for the world's fastest snail.

The goal is to get an answer out of people that reflects their own confidence level in their guess. Most respondents only get 4-6 questions correct—meaning they were overconfident in their ability to select an appropriate range.

This happens because most people have a positivity bias. Positivity bias has been found extensively in many studies. If you want to test it out for yourself, just ask anyone if they are better-looking than average, a better driver than average, or smarter than average in relation to their friends. I guarantee you will find that 50% of the people you ask do not believe themselves to be below average on any of those metrics, and yet half of them must be below average by definition. That's overconfidence and positive bias at work. However, on that crazy question test, there are people who do get 9 of 10 correct. The professor informed us that answering 9 of 10 questions correct does not correlate with intelligence, but instead with depression.

Research suggests that people who are depressed may be able to see the world more realistically[70]; they do not wear rose-colored glasses like most people. Furthermore, research suggests that the depression mechanism can be a powerful problem-solving mechanism[71]. I was intrigued, as this meant my depression, for all its negativity, may have some benefit to me both in terms of seeing reality as well as solving problems.

Though this research is controversial, it opened my mind to the possibility that both my ups and downs have functional aspects. During my "up" periods, I was able to explore crazy ideas and concepts that others would never see. But when I was down, I could look back at my crazy ideas and get rid of the garbage: the stuff that would likely never work in reality. Furthermore, my depression allowed me to linger on the problems longer than other people, giving me a chance to solve them. My depression had been a sorting mechanism for separating fantasy from real opportunities, and a focus mechanism to keep me at it. This got me thinking about how else my depression might be right.

Sometimes, my depression gets quite bad, as anyone with depression will know. During these times, my brain takes over and focuses on persistent messages, so I started to journal and capture these depressed thoughts. After journaling for a while, I went back to review my entries and noticed a pattern. Over and over, my depressed brain was telling me things like my life was useless, I was useless, there was no meaning and I would never find any, nothing I do is useful and so life is pointless. I have talked with other depressed people and they seem to have similar recurrent thoughts when depressed. To be sure, none of those thoughts are pleasant, and they are certainly not very functional in a person's life. But, armed with my new paradigm, I started looking at these thoughts and wondering if they were not correct in some way—a task I expected to depress me. But remember, when I am up, I am full of energy and optimism, so it was during those times I pursued the crazy ways these thoughts could be right. What I came up with was amazing. Maybe, just maybe, my depressed ideas were right—and maybe that was ok?

I did not have an *aha* moment of perfect insight. I started by researching Eastern and Western philosophies and religions and came out with the following idea: Life has no intrinsic purpose or meaning, until we add it. At first, this learning had me at a loss and was difficult to accept, but over time and with a significant amount of reflection, debate with friends, and experience, I started understanding the value of life from this point of view. As long as I am alive, and, as far as we know, only when I am alive, do I have the ability to create meaning and purpose in life. Everything in life has meaning and purpose *because* I (or we) put it there—both for myself and others. And since there is no intrinsic meaning or purpose to anything, it means nothing is truly important unless I make it important.

This paradigm gave me a power that I had never realized I had, and seemed both pragmatic and true.

When I started exploring this way of thinking in my life, I found it so freeing. It supersized the creative part of my up cycle because it played right into what that cycle already wanted to do, and opened lines of inquiry that were previously repressed. When it came to my down cycle, it neutered many of the most harmful parts: I no longer had to fight against these bad thoughts because I already knew and accepted that they were true. The truth of them just did not have as many teeth as it did before.

Furthermore, my purpose in life became more important and alive to me, and my physical death became less important. Through the process of exploring and including these base ideas into my everyday life, and figuring out how to express them to others, I rediscovered standard leadership lingo that I had heard a thousand times before: words like integrity, declaration, being, and mantra. These words started to make sense to me as part of a bigger and deeper truth than I had known before. These overused, yet underappreciated, pieces that were scattered all over the place started to fit together into a nice picture. They laid out a path to living a life of my choosing, and allowed me to build a life that I love. And this is how the concepts in this book were born.

The elephant in the room

I have always wondered if my experience and this discovery (or maybe rediscovery) could be helpful to other people. I had known people who suffered from depression throughout my life. And although I knew some of them ended up self-medicating, I had never known how big the problem was. The statistics are overwhelming. In 2017, the US Centers for Disease Control and Prevention estimated that 72,000 Americans died from drug overdoses[72]. As a comparison, according to the National Archives the U.S. lost 58,220 Americans during the whole Vietnam war[73]. Yes, in America, in one year, we lost more people to drug overdoses than we lost in the whole terrible Vietnam war. In Western Europe, and specifically in the UK, the number of drug-related deaths has been steadily on the rise[74]. I wondered how many of these drug-related deaths were due to people using drugs to deal with depression or anxiety. I wondered how many of them could have been prevented by someone explaining to them the things I had discovered. For sure, not all, but maybe some.

Around the Western world, the use of antidepressants has soared over the last 20 years, with Iceland in the lead at 1 person in 10 taking them[75]. It was estimated in 2014 that more than 322 million people globally were dealing with depression, and at that time, it was the leading cause of disability in the world[76]. Anxiety disorders add 264 million people to that list. The pharmaceutical industry says the anti-depressant drug market in the U.S. alone was 4.6 billion dollars in 2015 and expects it to grow to 7.3 billion over a decade. Globally, the anti-depressant market went from 15.2 billion in 2015 and is expected to grow significantly over the next decade[77]. It seemed that something was going on in the world, that so many people had these types of issues, and that it was forecast to increase at such an alarming rate.

Those statistics are both eye opening and devastating, especially to the families and friends who have been impacted by this epidemic. They strongly suggested to me that the world has a problem. More alarming is that the solutions being pursued, with a ton of money and resources, are from the pharmaceutical industry: the same industry generating the products that are killing more Americans each year than died in the Vietnam war. Now, I want to be clear that I am not an anti-drug person. There are times when drugs are critical to keeping people alive (Morphine, Epinephrine, Nitroglycerine), curing illness and disease (Penicillin, Polio vaccine, chemotherapy), improving the quality of life (Tylenol for any number of everyday pains), or even improving the quality of our intimate relationships (Viagra). The pharmaceutical industry has created many miracles that have benefited humanity by extending life and improving the quality of the life we have, so I am not willing to throw out the proverbial baby with the bathwater here. That being said, the expectation that the pharmaceutical industry will create pills that solve all of our problems puts an undue burden on them, and only serves to ignore our collective responsibility. A simple pill, as pleasant and dream-worthy as it sounds, is never going to solve all our problems.

Author's Note: How I See It

When it comes to our social problems like anxiety and depression, we appear to be primarily focused on a pill, and secondarily focused on trained psychologists. Not a lot of other mainstream methods exist to support people who desire to change, or to prevent people from falling into these conditions in the first place. I wondered if there was something that I had learned that could be useful to help with this global problem. I was on my way to seeing a reason to write this book.

A root of the problem

There has been a body of research that suggests one source of prevention, and maybe even a solution, for anxiety and depression already exists. That body of research is around meaning and purpose in life[78]. The research shows that meaningful living conditioned upon self-truth and self-responsibility is linked with better neuroendocrine regulation[79], better immune function[80], lower cardiovascular risk[81], better sleep[82], and more adaptive neural circuitry[83]. In young people, it is associated with higher grades[84]. In older people, it is associated with a lower risk of losing physical capabilities [85] and lower risk of dementia[86]. People who have purpose and meaning in life tend to be more optimistic and have better social relationships[87]. Unlike research around meat, or salt intake, or butter consumption, there is no conflicting research outcomes that suggest anything but positive benefits from having and living with a strong purpose and meaning in life.

Could it be that the depression and anxiety epidemics, rife through the world, are a sign that we are suffering from a crisis of empowerment towards meaning and purpose in life? Could it be that this crisis is showing up as a symptom in our health outcomes including everything from drug overdoses to premature age-related illness? Could it be that, for many people, anxiety and depression are a symptom of a deeper issue?

At this point, you should not be surprised the data shows that few people have mastered purpose and meaning in their lives. The Templeton Foundation reports that only one in five high school students have a clear sense of purpose in life. This increases to only one in three through the college years, then remains steady until mid-life when it begins to drop and never seems to recover. This research seemed strange to me, so I ran a quick survey with about 150 of my "friends" on Facebook. Though this quick survey was highly unscientific, these were people I knew personally. Many of them I had known since we were kids, some of them were former students in my classes at university, and others were parents of my friends, who I had close relationships with. So, though unscientific, the results were very personal.

I found that only 35% of my friends disagreed with the statement "I am struggling and need to find more meaning and purpose in life". This suggested that meaning and purpose were areas that two-thirds of my friends wanted to work on! I was surprised and a bit caught off guard, as their Facebook posts would lead any onlooker to believe their lives were both happy and full of purpose. Though I receive the random meme on my feed about anxiety or depression, I did not realize that my small friend community may be quite closely representative of the larger research, which suggested that purpose and meaning were a deeper and more complicated problem than I originally realized.

The complications were highlighted by the third question in my survey, "I have a strong sense of purpose and meaning in life". To this question, 83% of respondents agreed to some level. This suggested that one in five of my friends were seriously struggling, but overall this was a good and high percentage. That made me feel a little bit better but got me thinking. How could such a high percentage of people say they had a strong sense of purpose and meaning in life on one question, and then, in the same survey on another question, suggest they were struggling with purpose and meaning?

The answer came from another study that showed parents and others who care for someone else have a high sense of purpose but can struggle because caretaking can be challenging and stressful[88]. Unsurprisingly, when asked to rank in order the things that give them meaning and purpose in life, 86% of the respondents chose Family as #1 or 2.

The implications of this are mixed. Firstly, it means that about one in five of my personal connections are struggling with meaning and purpose in life at the most basic level. Second, it means that only about one in three have a meaning and purpose that excites and engages them. Thirdly, it means that 50% have meaning and purpose given by their families, which keeps them going, but does not provide them with the total fulfillment desired—in other words, something is missing!

At this point, I seriously started asking myself if what I had learned could help other people. I wondered if I could teach them about creating a life they love full of meaning and purpose, and then show them a path to execute on it with integrity such that it could be functional in their lives.

Living a life with purpose and meaning are important for the health, well-being, and success of an individual and society. It is for this reason that I decided to get off my butt and write this book.

Alignment Quotient

One's ability to declare and maintain integrity between who one is (being and purpose) and one's thoughts, emotions, behaviors, and actions despite the situation or circumstances.

APPENDIX 1: REASONABLE DOUBT IN A MATERIALIST VIEWPOINT

This argument is not meant to be totally exhaustive, but instead a brief overview of a much bigger and more detailed debate. There are a significant number of superfluous books written on this topic, and I will add some of the most scientifically and philosophically esteemed in the references for this appendix in the endnotes. That being said, I hope to have included enough of the argument below to create some doubt in the materialist view and inspire some interest in the debate. I have been careful to include all references so that you can do your own research and come to your own conclusions.

One might argue it is impossible to *be* before *having*, because one's subjective and practical experience of life demonstrates that *having* comes before anything else. Without a body, for example, one could not have thoughts, feelings, or emotions, nor could one observe them, making the idea of *being* preceding *having* impossible. This is no more than an attempted answer to the chicken-and-egg problem, which is often resolved with the simple materialist premise that *actuality* (the realized, and real, chicken) must come before the *potentiality* (the potential, and future, chicken). This is taken as a foundational argument raising doubts in any theory where *being* comes before *having*.

These doubts about the *Be-Do-Have* model are pervasive throughout Western culture. Materialism[89] is the belief that matter is fundamental, and nothing, including being and consciousness, exists outside of material interactions—i.e there is no spiritual world, or even a world of any kind, beyond material things. Reductionism[90] is the practice of explaining everything by breaking it down into its constituent material pieces. Many scientists look at the world and consciousness from a reductionist and materialist perspective: nothing can arise in isolation, hence, everything that exists is dependent upon other things—physical things—for that existence. They use previously gathered evidence as justification, and that evidence is compelling, at first glance.

A materialist will begin the argument with a clear and well-established set of scientific facts, none of which I argue with. Firstly, the great expansion, or some similar astrophysical event, happened, marking the beginning of the universe[91]. After, things cooled down enough for subatomic particles to form and eventually the first element, hydrogen, was born. There were enormous amounts of this hydrogen, which condensed into massive balls hundreds of millions of miles in diameter. As the mass increased, the atoms of hydrogen were pulled towards the center of the ball by gravity. Over time, the pressure at the center increased so much that the hydrogen atoms began to fuse together, creating helium. This fusion generated a massive energy release like millions of nuclear bombs, which created pressure that pushed outwards against the other hydrogen atoms preventing them from all collapsing onto the center. This is the same mechanism that causes our own sun to "burn" and provide energy to the planet Earth. But after the hydrogen was used up in the star, the helium started to fuse together into carbon, and then carbon fused into neon, and then neon fused into oxygen, and then oxygen fused into silicon, and then silicon fused into iron. As each new element is created it becomes a denser element (reflected by its higher atomic number on the periodic table) and migrates to the center of the star.

The smooth, stepwise process is disrupted when silicon fuses into iron. Until that point, all the atoms being fused together give off energy. The fusion reaction that turns hydrogen into helium can take billions of years.

The outward force caused by the energy release of the fusion reaction keeps the gravity created by billions of cubic miles of atoms in the star from rushing towards the center of the star. In contrast, the reaction that turns silicon to iron does not give off energy, and the silicon fuel available in the star can be burned through in a week or so. Iron is a very stable material and does not easily fuse to form elements higher on the periodic table. So, when the star reaches this stage, the iron sucks up all the energy instead of giving it off. This allows all the millions of miles of mass to succumb to gravity, and the outer layers of the star collapse into the center. With tens or hundreds of millions of miles of space in which to accelerate, the outer layers approach the speed of light before crashing into the iron core, where they ricochet off the iron and create a massive shockwave. This shockwave spreads back up through the other material in the star, fusing together elements such as gold, platinum, and uranium. This is known as a supernova. The first star supernovae occurred much faster than the current stars in the universe because they were much larger and burned through their fuel much faster.

The energy released from that one star can outshine an entire galaxy for a few days as all the newly created elements get shot out of the star and into the universe where they are free to recombine into other things like asteroids, planets, solar systems, and even human beings. In this theory of the universe's origins, supernovas and merging quasars (a special type of star) are responsible for the creation of all elements in the periodic table heavier than hydrogen[92].

Mathematical models, as well as replicable physics experiments, have confirmed this process, providing a compelling and elegant explanation for the creation of every element on the planet. How a supernova occurs and creates all of our elements requires no god, no heaven or hell, and no soul—in fact, nothing abstract is involved. It is a model that depends solely on known physical elements and processes.

The materialist will continue to build on this model. Because we know supernovas and merging quasars are the source of all elements, the thinking is that we can also estimate and measure the percentages of each element that must exist in the universe. Because of the Big Bang's ongoing influence, mass fraction shows hydrogen to be the most abundant element in the universe, followed by helium, carbon, oxygen, and nitrogen, in descending order. Any other elements are relatively and extraordinarily rare. Of the five most plentiful elements, 99.1% of the human body is made from four of them—only helium (a noble gas, and hence non-reactive) is not present in the human body. The other nine-tenths of one percent of the human body is comprised of very rare elements. In other words, the human body is composed of the exact type and quantities of elements that would be expected if humans emerged from star dust soup through some natural process.

Thus, the beautiful story about stars and supernovas that explains the creation of all the elements in the periodic table, also applies to the creation of the human body. No god was necessary, no heaven or hell, no soul, and nothing abstract. Only a simple group of processes that can be explained by the laws of physics and mathematics.

Beyond Body to Brain

The materialist view expanded its model to the brain. With technology such as the electroencephalogram (EEG) and functional magnetic resonance imaging (fMRI) machines, we can peer into the workings of the human brain. The results show that certain parts of our brain light up when we take an action, or are stimulated by an outside action. For example, when a person in an fMRI experiences social rejection or physical pain, a part of the brain called the anterior cingulate cortex (ACC) lights up[93]. When we are recalling the route to get from our work to home, a part of the brain called the hippocampus lights up[94]. When we are thinking about ourselves, a part of the brain called the medial prefrontal cortex lights up[95]. So, to a materialist there are parts of the brain that, alone or in combination, map to specific human behaviors. No abstraction is necessary in this conception. Anything that can be explained by an action or something observable can be explained by the operations of the physical brain. This tenet of the materialist model seems to be able to account for what is called the "easy problem of consciousness": a behavior can be explained by computational or neural mechanisms."[96]

But this is only one part of the consciousness problem. The other so-called "hard problem" is not so easy. How do computations in the brain explain our subjective experience of the world? How do they explain that a particular color of blue can, to a particular person, be beautiful? How do they explain my enjoyment when I hear my favorite symphony played? How do simple brain calculations explain how I can have a subjective experience of an emotion?

Because the materialist belief structure is founded upon *having* preceding *being*, they need to show some material connection to this hard problem of consciousness for their theory to be complete. This brings us to the edge of scientific and philosophical thought today, where the battle lines are being drawn and the challenging work is being done.

Emergence Theory: From Brain to Consciousness

A reductionist materialist would say that by understanding smaller and smaller parts of the brain, we will be led to an understanding of consciousness itself. One leading theory of human consciousness, which starts from this place, is known as "Emergence theory." Emergence refers to how collective properties or behaviors arise out of the properties of the constituent parts[97]. A traffic jam is a simple example of emergence, whereby too many cars on a joined network of roads combines to create a bottleneck down the road. Traffic jams are complex phenomena, which can be explained based on an understanding of the properties of their smaller parts (roads, vehicles, traffic laws, and so on). Emergence is evident everywhere in nature, from the movements of flocks of birds or schools of fish, to the way galaxies are formed as spirals. Emergence theory, when applied to consciousness, says that the complexity of consciousness arises from lots of simple things in the brain working together. It is the way materialists and reductionists rationalize consciousness into their paradigm of the world, and much research is occurring to help advance their thinking.

The nice thing about the theory of emergence of consciousness is that we can test it to see if it works in the real world. So, for example, one of the things that is suggested by emergence theory is, if we could build a computer with a large enough ability to calculate, then consciousness will automatically emerge. Basically, consciousness is an emergent property of having X number of calculations per second, and maybe some particular structure for those calculations—and nothing more. Using a reductionist perspective, let's start with small things and work up, and see if we can discover the flaws in the argument.

The definitional problem

> *"The idea that consciousness is an emergent property of brains is a metaphysical assumption, not a scientific fact"*
> —HIS HOLINESS THE DALAI LAMA.

If we want to challenge the materialist viewpoint, we need to look at the claim that consciousness emerges from any machine capable of a certain number of calculations per second. To do so, we need to first agree on a definition of consciousness—one that allows us to measure something. Unfortunately, no such definition exists, leading to a serious problem: you can't measure something you cannot define.

The scientific and philosophical communities have proposed various definitions of consciousness: at one extreme, the definition suggests that only self-aware creatures with language (such as humans) are conscious; while at the other extreme, consciousness is said to be fundamental and found virtually everywhere, including in inanimate objects and subatomic particles (such as quarks). This massive range allowed by the various definitions shows we really don't know what we are talking about when it comes to consciousness. This is our first hint there is something wrong with the materialist approach. Anyone suggesting that one theory is better than another is giving an opinion rather than facts. That being said, let's look at some facts and what they suggest about the materialist-reductionist perspective.

The Measurement Problem: Behaviors

The basic properties of consciousness that everyone (scientists and philosophers) seems to agree on is that it includes some sort of "awareness" and/or "understanding" that leads to a subjective experience of living. Though neither awareness nor understanding in themselves is expected to be synonymous with consciousness, there is hope that they can lead to a means to measure or explore consciousness through the observation of behaviors.

Following the materialist view that there must be a certain number of calculations per second for consciousness to emerge, only creatures and things that are able to do calculations should show behaviors suggesting awareness or understanding. In modern biological terms, this means any conscious creature must have neurons. Rocks, single-celled organisms, plants, and many other life forms must be eliminated from consideration.

The materialist discards these non-neuron things, even though there is some evidence for limited awareness and understanding by organisms without neurons. For example, unicellular organisms like paramecium can move towards food and away from danger. They can reproduce with other paramecia, and might even be said to enjoy reproduction by simply not moving during the process, all without a single neuron [98] (is this subjective experience?). Does this mean paramecia have awareness and understanding of their situation? And if so, are they conscious?

Many materialists would likely say they are not conscious, despite their observed behavior, which raises questions around behaviors as an appropriate measure of consciousness. What distinguishes the behaviors and possible subjective experience of a paramecium (which has no neurons) from a microscopic insect (which has neurons), or from more complex beings like mammals? Without the answer to this question, it seems problematic to use behaviors that suggest awareness or understanding as a means of finding or measuring consciousness.

But let's continue forward and see what we can discover. Knowing that materialist theories specify the inclusion of only animals with neurons as part of the explanation of consciousness, we might do well to turn our attention to a very special worm that may help us understand more about emergence theory and its calculations prediction.

The Animation Problem: The OpenWorm project

OpenWorm[99] is an open source project aimed at creating the first digital life form. Scientists, engineers and interested hobbyists from around the globe are working together to build a computational model of the *Caenorhabditis elegans* (*C. elegans*), a microscopic roundworm. *C. elegans* is the perfect candidate for such a project: it is well-studied, has a very consistent lifecycle, and has just under 1000 cells total, with 302 neurons and 95 muscle cells. With only those 1000 cells, *C. elegans* solves basic problems of feeding, mate-finding, and predator and toxin avoidance, using a nervous system-driving muscle on a body trying to survive in a complex world. It is the only animal with a fully mapped "connectome" identifying every single connection between neurons. This feat of mapping the connectome took 13 years of work including taking 20,000 very thin slices of the worm which were each imaged with a microscope and then assembled into a map like a giant jigsaw puzzle.

The goal of these scientists and engineers was to digitally reproduce the simplest and most studied animal so that the process of (re)creating digital life could ultimately be applied to other, more complex, life forms. The team spent years creating digital neurons, and then digitally wiring those neurons together in exactly the same configuration as in a living worm. Guess what happens when you hook up 302 digital neurons to a power source and then flip the "On" switch? In this case…nothing. Nothing happened at all.

Let's be clear: as simple as this organism is, this is a very ambitious project and can add a lot of important information to our understanding of the mechanics around a brain's calculations. That being said, the project founder, Dr. Steven Larson, has already conceded that the project is unable to create biological realism, as it is too complicated.[100] So instead, the team had to "fudge" the computer model to get it to work because organized neurons themselves did not create life.

By "fudging" the model, the programmers were able to animate the worm. This required coding rules and concepts into the model of neurons which said, these things are good and these other things are bad. The researchers had to, in effect, give the model a basic form of meaning and purpose before it started to act like a worm at the grossest and simplest levels—by, for example, moving away from things the researchers coded to simulate threat or towards things coded to simulate reward. Make no mistake, this is a fantastic achievement for the engineers and scientists, and much has been learned. But the neurons did not animate that simulation on their own, and the simulated worm cannot learn or exhibit other behaviors as a real worm can. Basically, a complete simulated neuronal brain showed neither awareness, understanding, nor subjective experience of the world on its own.

Donald Hoffman, a cognitive psychologist at the University of California, Irving outlines the problem that this example shows: no one has figured out how brain activity causes anything. Neurons have no causal powers. Brain causes none of our perceptions, behaviors, or emotions.[101] This suggests at the basic level that the idea of material coming before potential or abstraction may be flawed and that the focus on neurons, brain activity, or behaviors will never lead to answers as to the nature of consciousness. But let's keep going and look at the upper end of the range where emergence is expected to occur: Humans.

The Calculation Volume Problem: Human Awareness

According to emergence theory, consciousness emerges from calculations per second; and it could be thought that a worm simply does not have enough calculations per second for consciousness to emerge. For consciousness to emerge, then, we simply need to build a computer that can do as many calculations as a human brain—we know we are conscious, right? How many calculations is that? For humans, it is estimated to be 1 exaFLOPS, or 10^{18} floating-point operations per second[102]. That is a billion billion calculations per second. Keep in mind, a single floating-point operation is the ability to calculate 4.387 multiplied by 7.846, which is already much harder than multiplying a simple 5 by 7. This is the limit that must be achieved according to the most extreme version of the definition, which only includes humans.

Today, a U.S.-based machine named "Summit" is the fastest computer in the world, and can perform at 200 petaFLOPS, or 2 times 10^{17} calculations per second[103]. The U.S. Department of Energy has commissioned a faster computer to come online in 2021 that will reach 1.5 exaFLOPS (1.5 times 10^{18})[104] . If we take emergence theory at face value, then we should have a computer that is conscious by 2021. Should we be worried about the much-feared *technical singularity* threatening to take over the world in 2021? Don't worry, we have nothing to fear. Split brain research suggests that if it was going to happen, if calculations per second was the metric we should be using, we would already have conscious computers.

Split Brain Research and Consciousness

In observing split brain human patients, in whom a mechanical separation has been created via surgery between the right and left parts of the brain to stop seizures, it seems a person can have two distinct consciousnesses. Scientists discovered this by supplying different information to each side of the brain, and then observing that each has a different experience independent of the other side.[105]

In one experiment, scientists put up a physical divider so that the subject's right eye saw a picture of a pencil, and the left eye saw a picture of a cup. The right eye feeds information to the left brain, and the left eye feeds information to the right brain. Language is controlled by only the left brain. So, when asked what picture was shown, the left brain responded "pencil." However, when the left eye was shown a range of objects and the subject was asked to select a complementary object, the right brain "told" the left arm to choose the saucer: an object that is associated more with the cup than with the pencil. When asked why the person picked the saucer, the left brain then provided a logical reason for this mis-association. The explanation was totally disconnected from the fact that the right brain had seen the cup, since the language part of the brain had only seen the pencil.

Remember, the challenge of consciousness is related to our subjective experience of the world, and each side of the brain has its own subjective experience of the world independent of the other side.

There are many experiments that have been done on split brain patients that seem to suggest each side of the brain experiences consciousness independent of the other. Some research shows the different sides having different personalities and belief structures. For example, one side can be Catholic, and the other Atheist. Considering this information, the human with the split brain seems to have no limitation of their sense of their own consciousness. Each side of the brain feels it is fully conscious and does not recognize a difference between its state of consciousness before the surgery and after the surgery. Furthermore, other humans around these split-brain patients would not suggest they were any less conscious than they were either prior to surgery, or in comparison to anyone else.

So, what does this mean for our estimates of the number of calculations required to achieve consciousness? Does this mean consciousness actually only requires half the calculations per second of a human brain? If so, a computer has already surpassed this half brain calculating capability, and therefore should be conscious. Yet, as far as we know, we have no conscious computers, and are unlikely to have conscious computers anytime soon.

Artificial Intelligence and consciousness

From here, one may argue that maybe these super-fast computers don't have the right structure or organization to be conscious. In the OpenWorm project, we learned that "rules" seemed to make a difference in animating the worm, so maybe these fast computers simply need to be organized with some proper rules for awareness and understanding to emerge—like may be possible with neuro-networks and the advances of artificial intelligence. In the 1980s, a philosopher named John Searle came up with a famous thought experiment called "the Chinese room" [106] that suggests this will not cause consciousness either.

The Chinese room argument

Imagine that an English speaker, who only speaks English, is placed into a room that holds a series of books. Inside these books lie instructions that, if followed perfectly, will allow the English speaker to correlate any series of Chinese characters with a set of response characters (i.e. the books are an algorithm). Functionally, if the instructions are followed correctly then the English speaker would be able to give to a Chinese speaker an appropriate response to any question in Chinese characters.

Outside of this room is a set of Chinese people who want to discover if the *room* understands Chinese. They do not know that the English-speaking person is inside. They "interrogate" the room by asking questions via pieces of paper with Chinese characters written on them that are passed through a slot in the wall of the room. The questions include topics about subjective experience of life.

The person inside takes in the pieces of paper with Chinese symbols and looks through the books. Using the information in the books, they send responses written in Chinese characters back through the slot. The Chinese people are amazed! Wow, the room understands my questions—it must be conscious!

Then, these Chinese people, acting very much like neuroscientists, come up with a crazy idea to find a way to see which parts of the room have activity when they ask a question. Without realizing it, they find a way to track the "activation" of the individual books (They did not know they were books; they only found a way to measure movement, which turned out to be the opening and closing of books). When they send a piece of paper with Chinese characters to the room, they see which parts of the room are activated (the books) and determine that this part or that part is responsible for a certain type of "thought".

As we think through this example, it is easy to see that the English speaker had no understanding of neither the questions nor the responses. Neither did the books have an understanding. But all the measurements that were being done provided more and more data supporting the conclusion that the room itself understood Chinese and maybe was even conscious.

This thought experiment highlights the problem we face with measuring consciousness via neurons or behaviors. Our science seems to break down when it comes to pinpointing consciousness. Why? Because scientific interrogation can only look at observable behaviors—not essence—hence, at best we can show correlation between matter and behaviors, but not causation. We miss the man in the machine!

We have reached the limits

To summarize what we have seen so far in this argument: our top minds have been unable to define or agree on a basic definition of consciousness. Through the OpenWorm project, we have seen failure to use the most basic material brain to create even the most simplistic behaviors, without having to add rules and concepts that exist beyond the meat-based machine made of neurons. We have seen a disconnect between the number of calculations in a brain and consciousness; hence, simple calculations per second cannot be the solution. And we have shown that measuring behaviors and even simple measurements of brain cannot show understanding and will; they correlation but not causation when it comes to consciousness.

There are no theories that attempt to explain how neurons, rules, or calculations per second can create feelings such as love, compassion, or anger. Even though neuroscientists have shown there are parts of the brain that light up when a person has such feelings, they are unable to prove their measurements are showing the *cause* of an emotion rather than correlation to an emotion. When it comes to consciousness, let's face it—we are at a loss.

These facts suggest that we do not have the proper tools, language, mathematics, science, or paradigms to capture or understand what consciousness is. We need a revolution in one or all of these areas: something completely new and unknown to aid in the understanding of consciousness. If that is the case, then the materialist's generalizations based on existing science and the physical world must be incorrect. And if they are incorrect, then it means that consciousness may not flow from the things we *have*.

Which, for the doubter, should be enough to open the door to consider the Be-Do-Have model over the Have-Do-Be model.

Revisiting the Definition Problem

Sir Roger Penrose, Professor Emeritus at Oxford University, has proposed that an obscure mathematical proof may suggest why consciousness can never be measured via a materialist viewpoint, and that a revolution is necessary in order to appropriately define and explore consciousness. Penrose is a mathematical physicist, mathematician, and philosopher of science. He has won numerous awards for his groundbreaking work. In his brilliant book *The Emperor's New Mind*[107], Penrose dives into the topic of mathematics and the known physics around consciousness. I will not get into his complete arguments here, but if you are interested in the topic I highly recommend his book. I will explore one part of his argument in brief, which should serve to open the cracks we have developed in the previous arguments into much wider chasms, thereby solidifying reasonable doubt that the materialist viewpoint will ever be able to offer a solution to the problem of consciousness.

One of Penrose's most interesting arguments is the problem of defining "truth." Truth is supposed to be something you can conclude via pure logic, and mathematical truth is supposed to be both universal and non-contradictory (in other words, it cannot be both true and false at the same time). Penrose uses Gödel's theorem[108] to lay out this argument. The first part of this theorem states that no consistent system of axioms whose theorems can be listed by an effective procedure (i.e. an algorithm) is capable of proving all truths about the arithmetic of natural numbers. For any such consistent formal system, there will always be statements about natural numbers that are true, but that are unprovable within the system. The second part of the overall theorem, an extension of the first, shows that the system cannot demonstrate its own consistency. Therefore, when a mathematician creates the rules for discovering truths inside a system, and if those rules are complete such that they disallow contradictions, then there will be things that are known to be true but can never be proven as such inside the system.

A simple analogy might add clarity. Imagine you wanted to write a set of strict rules to define what is a chair. These rules would be written in such a way that anything that is *not* a chair could never be named a chair. Gödel's theorem suggests that if the rules are written perfectly, they will guarantee that there will be things that *you know to be chairs* that, according to the strict rules you outlined, you would not be able to call "chair." Gödel's theorem also suggests that if you create rules such that anything that is a chair will be able to be named chair, then you are certain to allow things that are *not chairs* to be *named a chair*. An example of this would be the fallen tree that you sat on to rest that time you were camping. If you want to explore this theorem for yourself, go ahead and create rules for a chair such that nothing that is not a chair will ever be mistaken as one—and then see if you can find things that are, in fact, seen as chairs by yourself and others, but would not meet your definitional requirements.

Defining what is a chair, and what is not, may not be the most high-stakes exercise one can imagine, but when we are talking about scientific discovery—truth matters. If we extend Gödel's theorem to the scientific method as the rules and procedures of discovering truth inside our universe, then by using only the scientific method as our way of knowing truth in the universe, things will exist that we know to be true, but can never prove true. Though the scientific method has been fantastic as a means to understand and codify the behaviors of things in our universe, it has so far failed to uncover anything about the nature of our reality beyond the categorization of behaviors. Does this mean that consciousness could be a thing we know to be true, but can never prove to be true inside of our existing tools and paradigms for proving truth?

The Materialist approach fails to even understand material.

Consciousness is not the only thing that evades full understanding inside our existing mathematic and scientific frameworks. There is another critical phenomenon in our physical world that evades science's ability to appropriately model and capture it: matter itself. Quantum mechanics (the mechanical workings of tiny bits of matter) underlies the workings of everything in our universe: from the black holes at the center of our galaxy, to the cell phone in your pocket. Scientists have been probing these tiny bits of matter since 1897, when J.J. Thomson discovered the electron. Later, Albert Einstein declared matter to be nothing more than energy divided by the speed of light squared ($E=MC^2$ or also written as $M=E/C^2$).

Think about Einstein's equation for a second. Matter—the stuff that makes up everything we see, feel, and interact with—is simply energy divided by a really fast speed, squared. And what is energy? It is the capacity to do work; or said another way, the potential to do something or behave. This answer about matter is no more comforting than the ones we have about consciousness. Since speed is not a physical thing, and energy is just a potential to do something (not a thing but a potential doing), then mathematically does matter exist? From our experience of the world, it seems so—but science has not been able to really help us understand its nature beyond its behaviors.

For example, matter has mass...but what is mass? It is a behavior that matter exhibits that resists change in speed or direction when a force is applied[109]. Basically, when we apply a force to a bit of matter, we measure the amount of resistance that matter creates to that force. This is nothing more than a behavior that we call mass. If it were a human, we may call that behavior stubbornness.

When we get down to the subatomic level, we account for matter based on behaviors such as charge and spin. Charge is simply the behavior that a tiny bit of matter exhibits towards or away from an interaction with another charge. Spin is nothing more than a behavioral characteristic that we do not really understand either.[110]

In fact, particle accelerators are big machines that observe the behaviors of small bits of matter as they are smashed against other small bits of matter. Let's face it, we don't even know what matter "is" except for the behavioral characteristics that it exhibits as it interacts with other matter. And we do not even fully understand these behavioral characteristics.

To make our lack of understanding of matter even clearer, let's briefly look at what mathematics tells us about the location of matter. In 1935,

Appendix 1: Reasonable doubt in a materialist viewpoint

Austrian physicist Erwin Schrödinger made the science of *tiny bits of matter* memorable by explaining the craziness of the position of those electrons with an analogy that became one of his namesakes: Schrödinger's cat[111].

The Schrödinger's cat is a thought experiment in which a cat is put in a box with some kind of poison. A mechanism is added that will trigger the poison's release by the radioactive decay of a subatomic particle. Scientists know that these tiny particles are capable of being in multiple states at once, meaning that a particle could be decaying or not decaying at the same time. It follows that the poison could simultaneously be released and not released, and by extension, the cat would be both dead and not dead at the same time. So, until the box is opened and the cat is observed, it exists in a state of being BOTH alive and dead at the same time—basically nothing more than a potential of either. And this is how our science shows how tiny bits of matter actually behave.

Schrödinger's analogy is a brilliant, though somewhat unsavory, way of showing—through mathematical expression— that the simple act of making measurements changes the nature of the thing that is being measured. Hence, measurement of behavior will never be the appropriate way to understand the real underlying nature of matter. And although both Schrodinger and Einstein disliked what these equations meant about the fundamental uncertainty of matter, calling it "quantum weirdness", the equations seem to be sound.

So, if science, with its existing rules, frameworks, and theories, cannot be certain about something as basic as the nature of the building blocks that make up everything physical in the world, how can we be certain about materialist scientists' ability to locate an abstract consciousness within those same rules, frameworks, and theories?

Conclusion

It seems that we are nothing more than blind creatures, walking around, interacting with things. Based on what we "measure", we then classify common measurements of things that exude similar behaviors into a group and then give them a name. The name we give something does not tell us about its underlying nature. It only acts as a notational means for us to make sense of the world. And this is our limit—which we may never be able to be overcome.

Everything science knows about you is based on categorized behaviors. Your physical characteristics are a mix between the behaviors of your genes (e.g. blue eyes) and the behaviors of your body (e.g. big muscles) as it interacts with your environment. Your mental characteristics are also classified through your behaviors (e.g. extroverted or introverted). Even the titles we give one another are based upon previous behaviors or expectations of future behaviors (parent, soldier, doctor). But I think we all understand that we are not simply a summation or categorization of our behaviors.

As our scientific tools are designed to interrogate nature via categorization of behaviors, materialist-based science will likely never be appropriate for saying what we are and uncovering our underlying essence or consciousness. Therefore, analogous to matter, could consciousness, as an underlying nature of what makes us who we are, be one of those things that is true, but which our current rules around discovering truth prevent us from fully understanding? Based on the arguments laid out above, I leave the answer to you.

For anyone still thinking that consciousness is located straightforwardly inside the skull, I hope I have opened a door for you to consider that, when it comes to consciousness, the materialist view is nothing more than a belief structure, and this belief structure has serious flaws. If you can concede that, then you can be open to the possibility that consciousness lies beyond material things, and there is a reasonable chance that *Being* can, in fact, come before *Having*.

APPENDIX 2: BEING DEFINITIONS AND QUESTIONS

This list of 35 "being" nouns and their definitions can serve as a place to start for your own declaration. The questions below each definition are suggestions to get you started using the feedback tool that can be found at www.thealignmentquotient.com. You are free to change or combine these questions, or even create your own.

Notice there are two definitions for each "being" word. First is a noun: this is the word you are going to put in your declaration of being. Below that is a description of what it means to "be" your declared noun. The second definition is included to help you understand how you will show up—for yourself and in the world.

You may find it useful to read the questions first. They will give you a sense of how each declared being may show up for others, and the behaviors that a person who has integrity with each being will exude.

I suggest choosing one of the scales below for answering the questions:

a. Strongly agree
b. Agree
c. Slightly agree
d. Neither agree nor disagree

e. Slightly disagree
f. Disagree
g. Strongly disagree

OR

a. Rarely
b. From time to time
c. Sometimes

d. Often
e. Most of the time
f. Always

1. Enthusiasm
2. Joy
3. Inspiration
4. Excellence
5. Love
6. Compassion
7. Freedom
8. Self-Expression
9. Integrity
10. Resilience
11. Dependability
12. Courage
13. Responsibility
14. Authenticity
15. Present
16. Cause
17. Grace
18. Peace
19. Hope
20. Ambition
21. Persistence
22. Curiosity
23. Adventure
24. Creativity
25. Conscientiousness
26. Generosity
27. Abundance
28. Determination
29. Fun
30. Passion
31. Humility
32. Optimism
33. Thoughtfulness
34. Kindness
35. Unreasonableness

1. Enthusiasm

Intense and eager excitement, enjoyment and approval; something that inspires zeal or fervor.

Being Enthusiastic: A way of Being that supports one's own eagerness in pursuit of a passion and an intensity of purpose and direction.

Social Feedback Question Suggestions

How much do you agree with the following statements?

1. I am a person driven with an intensity of purpose, clear about what direction I want to go in my life.

2. My level of enthusiasm is infectious: I cause others to be excited about areas of their own life.

3. I am eager to accomplish projects that I am passionate about.

2. Joy

Great delight or happiness; elation.

Being Joyful: A way of Being that transcends happiness to a persistent quality of contentment and appreciation, given any circumstance or situation.

Social Feedback Question Suggestions

How much do you agree with the following statements?

1. I am more than happy, more often than not. My energy seems to come from within, with a strong emphasis on enjoying life.

2. My way of enjoying life is infectious. I cause those around me to be in a good mood.

3. I am the type of person that sees how easy and fun it is to make lemonade when life gives you lemons. As long as we get to be alive, let's enjoy it.

3. Inspiration

The quality of being a "creative breath" that stimulates or animates feelings or actions.

Being Inspired: A way of Being that calls forth a life-giving way of Being from others, such that they are touched, moved, and inspired into action in their own lives for the benefit of others.

Social Feedback Question Suggestions

How much do you agree with the following statements?

1. I am the type of person that encourages others to move beyond their limitations. When they do, it makes a difference for themselves and others.

2. I inspire others to be their best through my own actions and behaviors.

Open-ended question:

What advice would you give me to help me become more inspiring?

4. Excellence

The quality of being outstanding or extremely good. The fact or state of excelling; superiority; eminence.

Being Excellent: A way of Being that propels one to a level of mastery, to accomplish one's task for every reason possible, not just the perceived reasons as stated by others.

Social Feedback Question Suggestions

How much do you agree with the following statements?

1. I strive to be the best I can be in everything I take on.
2. I am driven from an internal motivation that seeks continuous improvement towards excellence.
3. When I am handed a project or activity, I can be counted on to deliver a result of the highest quality.

Open-ended question:

Where have I fallen short on being excellent in the last two weeks, and what advice could you give me to avoid that shortfall in the future?

5. Love

Feeling of strong or constant regard for and dedication to someone or something.

Being Loving: A way of Being that takes a stand for and is dedicated to others' experience of life, including the experience of peace, love, joy, and freedom.

Social Feedback Question Suggestions

How much do you agree with the following statements?

1. I desire other people's lives to work out well—I am always concerned with others' well-being.

2. I am a pleasure to work with because I make everyone's experience of the project so rewarding.

3. You can count on me to consider your needs over mine. I seem to get satisfaction from your success.

6. Compassion

A feeling of deep sympathy and sorrow for another who is stricken by misfortune, accompanied by a strong desire to alleviate the suffering.

Being Compassionate: A way of Being that allows one to relate to the being and actions of others in a way that brings understanding for others in any given situation.

Social Feedback Question Suggestions

How much do you agree with the following statements?

1. I am a champion for those who need one. I take up a cause because I can, when others can't.

2. I am the type of person who won't turn a blind eye to someone in need, and will take action to assist.

3. You can count on me to walk in another person's shoes and see what they need, and then do what it takes to fill that need.

Open-ended question:

Would you tell other people that I am a compassionate person?

7. Freedom

The power or right to act, speak, or think as one wants; a state of not being imprisoned or enslaved.

Being Free: A way of Being that allows every other way of Being as well as the actions that come from them. It exists in a space where things are neither wrong nor right, they are simply possible. It is a way of Being that considers the bigger picture and works with that view in mind.

Social Feedback Question Suggestions

How much do you agree with the following statements?

1. I allow people to be who they are without criticism.

2. I am willing to give people space to generate their own rewards and make their own mistakes.

3. You can count on me to not micromanage or behave in a controlling way.

How do you think I could enable others to feel freer in who they are and what they do?

8. Self-Expression

The expression into the world of one's feelings, thoughts, or ideas.

Being Self-expressive: A way of Being that gives the self the freedom to be whatever there is to be. It considers decorum, social norms, and what is usually accepted behavior...and then makes its own choice. A way of Being that exists as a passionate response to the wonders of life, while holding nothing back.

Social Feedback Question Suggestions

How much do you agree with the following statements?

1. I can express myself freely. More than a free spirit, I can articulate my wishes, wants, and desires in a wonderful way.

2. I have the ability to dance when what there is to do is dance; to cry when what there is to do is cry; to laugh when what there is to do is laugh; and work when what there is to do is get things done.

3. You can count on me to say what there is to say, do what there is to do, and be completely authentic no matter the situation.

9. Integrity

Honoring yourself as your word. Being whole and complete.

Being Integrous: A way of Being that brings honor and agreement to one's own words and promises—even your unspoken words and your own expectations of yourself.

Social Feedback Question Suggestions

How much do you agree with the following statements?

1. I am honest, authentic, and genuine. What you see is what you get, without pretense or deceit.

2. I fulfill my promises. If I say I will do it, then you know I will. If I say I can't, I'll tell you what my new promise is and give you enough notice so that you can make an adjustment.

3. You can count on me to give my word and keep it. I will move beyond that which would stop others, in order to keep my word.

10. Resilience

The capacity to face and recover quickly from difficulties or adversity; toughness.

Being Resilient: A way of Being that seeks possibility in the face of adversity or non-agreement, and is able to see beyond setbacks to maintain forward momentum with the wholeness and completeness of one's own declaration. An unshakable force that defies resistance and opposition through flexibility, determination, and creativity.

Social Feedback Question Suggestions

How much do you agree with the following statements?

1. I recover quickly from perceived setbacks, and get on with business, whatever that may be for me.

2. You can count on me to be a champion for a cause while standing firm in the face of non-agreement.

3. I always find a way of looking at people, situations, and the world so that adverse things don't seem to negatively impact me.

4. When facing change, I am readily able to adapt and move forward without allowing the disruption to unsettle me or affect me negatively.

11. Dependability

The quality of being trustworthy and reliable.

Being Dependable: A way of Being that others see you as being your word and your promises. Who you are is "count-on-able."

Social Feedback Question Suggestions

How much do you agree with the following statements?

1. I always do what I say I will do. Once I have given my word to do something, it is as good as done.

2. I only make promises that I have the ability to fulfill.

3. When I give my word, I move beyond that which would stop others. I don't whine, complain, or make a big deal about it—I just get it done.

Open-ended question:

What actions or behaviors would you advise me to take to improve my dependability?

12. Courage

The quality of mind or spirit that enables a person to face difficulty, danger, pain, and the like, in spite of fear; bravery.

Being Courageous: A way of Being that can be in the presence of a threat yet maintain forward momentum towards any commitment that is at risk due to this threat.

Social Feedback Question Suggestions

How much do you agree with the following statements?

1. I do not allow my fears to stop me from doing the things I love or taking actions that I feel are right.

2. I am a person who doesn't back down just because something seems difficult.

13. Responsibility

The state or fact of having a duty to deal with something or of having control over someone.

Being Responsible: A way of Being that will respond, when it is possible to respond, to any circumstance or situation; to be willing to take on what others have given up on.

Social Feedback Question Suggestions

How much do you agree with the following statements?

1. I am the type of person who finds freedom in the word *responsibility*. I am okay with the buck stopping with me.

2. I am always ready to step up when the situation requires; I take ownership and get things done.

3. I don't put blame on others for my shortfalls; I take responsibility and then set out to make it right.

14. Authenticity

The quality of being genuine, not false, copied or corrupted.

Being Authentic: A way of Being that wholly represents one's declared self with full expression.

Social Feedback Question Suggestions

How much do you agree with the following statements?

1. I am who I am without apology; I am not a person who fakes it 'til they make it.
2. I carry no pretense. What you see is what you get.

Open-ended question:
What advice could you give me on how I could be more authentic?

15. Present

Being, existing, or occurring at this time, right now.

Being Present: A way of Being that honors the past, acknowledges the future, but only deals with what is so right now, allowing life to sit calmly within one's self.

Social Feedback Question Suggestions

How much do you agree with the following statements?

1. I am at peace with life as it is, and unconcerned by the drama that whirls around me.
2. I am not one who panics, but instead acknowledges the situation, and moves forward step by step.
3. I am not stuck or focused on the past, nor always worried about the future. I seem to be right here in the moment with whatever I am doing.

16. Cause

A person or thing that gives rise to an action, phenomenon, or condition; the producer of an effect.

Being at Cause: A way of Being that generates results that allow for the experience of life (the experience of peace, love, and joy).

Social Feedback Question Suggestions

How much do you agree with the following statements?

1. I am a catalyst who makes things happen. It is not that I necessarily do it myself, but when you need to get something done, I can be counted on to assure results are delivered.

2. I have the ability to get people to support what I am up to.

3. I can get people to support what other people are up to.

4. I am able to see what needs to be done, figure out who to talk with in order to get things done, and work out how to put resources together to make it happen.

17. Grace

Exuding the qualities of elegance, kindness, courtesy, and tact: characterized by generosity of spirit.

Being Gracious: A way of Being that generously dignifies others. It appreciates and acknowledges the time, costs, and efforts others put forth. It gives the benefit of the doubt instead of skepticism.

Social Feedback Question Suggestions

How much do you agree with the following statements?

1. I have a generous way of judging people's actions and intentions so that I make them feel validated and worthy—even when others (or even they themselves) judge their actions to be failed or unworthy.

2. I have the ability to see things from different points of view. This allows me to respond to those with whom I disagree with tact, giving them the benefit of the doubt regarding their intentions.

3. Working with me is pleasurable because I give credit where it is due and make everyone feel validated and accepted, even if they think differently from me.

Open-ended question:

What advice would you give to help me become more gracious?

18. Peace

The state of being free from disturbance; without engagement with internal or external conflict; tranquility.

Being Peaceful: A way of Being that stands in the present and can be with what's so, in a way that allows for the freedom to experience all the goodness life has to offer.

Social Feedback Question Suggestions

How much do you agree with the following statements?

1. I am a tranquil person with the ability to calm other people down and diffuse tense situations simply by being in the room.

2. I am neither excitable nor prone to panic. I exude peace and tranquility in everything I do.

Open-ended question:

What advice would you give me that could help me become more peaceful?

19. Hope

The optimistic sense that what is wanted can be had, or that events will turn out for the best.

Being Hopeful: A way of Being that generates optimism about the future, and prioritizes thoughts, behaviors, and intentions towards the possibilities that will result in desirable future outcomes—without ignoring what is so.

Social Feedback Question Suggestions

How much do you agree with the following statements?

1. No matter how difficult the situation appears, I have a way to chart a course to a positive outcome on the other side.

2. When the chips are down and times are tough, I am able to inspire others to continue moving forward towards a vision of success.

Open-ended question:

What do you think I could do, or how could I behave, so you would see me as a hopeful person?

20. Ambition

An earnest desire for some type of achievement or distinction, and the willingness to strive for its attainment.

Being Ambitious: A way of Being that unendingly seeks to achieve and generates energy towards that pursuit, and inspires others towards their own ambitions.

Social Feedback Question Suggestions

How much do you agree with the following statements?

1. I never miss an opportunity to advance myself, whether in building a relationship or taking on a responsibility that can propel me towards my commitment.

2. I am focused and have an unending motivation for moving forward and achieving in my life.

3. I am a person you want to be around because you can see I am going places, and you hope to be able to learn something from me so you can accomplish your own ambitions.

21. Persistence

The quality of continuing in an opinion or course of action despite difficulty, obstacles, discouragement, or opposition.

Being Persistent: A way of Being that never quits or gives up, allowing for multiple do-overs and endless endurance while living in unreasonableness.

Social Feedback Question Suggestions

How much do you agree with the following statements?

1. I seem to keep going towards my vision no matter what obstacles I face.

2. When I get knocked down, I keep getting up. Other people see me as an unstoppable force because I never seem to quit.

3. I not only do not give up on my goals, I also don't give up on other people. I go out of my way to be there for them when they need, guide them when asked, and stand by their side no matter what.

22. Curiosity

An eagerness to learn, explore, or know; inquisitive.

Being Curious: A way of Being that unendingly seeks knowledge and awareness, ready to explore the unknown of the unknown.

Social Feedback Question Suggestions

How much do you agree with the following statements?

1. I am the type of person that can never stop learning. I always seem to be well informed, and I love figuring things out.

2. In situations that others see as problems or impossible obstacles, I find an interesting puzzle and the possibility to explore or learn.

3. I tend to go towards the unknown, unexplored, or new, where other people are more likely to avoid, stay away, or wait. This can show up in the form of attacking new problems, or testing new solutions or technologies.

23. Adventure

One who creates exciting or unusual experiences or finds experiences to be exciting or unusual.

Being Adventurous: A way of Being that allows for the risk of and celebrates untried activities, paradigms, or experiences. It moves beyond the need to survive and seeks out life experiences to transcend the mundane or usual, without being reckless or self-destructive.

Social Feedback Question Suggestions

How much do you agree with the following statements?

1. I see the adventure in any situation or circumstance. For me, life never seems to be boring or mundane.

2. I take an unreasonable approach to life, in the sense that I am not a "should be" type person, instead always seeing what "could be" and enthusiastically going towards that vision.

3. Some people may see me as reckless, but my risks are measured and calculated, ensuring that the adventure is positive and sustainable.

24. Creativity

One who can transcend traditional ideas, rules, patterns, relationships, or the like, and bring into being meaningful new ideas, forms, methods, and interpretations.

Being Creative: A way of Being that takes what is and brings forth that which has yet to be. An unstoppable force of possibilities that goes beyond that which already exists.

Social Feedback Question Suggestions

How much do you agree with the following statements?

1. I have the ability to take the simple things around me and make something wonderful.

2. I bring things to life that nobody else would have thought of. It is always a delight to watch me work this magic.

3. You can count on me to work with any type of person, in any given situation, and discover what is possible rather than what is not possible.

25. Conscientiousness

A way of being that exudes an inner sense of what is right or principled in one's conduct or motives, impelling one toward right action.

Being Conscientious: A way of Being that considers both the details and the big picture in order to honor oneself, others, and the circumstances and situations that arise, in order to maintain integrity with who one is, while assisting others in maintaining their own integrity.

Social Feedback Question Suggestions

How much do you agree with the following statements?

1. I go out of my way to consider many viewpoints and angles to ensure I make the best decisions possible for myself, others, and society overall.

2. I do a good job because that's what there is to do, and a good job for me includes both outstanding results and outstanding relationships with those I work with. I act in such a way that I do not sacrifice one for the other.

26. Generosity

Liberal in giving or sharing; unselfish.

Being Generous: A way of Being that seeks and celebrates the opportunity to give, and the act of sharing. A person being generosity tends to relate to the world as abundant in contrast to seeing loss, lack, or scarcity.

Social Feedback Question Suggestions

How much do you agree with the following statements?

1. I will give you the shirt off my back. I am always willing to contribute to a worthy cause and never say no when asked to help.

2. I always seem to find a way to help out with my time, money, access to other resources, or even emotional availability.

3. I am a person who is likely to offer to help before the request is made.

27. Abundance

Overflowing fullness; plentifulness.

Being Abundance: A way of Being that always sees, discovers, and finds more and never lacks or faces scarcity.

Social Feedback Question Suggestions

How much do you agree with the following statements?

1. I seem to create opportunity where there did not appear to be any.
2. I always find a way to gain the resources needed to get things done. I never seem to be without, even when times get tough—I am always able to generate a path to plenty.

Open-ended question:

What behavioral habits, perspectives, or paradigms do I have that hold me back from embodying abundance in my life?

28. Determination

The quality of being resolute and unwavering with firmness of purpose.

Being Determined: A way of being that remains steady, committed, and moving forward towards an admirable purpose. An unshakable and unstoppable force in the face of odds that appear unreasonable.

Social Feedback Question Suggestions

How much do you agree with the following statements?

1. Once I set myself on a course or in a direction, I am unstoppable.
2. Setbacks or being knocked down never hold me back for long because I get up and get going again.
3. I never give up.

29. Fun

One who provides amusement or enjoyment; playfulness.

Being Fun: A playful way of Being that allows for the enjoyment of all the situations and circumstances of life and inspires others to join in.

Social Feedback Question Suggestions

How much do you agree with the following statements?

1. I always find opportunities to celebrate and create great memories with those around me.

2. My way of valuing the enjoyment of life is infectious. I cause those around me to want to enjoy the life we have.

3. I look for opportunities to play, celebrate, and create great memories.

30. Passion

One who is capable of generating powerful or compelling emotions or feelings.

Being Passionate: A way of being that can generate directional energy (towards or away) that goes beyond purpose, stays unreasonable, and requires no justification.

Social Feedback Question Suggestions

How much do you agree with the following statements?

1. I am a person who seems to experience life at a different level. I think deeper, feel more, and express life as more vivid and alive than others.

2. I have the ability to generate energy and excitement around any idea I connect with—and it is contagious.

What advice would you give me to help me express more passion in my life?

31. Humility

The quality or condition of being humble; having a modest opinion or estimate of one's own importance, rank, etc.

Being Humble: A way of Being that appropriately and peacefully values its own importance, accomplishment, and significance in the context of the infinite universe where nothing is meant to last. It also appropriately values the experience and effort of others so that they feel respected and honored.

Social Feedback Question Suggestions

How much do you agree with the following statements?

1. I am the type of person that sees high value in everyone (equivalent to, or higher than myself) and I treat them honorably and with dignity.

2. When I interact with people, I make them feel good about themselves and their significance by honestly considering their thoughts, ideas, and experiences and giving them credit where it is due without hesitation or reservation.

3. I do not seem to need to be better than others. Others would say I am a humble person.

32. Optimism

A disposition or tendency to hope for and look on the more favorable side of events or conditions and to expect the most favorable outcome.

Being Optimistic: A way of Being that sees the future for all the glorious possibilities that it holds. Unmoved by the constraints of the past, it sits in the present, and creates a future that anyone would want to walk into.

Social Feedback Question Suggestions

How much do you agree with the following statements?

1. I take an upbeat approach to any situation, and things that others would see as negative, never get me down.

2. My positive outlook does not seem to be affected by naysayers. I can always argue for a positive way of looking at a future, no matter the circumstances.

3. I do not get stuck in past circumstances. if there's a light at the end of the tunnel, I will spot it and make it my purpose to get to it.

Open ended question:

What can I do to inspire more optimism around me?

33. Thoughtfulness

Showing consideration for the needs of others.

Being Thoughtful: A way of Being that generates actions towards others that reflect a consideration and understanding of the world from others' perspective. This way of being allows for the treatment of others with dignity and respect because it is seeking to understand others without judgement.

Social Feedback Question Suggestions

How much do you agree with the following statements?

1. I can see the humanity in every individual. I do not put people into general categories, nor do I place a person's situation or circumstance above who they are as a unique human being.

2. I make others feel like I really know them through all my interactions, both big and small—whether that be in giving a compliment, feedback for improvement, a gift, or a hand with a project, my actions always consider others' needs.

3. Others see me as an example for how to treat each other. I make others want to be more empathetic and compassionate in their interactions.

34. Kindness

The quality of being gentle, caring, generous, helpful, and considerate.

Being Kind: A way of Being that takes actions that consider others' needs equal to or ahead of one's own.

Social Feedback Question Suggestions

How much do you agree with the following statements?

1. I never seem to say anything bad about anyone else. I tend to give everyone the benefit of the doubt.

2. I will go out of my way to help people in need. That may be crossing the road to help a stranger, or giving a ride to a co-worker who is feeling ill. I simply seem to be the type of person that is looking out for others.

3. I make other people want to be kinder themselves.

35. Unreasonableness

Not reasonable or rational; acting at variance with or contrary to reason; not guided by reason.

Being Unreasonable: A way of Being that uncompromisingly honors who you are. It pushes aside your wants, or your not-wants, as well as predominant worldviews. It moves forward unimpeded by any circumstance or situation. When asked why, it answers, "because that's how it is."

Social Feedback Question Suggestions

How much do you agree with the following statements?

1. In many areas of my life, I could be compared to Don Quixote tilting at windmills. I have my ideas and I go at them with my whole being, without compromise—and I take the associated hits for being this way.

2. I take on projects that seem like mission impossible and I find ways forward with a level of stubbornness and tenacity that borders on unbelievable. I never allow the reasons of being tired, or low on resources, or low on available time, to get in the way of going for whatever I set my mind to.

3. When I set my mind to something, there is nothing that can get in my way or change my course. This allows me to show ways to others that they never imagined possible.

4. I am the type of person who lives life without excuses. Where others have reasons why they can't, I ignore these reasons so that I can make sure I fulfill the promises that I have made.

An important note about being Unreasonableness:

Of all the beings, unreasonableness is one of the most counter-intuitive. But it is this being that is the foundation of all our most interesting love stories, our finest explorers or entrepreneurs, and even our greatest friendships. It is characterized by sticking by someone or some belief, come hell or high water.

Furthermore, if the definition of a reasonable person is one who conforms themselves to the world, and an unreasonable person is one who seeks to conform the world to themselves, then all human advancement can only come from unreasonable people!

ENDNOTES

Introduction

1. (2017, November 2). "Readiness for College, Career and Life: The Purpose of K-12 Public Education Today." Retrieved from https://www.inacol.org/news/readiness-for-college-career-and-life-the-purpose-of-k-12-public-education-today/

2. Krok, Dariusz. "The role of meaning in life within the relations of religious coping and psychological well-being." *Journal of Religion and Health* 54.6 (2015): 2292-2308.

3. Petersen, Larry R., and Anita Roy. "Religiosity, anxiety, and meaning and purpose: Religion's consequences for psychological well-being." *Review of Religious Research* (1985): 49-62.

4. F. Karpowitz, C. F., & Pope, J. C. (2018). *American Family Survey 2018 Summary Report:* "Identities, Opportunities and Challenges". (pp. 1–114). Deseret News and The Center for the Study of Elections and Democracy at Brigham Young University.

5. Sherwood, H. (2018, March 21). " 'Christianity as default is gone': the rise of a non-Christian Europe". Retrieved from https://www.theguardian.com/world/2018/mar/21/christianity-non-christian-europe-young-people-survey-religion

Alignment Quotient

6. Makos, A., & Alexander, L. (2013). *A higher call*. New York: Berkley Books.

7. Goleman, Daniel. *Emotional Intelligence: Why It Can Matter More Than IQ*. New York: Bantam Books, 1995.

Part 1

8. The definition of being is a composite one from multiple dictionaries such that I could make it as complete and understandable as possible.

9. 1 Corinthians 13:4-8 NIV

10 The Everly Brothers, "Love Hurts" on album *A date with the Everly Brothers,* Warner Brothers, 1961

11 Rene Descartes, *Discourse on the Method of Rightly Conducting One's Reason and of Seeking Truth in the Sciences, Part 4*, Rene Descartes, 1637

12 Rene Descartes, *La Recherche de la Vérité par La Lumiere Naturale (The Search for Truth by Natural Light)* 1647

13 1. Falk, Dan. "Cosmos, Quantum and Consciousness: Is Science Doomed to Leave Some Questions Unanswered?" *Scientific American*, 1 May 2019, https://www.scientificamerican.com/article/cosmos-quantum-and-consciousness-is-science-doomed-to-leave-some-questions-unanswered/.

2. Overgaard, Morten. "The Status and Future of Consciousness Research." *Frontiers in Psychology* vol. 8 1719. 10 Oct. 2017, doi:10.3389/fpsyg.2017.01719

3. Burkeman, Oliver. "Why Can't the World's Greatest Minds Solve the Mystery of Consciousness? | Oliver Burkeman." *The Guardian*, Guardian News and Media, 21 Jan. 2015, https://www.theguardian.com/science/2015/jan/21/-sp-why-cant-worlds-greatest-minds-solve-mystery-consciousness.

14 Taren, A. A., Creswell, J. D., & Gianaros, P. J. (2013). "Dispositional mindfulness co-varies with smaller amygdala and caudate volumes in community adults." *PloS one*, 8(5), e64574.

15 Primacy effect - Biases & Heuristics. (n.d.). Retrieved from https://thedecisionlab.com/biases/primacy-effect.

16 Lieberman, M. D. (2013). *Social: Why our brains are wired to connect.* OUP Oxford.

17 1. Kruger, J., & Dunning, D. (1999). "Unskilled and unaware of it: how difficulties in recognizing one's own incompetence lead to inflated self-assessments". *Journal of Personality and Social psychology*, 77(6), 1121.

2. Zuckerman, E. W., & Jost, J. T. (2001). "What makes you think you're so popular? Self-evaluation maintenance and the subjective side of the friendship paradox". *Social Psychology Quarterly*, 207-223.

18 Frankl, V. E. (1985). *Man's search for meaning.* Simon and Schuster.

19 Siegel, D. J. (2016). *Mind: A Journey to the Heart of Being Human* (Norton Series on Interpersonal Neurobiology). WW Norton & Company.

20 Value: Definition of Value by Lexico. (n.d.). Retrieved from https://www.lexico.com/en/definition/value. *The Oxford English Dictionary* defines "values" as: "principles or standards of behavior; one's judgement of what is important in life."

21 Locher, Christine (2018) *Values-based: Career and Life Changes that make Sense*, Christine Locher Ltd.

22 Pembrey, M. E. (2002). "Time to take epigenetic inheritance seriously." *European Journal of Human Genetics*, 10(11), 669.

23 Hare, R. D. (1999). *Without conscience: The disturbing world of the psychopaths among us.* Guilford Press.

24 1. Meyer-Lindenberg, A., Buckholtz, J. W., Kolachana, B., Hariri, A. R., Pezawas, L., Blasi, G., ... & Egan, M. (2006). "Neural mechanisms of genetic risk for impulsivity and violence in humans." *Proceedings of the National Academy of Sciences*, 103(16), 6269-6274.

2. Caspi, A., McClay, J., Moffitt, T. E., Mill, J., Martin, J., Craig, I. W., ... & Poulton, R. (2005). "Role of genotype in the cycle of violence in maltreated children. Fears of the future in children and young people." *ZSE: Zeitschrift für Soziologie der Erziehung und Sozialisation*, 25(2), 133-145.

25 1. Darley, J. M., & Gross, P. H. (1983). "A hypothesis-confirming bias in labeling effects". *Journal of Personality and Social Psychology*, 44(1), 20.

2. Rosenthal, R., & Jacobson, L. (1992). *Pygmalion in the classroom*. Expanded edition. New York: Irvington, 382.

26 Fallon, James. *The psychopath inside: A neuroscientist's personal journey into the dark side of the brain.* Current, 2014.

27 Johnson, W., Turkheimer, E., Gottesman, I. I., & Bouchard Jr, T. J. (2009). "Beyond heritability: Twin studies in behavioral research." *Current directions in psychological science*, 18(4), 217-220.

28 Derringer, J., Krueger, R. F., Dick, D. M., Saccone, S., Grucza, R. A., Agrawal, A., ... & Nurnberger Jr, J. I. (2010). "Predicting sensation seeking from dopamine genes: A candidate-system approach." *Psychological Science*, 21(9), 1282-1290.

29 Fuchs, E., & Flügge, G. (2014). "Adult neuroplasticity: more than 40 years of research." *Neural plasticity*, 2014.

30 Goleman, D., & Davidson, R. J. (2017). Altered traits: Science reveals how meditation changes your mind, brain, and body. Penguin.

31 Reardon, S. F. (2011). "The widening academic achievement gap between the rich and the poor: New evidence and possible explanations." *Whither opportunity*, 91-116.

32 Claro, S., Paunesku, D., & Dweck, C. S. (2016). "Growth mindset tempers the effects of poverty on academic achievement." *Proceedings of the National Academy of Sciences*, 113(31), 8664-8668.

33 Shepherd, J. (2015). "Consciousness, free will, and moral responsibility: Taking the folk seriously." *Philosophical psychology*, 28(7), 929-946.

PART 2

34 Siegel, E. (2017, February 10). "Why Science Will Never Know Everything About Our Universe." Retrieved from https://www.forbes.com/sites/startswithabang/2017/02/10/why-science-will-never-know-everything-about-our-universe/.

35 Carnal, O., & Mlynek, J. (1991). "Young's double-slit experiment with atoms: A simple atom interferometer." *Physical review letters*, 66(21), 2689.

36 1. Emspak, J. (2016, February 14). "Quantum Entanglement: Love on a Subatomic Scale." Retrieved from https://www.space.com/31933-quantum-entanglement-action-at-a-distance.html.

2. Zeilinger, A. (1999). "Experiment and the foundations of quantum physics. In More Things in Heaven and Earth" (pp. 482-498). *Springer*, New York, NY.

37 Kwiat, P. G., Steinberg, A. M., & Chiao, R. Y. (1992). "Observation of a "quantum eraser": A revival of coherence in a two-photon interference experiment." *Physical Review A*, 45(11), 7729.

38 Tang, J. S., Li, Y. L., Xu, X. Y., Xiang, G. Y., Li, C. F., & Guo, G. C. (2012). "Realization of quantum Wheeler's delayed-choice experiment." *Nature Photonics*, 6(9), 600.

39 1. Nairz, O., Arndt, M., & Zeilinger, A. (2003). "Quantum interference experiments with large molecules." *American Journal of Physics*, 71(4), 319-325.

2. arXiv, E. T. from the. (2019, November 9). "A natural biomolecule has been measured acting like a quantum wave for the first time." Retrieved from https://www.technologyreview.com/s/614688/a-natural-biomolecule-has-been-measured-acting-in-a-quantum-wave-for-the-first-time/.

40 (n.d.). Retrieved from https://archive.org/stream/TheBornEinsteinLetters/Born-TheBornEinsteinLetters_djvu.txt.

41 1. Aron, J. (2016, May 4). "Try your hand at programming IBM's online quantum computer." Retrieved January 10, 2020, from https://www.newscientist.com/article/2086702-try-your-hand-at-programming-ibms-online-quantum-computer/.

2. Fisher, C. (2009, April 2). "Quantum Starts Here." Retrieved January 10, 2020, from https://www.ibm.com/quantum-computing/.

3. IBL News, & IBL News. (2019, September 18). IBL News. Retrieved January 10, 2020, from https://iblnews.org/ibm-releases-a-video-tutorial-series-and-textbook-to-educate-on-quantum-computing/.

42 Conroy, G. (n.d.). "Physicists Just Smashed a Record to Achieve Quantum Entanglement in Space." Retrieved from https://www.sciencealert.com/physicists-just-quantum-entangled-photons-between-earth-and-space.

43 Composition definition from multiple sources, Lexico.com being primary

44 Ware, B. (2012). "The top five regrets of the dying: A life transformed by the dearly departing." Carlsbad, Calif.: Hay House.

45 Elek, S. D. (1966). "Semmelweis Commemoration: Semmelweis and the Oath of Hippocrates."https://www.loebclassics.com/view/hippocrates_cos-oath/1923/pb_LCL147.299.xml

46 Loeb, J., & Henderson, J. (2019, June 24). "HIPPOCRATES OF COS, The Oath." Retrieved from https://www.loebclassics.com/view/hippocrates_cos-oath/1923/pb_LCL147.299.xml.

47 Compilation of information from Google via dictionary.com and Oxford.

48 Compilation definition from multiple dictionaries

49 Awakin.org. (n.d.). Retrieved November 12, 2019, from http://www.awakin.org/read/view.php?tid=668.

50 Langer, E., Blank, A., & Chanowitz, B. (1978). "The mindlessness of Ostensibly Thoughtful Action: The Role of "Placebic" Information in Interpersonal Interaction." *Journal of Personality and Social Psychology*, 36(6), 635-642

51 Musich, S., Wang, S. S., Kraemer, S., Hawkins, K., & Wicker, E. (2018). "Purpose in life and positive health outcomes among older adults." *Population health management*, 21(2), 139-147.

52 Ryff, C. D., Singer, B. H., & Dienberg Love, G. (2004). "Positive health: connecting well-being with biology." *Philosophical Transactions of the Royal Society of London. Series B: Biological Sciences*, 359(1449), 1383-1394.

53 Boyle, P. A., Buchman, A. S., & Bennett, D. A. (2010). "Purpose in life is associated with a reduced risk of incident disability among community-dwelling older persons." *The American Journal of Geriatric Psychiatry*, 18(12), 1093-1102.

54 Boyle, P. A., Buchman, A. S., Barnes, L. L., & Bennett, D. A. (2010). "Effect of a purpose in life on risk of incident Alzheimer disease and mild cognitive impairment in community-dwelling older persons." *Archives of general psychiatry*, 67(3), 304-310.

55 Lee, V., Cohen, S. R., Edgar, L., Laizner, A. M., & Gagnon, A. J. (2006). "Meaning-making intervention during breast or colorectal cancer treatment improves self-esteem, optimism, and self-efficacy." *Social science & medicine*, 62(12), 3133-3145.

56 1. Damon, W., Menon, J., & Cotton Bronk, K. (2003). "The development of purpose during adolescence." *Applied developmental science*, 7(3), 119-128.

2. "The Psychology of Purpose." (n.d.). Retrieved from https://www.templeton.org/discoveries/the-psychology-of-purpose.

57 Vicedo, M. (2010). "The evolution of Harry Harlow: from the nature to the nurture of love." *History of psychiatry*, 21(2), 190-205.

58 Russek, L. G., & Schwartz, G. E. (1997). "Feeling of parental caring predict health status in midlife: A 35-year follow-up of the Harvard Mastery of Stress Study." *Journal of behavioral medicine*, 20(1), 1-13.

59 Holt-Lunstad, J., Smith, T. B., & Layton, J. B. (2010). "Social relationships and mortality risk: a meta-analytic review." *PLoS medicine*, 7(7), e1000316.

60 Blaine, D. (n.d.). Retrieved November 12, 2019, from https://www.ted.com/talks/david_blaine_how_i_held_my_breath_for_17_min?language=en.

Part 3

61 "14 Incredible Mantis Shrimp Facts." (n.d.). Retrieved from https://factanimal.com/mantis-shrimp/.

62 "Cognitive Distortions: When Your Brain Lies to You" (PDF Worksheets). (2019, October 10). Retrieved from https://positivepsychology.com/cognitive-distortions/.

63 Quinn, J. (2017, April 7). "Story Of The Old Farmer." Retrieved November 13, 2019, from http://emptygatezen.com/teaching/2017/4/7/story-of-the-old-farmer.

64 "Definition of integrity in English". Oxford Living Dictionaries. Oxford University Press. Retrieved February 26, 2019.

65   Integrity. (n.d.). Retrieved November 13, 2019, from https://www.dictionary.com/browse/integrity.

66   Grossmann, I., Dorfman, A., Oakes, H., Santos, H. C., Vohs, K. D., & Scholer, A. (2019). "Training for Wisdom: The Illeist Diary Method."

67   Purcell, M. (2018, October 8). "The Health Benefits of Journaling." Retrieved from https://psychcentral.com/lib/the-health-benefits-of-journaling/.

Part 4

68   Fairchild, M. D. (2013). *Color appearance models.* John Wiley & Sons.

69   "Acceptance and Commitment Therapy." (n.d.). Retrieved from https://www.psychologytoday.com/intl/therapy-types/acceptance-and-commitment-therapy.

Authors Note

70   1. Alloy, Lauren B., and Lyn Y. Abramson. "Depressive realism: Four theoretical perspectives." (1988).

  2 . Moore, Michael T., and David M. Fresco. "Depressive realism: A meta-analytic review." *Clinical psychology review* 32.6 (2012): 496-509.

71   Andrews, P. W. (2009, August 25). "Depression's Evolutionary Roots." Retrieved from https://www.scientificamerican.com/article/depressions-evolutionary/

72   (n.d.). Products - Vital Statistics Rapid Release - Provisional Drug Overdose Data. Retrieved from https://www.cdc.gov/nchs/nvss/vsrr/drug-overdose-data.htm

73   (n.d.). "Vietnam War U.S. Military Fatal Casualty Statistics." Retrieved from https://www.archives.gov/research/military/vietnam-war/casualty-statistics

74   "Deaths related to drug poisoning in England and Wales: 2017 registrations." (n.d.). Retrieved November 20, 2019, from https://www.ons.gov.uk/peoplepopulationandcommunity/birthsdeathsandmarriages/deaths/bulletins/deathsrelatedtodrugpoisoninginenglandandwales/2017registrations.

75   Chalabi, M. (2013, November 20). Antidepressants: global trends. Retrieved from https://www.theguardian.com/news/2013/nov/20/mental-health-antidepressants-global-trends

76   Chalabi, M. (2013, November 20). Antidepressants: global trends. Retrieved from https://www.theguardian.com/news/2013/nov/20/mental-health-antidepressants-global-trends

77   "Anxiety Disorders And Depression Treatment Market Report, 2018-2025." Anxiety Disorders And Depression Treatment Market Report, 2018-2025, www.grandviewresearch.com/industry-analysis/anxiety-disorders-and-depression-treatment-market.

78   "The Psychology of Purpose." (n.d.). Retrieved from https://www.templeton.org/discoveries/the-psychology-of-purpose..

79 Ryff, C. D., & Singer, B. H. (2008). "Know thyself and become what you are: A eudaimonic approach to psychological well-being." *Journal of happiness studies*, 9(1), 13-39.

80 Fredrickson, B. L., Grewen, K. M., Coffey, K. A., Algoe, S. B., Firestine, A. M., Arevalo, J. M., ... & Cole, S. W. (2013). A functional genomic perspective on human well-being. *Proceedings of the National Academy of Sciences*, 110(33), 13684-13689.

81 Mount Sinai Medical Center. "Have a sense of purpose in life? It may protect your heart." *ScienceDaily*, 6 March 2015. <www.sciencedaily.com/releases/2015/03/150306132538.htm>.

82 Turner, A. D., Smith, C. E., & Ong, J. C. (2017). Is purpose in life associated with less sleep disturbance in older adults?" *Sleep Science and Practice*, 1(1), 14.

83 Schaefer, S. M., Boylan, J. M., Van Reekum, C. M., Lapate, R. C., Norris, C. J., Ryff, C. D., & Davidson, R. J. (2013). "Purpose in life predicts better emotional recovery from negative stimuli." *PloS one*, 8(11), e80329.

84 Yeager, D. S., & Bundick, M. J. (2009). "The role of purposeful work goals in promoting meaning in life and in schoolwork during adolescence." *Journal of Adolescent Research*, 24(4), 423-452.

85 Boyle, P. A., Buchman, A. S., & Bennett, D. A. (2010). "Purpose in life is associated with a reduced risk of incident disability among community-dwelling older persons." *The American Journal of Geriatric Psychiatry*, 18(12), 1093-1102.

86 Boyle, P. A., Buchman, A. S., Barnes, L. L., & Bennett, D. A. (2010). "Effect of a purpose in life on risk of incident Alzheimer disease and mild cognitive impairment in community-dwelling older persons." *Archives of general psychiatry*, 67(3), 304-310.

87 Kashdan, T. B., & McKnight, P. E. (2013). "Commitment to a purpose in life: An antidote to the suffering by individuals with social anxiety disorder." *Emotion*, 13(6), 1150.

88 Stetz, K. M. (1989). "The relationship among background characteristics, purpose in life, and caregiving demands on perceived health of spouse caregivers." *Sch Inq Nurs Pract*, 3(2), 133-153.

Appendix 1: Reasonable doubt in a materialist viewpoint

89 Smart, J. J. C. (2016, April 28). Materialism. Retrieved from https://www.britannica.com/topic/materialism-philosophy.

90 The Editors of Encyclopaedia Britannica. (2017, June 12). Reductionism. Retrieved from https://www.britannica.com/topic/reductionism.

91 Greshko, M. (2019, March 28). "The origins of the universe, explained." Retrieved from https://www.nationalgeographic.com/science/space/universe/origins-of-the-universe/.

92 (n.d.). Retrieved from http://abyss.uoregon.edu/~js/ast122/lectures/lec18.html.

93 Eisenberger, N. I., Lieberman, M. D., & Williams, K. D. (2003). "Does rejection hurt? An fMRI study of social exclusion." *Science*, 302(5643), 290-292.

94 Maguire, E. A., Frackowiak, R. S., & Frith, C. D. (1997). "Recalling routes around London: activation of the right hippocampus in taxi drivers." *Journal of neuroscience*, 17(18), 7103-7110.

95 Philippi, C. L., Duff, M. C., Denburg, N. L., Tranel, D., & Rudrauf, D. (2012). "Medial PFC damage abolishes the self-reference effect." *Journal of cognitive neuroscience*, 24(2), 475-481.

96 Chalmers, D. J. (1995). "Facing up to the problem of consciousness." *Journal of consciousness studies*, 2(3), 200-219.

97 O'Connor, T., & Wong, H. Y. (2015, June 3). "Emergent Properties." Retrieved from https://plato.stanford.edu/entries/properties-emergent/.

98 Dr. Stuart Hameroff. Retrieved November 18, 2019, from https://www.youtube.com/watch?v=Xx0SsffdMBw.

99 OpenWorm. (n.d.). Retrieved from http://openworm.org/.

100 Albo, M. (2017, June 1). "The fascinatingly complex feat of trying to build a virtual worm." Retrieved from https://ideas.ted.com/the-fascinatingly-complex-feat-of-trying-to-build-a-virtual-worm/.

101 Hoffman, D. (2008). "Conscious realism and the mind-body problem." *Mind and Matter*, 6(1), 87-121.

102 Malickas, A. [1996] "Gradual uploading as a cognition of mind." http://www.aleph.se/Trans/Global/Uploading/gupload.html

103 "ORNL Launches Summit Supercomputer." (2018, June 8). Retrieved November 15, 2019, from https://www.ornl.gov/news/ornl-launches-summit-supercomputer.

104 "U.S. Department of Energy and Cray to Deliver Record-Setting Frontier Supercomputer at ORNL." (n.d.). Retrieved from https://www.energy.gov/articles/us-department-energy-and-cray-deliver-record-setting-frontier-supercomputer-ornl.

105 Gazzaniga, M. (2012). "Who's in Charge?: Free Will and the Science of the Brain." *Hachette UK*.

106 (n.d.). Retrieved November 15, 2019, from https://www.iep.utm.edu/chineser/

107 Penrose, R. (1989). "The emperor's new mind: concerning computers, minds, and the laws of physics" Oxford Univ.

108 Raatikainen, P. (2015, January 20). "Gödel's Incompleteness Theorems." Retrieved from https://plato.stanford.edu/entries/goedel-incompleteness/.

109 "The True nature of matter and mass by PBS Spacetime". Retrieved November 18, 2019, from https://www.youtube.com/watch?v=gSKzgpt4HBU.

110 "What is Spin Retrieved" Nov 18, 2019 from https://www.youtube.com/watch?v=cd2Ua9dKEl8&t=541s

111 Kramer, M. (2013, August 14). "The Physics Behind Schrödinger's Cat Paradox." Retrieved from https://www.nationalgeographic.com/news/2013/8/130812-physics-schrodinger-erwin-google-doodle-cat-paradox-science/.

www.ingramcontent.com/pod-product-compliance
Lightning Source LLC
Chambersburg PA
CBHW030313080526
44584CB00012B/552